# A CENTURY OF
# MORAL PHILOSOPHY

To
Rebecca, Katie and Peter
with much love

# A CENTURY OF
# MORAL PHILOSOPHY

by
W. D. Hudson

LUTTERWORTH PRESS
GUILDFORD AND LONDON

First published in 1980

ISBN 0 7188 2429 6

Set in 10/12 pt Plantin
Printed by Butler & Tanner Ltd,
Frome and London

# Contents

# Introduction

Moral philosophy is the attempt to understand the kind of thinking normally called moral judgement. This is a kind of thinking in which we all engage. Where is the man who has never wondered what he ought to do? Even if we could find him, we should soon discover that he had, at any rate, thought a good deal about what other people ought to do. For where is the man who has never felt that he was being treated unfairly, inconsiderately, less than honourably, by his fellow men? Moral judgement is not a mental activity in which only a select few take part, like scientific investigation or artistic criticism. It is not only bishops, judges, schoolmasters or parents who go in for it. We are all moralists. This book is about something we all do.

A distinction can be drawn between the *meaning* and the *measure* of morality. Suppose a man complains that his wage is unfair. In order to understand him we need to know at least two things. One is what he *means* by 'unfair'; the other, how he *measures* unfairness. They are not the same thing. If he is using the word in the normal sense, he will mean by 'unfair' that his wage falls short of some standard to which in his opinion it ought to conform; but what he takes this standard to be may differ from what some other people would take it to be. If we do not know whether or not he is using 'unfair' in a normal sense, we shall be in the dark. But equally, if we do not know how he measures unfairness, we shall not be able to understand him—not, at least, sufficiently to decide whether what he says is sensible or not.

Once these conditions are fulfilled and we do understand him, there are two kinds of question which we can ask, two sorts of interest which we can take in what he has said. To mark the difference between these two kinds of question or interest, they are sometimes called the ethical and the metaethical respectively. We can take an *ethical* interest in what the man has said by asking ourselves whether or not we agree with it. Do we think his wage unfair? If we do, we can further display this kind of interest by making speeches against low pay, contributing to his strike fund, coming out in sympathy with him, and so on. Alternatively, we can take a *metaethical* interest in his moral judgement by raising the following kinds of question about it. How precisely does what he *means* by saying that his wage is unfair differ from what he would have meant if he had simply told us that it amounts to no more than, say, thirty-five pounds a week? How is the meaning, which moral judgements have, like—and how unlike—the meaning which factual statements have? Or again, we may ask how the *measure* of unfairness to which this man appeals is related to the fact that his judgement is a *moral* one. Can people choose *any* standard of measurement at all and their judgements still be moral ones? Or are there only certain criteria which we can intelligibly invoke when we are using words like 'unfair'? And if so, what are these criteria, and why?

It is metaethical questions such as these with which moral philosophy—as distinct from moral preaching or pamphleteering—is concerned. Regrettably, there is no guarantee that those who engage in it will become better men in consequence. But there is a hope that they may become a little clearer in the head about what moral judgement is and so perhaps—should they choose to think about their duty—do so with a little less confusion.

A book like this is necessarily selective. It represents one man's view of a century of reflection upon the nature of moral judgement. I have made it even more selective than it might have been by deliberately choosing not to offer an encyclopaedic digest of all the moral philosophers from the last hundred years or so of whom I have heard, but rather to trace what seems to me to be the most important thread of argument and counter-argument in this branch of philosophy, during the period assigned to me. It would be too much to hope that others who work professionally in the same field will all agree with me about what has been most important. But I can only tell the story as I see it. In the attempt to do so I have received help from friends and pupils. In particular, I must thank Professor R. M. Hare, who let me see some of his recent work ahead of publication and also cast an eye over the last part of chapter 8 to ensure that I had not seriously misrepresented his opinions; Mrs. Eugénie Ridgeon, who, as always, has given me invaluable secretarial assistance, and Mrs. Christine Channon, who took time off from post-graduate studies to help with checking references and reading proofs.

People, who come new to philosophy, sometimes complain that philosophers go round in circles. They keep coming back to the questions from which they started, age after age, in book after book. But this, in so far as it is true, is of the nature of the philosophical enterprise and the hope which inspires it. One thing philosophers try to do is to define the questions which they are asking ever more clearly in the hope that they will eventually answer themselves.

> *We shall not cease from exploration*
> *And the end of all our exploring*
> *Will be to arrive where we started*
> *And know the place for the first time.**

*T. S. Eliot, *Little Gidding*.

## 1

# Two conflicting schools of thought

At the time when our story begins two schools of thought—namely intuitionism and utilitarianism—dominated moral philosophy. In order to understand the developments in the subject which have taken place since then, we need to know how things stood between these two conflicting schools of thought a little over a hundred years ago. I will, therefore, say something in this chapter about each of them, indicating what, respectively, their main ideas were and concluding with an account of the controversial exchange which took place between two of their protagonists, William Whewell and John Stuart Mill.

### Intuitionism

Intuitionism is the view that human beings possess a faculty, commonly called conscience, which enables them to discern directly what is morally right or wrong, good or evil. But those who have taken this view have not always agreed among themselves in their account of the faculty concerned.

In the seventeenth and eighteenth centuries there was a great deal of debate amongst intuitionists as to whether conscience should be conceived as a kind of sense or an aspect of reason. Some, like the third Earl of Shaftesbury (1671–1713) and Francis Hutcheson (1694–1746), were of the former opinion. Under the influence of Locke's empiricist epistemology, according to which the ultimate constituents of our knowledge are simple ideas of sensation, they inferred that the faculty which apprehends the moral properties of actions or states of affairs must be some sort of sense; just as all we know about the physical world comes to us through the perceptions of our physical senses, so, they thought, all we know about right and wrong, good and evil, must come to us through the intuitions of a moral sense. Other intuitionists, such as Ralph Cudworth (1617–88), Samuel Clarke (1675–1729), John Balguy (1686–1748) and Richard Price (1723–1791) took the view that the moral faculty is reason. Influenced by Cartesian philosophy, according to which the ultimate constituents of our knowledge are clear and distinct ideas supplied by the understanding, they concluded that conscience must be reason in its intuitive aspect; just as the equality of two angles, made by a right line, standing at any angle upon another, to two right angles is a new, simple mathematical idea supplied by the understanding, so, they claimed, the rightness of an act which e.g. fulfils a promise must be a new simple moral idea supplied by the understanding.

Both these kinds of intuitionists thought that moral properties are objectively *real* and *intrinsic* to the actions or states of affairs which they characterise. When we say that an act is right, we are not simply registering an effect which it has had upon us. We are saying that it is *really* right *in itself*. It has the objective property of rightness, considered as an end in itself and not simply as a means to some end. So much was common ground. But differences arose about what this implies concerning conscience.[1] The kind of point which the moral sense philosophers made was that, since reason is the faculty which discerns appropriate or effective means to given ends, rather than the properties which these ends possess in themselves, conscience, which discerns *intrinsic* moral properties, cannot be an aspect of reason but must be some kind of sense. To which the rational intuitionists replied that, since reason is the faculty which apprehends the essence, or real nature, of things, as distinct from what they merely appear to be, conscience which discerns whether actions are *really* right or wrong, cannot be a sort of sense but must be an aspect of reason.

Some philosophers took the view that conscience may be described as *both* reason *and* sense. Bishop Joseph Butler (1692–1752) spoke of it as 'our moral understanding and moral sense';[2] and the Scottish intuitionist, Thomas Reid (1710–96) said, in

2

similar vein, that conscience is 'an original power of the mind' which supplies us in the first place with our 'original conceptions of right and wrong in conduct' and is comparable in this regard to a sense such as sight or hearing; and supplies us in the second place with our 'original judgements that this conduct is right and that is wrong' and is comparable in this respect to the understanding which makes us aware of mathematical axioms.[3] If, for instance, I were to say that you were wrong to tell someone something which you knew to be false, I would be 'sensing' in your action the characteristic of wrongness and 'understanding' it to possess this characteristic because it comes under the axiom that it is wrong to tell lies. My conscience can and does function in both ways. Butler and Reid were not, however, mainly concerned to discuss whether conscience is sense or reason but to insist upon its magisterial authority. What they wanted to emphasise above all else was, to quote Reid, that conscience has 'an authority which belongs to no other principle of the human mind,'[4] or, as Butler put it in words which have become famous, 'Had it strength, as it had right; had it power as it had manifest authority, it would absolutely govern the world.'[5]

One of the most distinguished representatives of intuitionism in the latter part of the nineteenth century was William Whewell (1794–1866), an able scientist who became professor of moral philosophy at Cambridge. His *Elements of Morality* was published in 1845 and had run into four editions by 1864. Whewell was totally committed to the view that the moral faculty is reason.[6] Reason 'directs us to rules,' he said, and the adjective 'right' 'signifies conformable to rule'. Reason's moral function is to direct us to: (i) a 'supreme' rule of human action 'to do what is right and to abstain from doing what is wrong', and (ii) various 'subordinate' rules 'which determine what is right and what is wrong'. The 'subordinate' rules are those embodied in conventional morality and positive law at any given time. It is important to obey them; but they must never be equated with the 'supreme' rule. They simply represent as much as people in the given society have so far understood of moral truth—that is, of what the 'supreme' rule requires of us. Room is always left for reason to reveal more of this. Because it is reason which does so, the revelation is self-authenticating. Reason is 'the light of man's constitution which reveals him to himself ... this light by being light, is fit to guide us; as in the

3

world without, so in the world within us, the light, by guiding us, proves that it is its office to guide us.'

The intuitionists, to whom I have referred, all agreed that an action, in order to be virtuous, must be one which the agent has freely chosen to do because his conscience approves of it. But they differed among themselves as to precisely what it is of which an enlightened conscience will approve. The moral sense philosophers thought that the motive or intention with which certain kinds of action are done is what conscience judges. Hutcheson,[7] for example, said that actions are virtuous if they aim at producing as much general happiness as possible. Against his exclusive approval of benevolence, Butler[8] argued that if we could make either of two men happy and only one of them was our friend or benefactor, then it would be our duty to make him happy rather than the other man—a fact from which he concluded that motives such as friendship or gratitude, as well as benevolence, can make actions right; and others such as deceit, violence or injustice, as well as malevolence, can make them wrong. The rational intuitionists for their part took the view that what conscience approves of is actions which instantiate certain first principles of morality; but there was some slight difference of opinion among them as to what exactly these first principles are. Clarke[9] listed three: duty to God, which consists in worshipping and obeying him; duty to others, which comprises both equity and love; and duty to self, which is the duty to preserve one's own life and develop one's own talents. Price[10] added to this list gratitude, which is duty to benefactors; veracity, which includes promise-keeping; and justice.

Reid,[11] for his part, said that there are three kinds of moral axioms. First, there are some very general ones, such as that some acts merit praise and others blame, that only voluntary acts merit either, etc. These constitute the necessary conditions of morality. Secondly, there are some more particular axioms, such as that we ought always to prefer a greater to a lesser good and a lesser to a greater evil, that we ought to live in accordance with our nature, that we ought to do to others what we would judge it right for them to do to us if they were in our circumstances and we in theirs, etc. Implicit within these particular principles, Reid said, are such virtues as prudence, benevolence, family affection, gratitude, generosity, justice, etc., which constitute the basic content of morality. Thirdly, there are axioms which guide us when we find

4

ourselves in a conflict of obligations, such as the principles that unmerited generosity should always yield to gratitude and both to justice. These are, so to speak, arbiters within morality.

None of the intuitionists would have denied that the moral faculty, though intuitive, may need educating; nor that, however well trained it has become, it may from time to time make mistakes. The idea of development towards greater clarity and correctness in the deliverances of conscience is accepted by all of them, but it is particularly evident in Whewell.[12] In working out this idea he showed affinities both with his Platonic predecessors in British intuitionism and with Kant, whose writings he was one of the earliest British philosophers to study. Like Cudworth or Clarke, he thought of moral intuition as a faculty which perceives the eternal and immutable ideas of rightness and goodness existing in the mind of God; but, like Kant, he also thought of it as a faculty which imposes rules upon the other elements in human nature. Every science, he held, is constituted by a Platonic Idea (or Ideas); as, for instance, mechanics by that of force. The relevant Idea is explicated in the axioms of the science concerned. These are in themselves self-evident, though their content may only gradually become apparent to us. In any science, we proceed by using what we know of its axioms in order to interpret empirically observed facts in its particular field. When we have so interpreted any given facts, our understanding of the axioms invoked in order to do so, will be more completely clarified. By the light of this clearer understanding, we shall then be able to interpret further facts. And so on. That is how science progresses—through the interplay of Platonic Idea and fact, theory and observation.

Now, said Whewell, it is just the same in the case of morality. We apprehend its eternal and immutable first principles more and more clearly as we use what we know of them to judge men and affairs. Such development, he went on—here following his Kantian as well as his Platonic line of thought—comes about as the 'subordinate' rules of morality are brought ever more fully into line with its 'supreme' rule. These two kinds of rule control desire. The five main kinds of desire in human nature are,

(i) the desire of *safety*, which includes that of free agency;
(ii) the desire of *having*, which is satisfied by the ownership of things;
(iii) the desire of *mutual understanding*, which requires for its satisfaction that promises be kept;

5

   (iv)  the desire of *family affection*;

   (v)  the desire of *civil society*.

Reason must control these desires so that every man may enjoy a 'tranquil gratification' of them and society be preserved from becoming 'disturbed, unbalanced, painful'.

To this end, it is an essential element in Whewell's moral philosophy that we must obey the positive laws of our society. These laws define for us the five 'primary and universal rights of man', which correspond to the five kinds of desire: namely the rights of security, property, contract, family life and civil order. They also defend these rights by forbidding violence, theft, breach of contract, adultery and civil disorder. In Whewell's view, as we have already noted, subordinate rules are always subject to the supreme rule 'to do what is right and to abstain from doing what is wrong'. This rule, in turn, breaks down into five 'cardinal virtues'. These are: benevolence, justice, truth, purity and order. They correspond to the five kinds of desire and the five primary rights. In applying positive laws to actual situations, mankind's understanding of the supreme rule is progressively clarified. So morality gradually advances in a five-fold way, from mere prohibitions of violence to the recommendation of benevolence; from the mere condemnation of theft to enriched conceptions of distributive justice; from mere penalties for breach of contract to the awareness that people should be able to rely on each other's truthfulness in every situation; from mere commandments forbidding adultery or civil disobedience to a pure, wholehearted love of family and country. There is no limit to the development of conscience. As Whewell has it, 'We must labour to *enlighten* and *instruct* our Conscience. This task can never be ended. So long as life and powers of thought remain to us, we may always be able to acquire a still clearer and higher view than we yet possess, of the Supreme Law of our Being.... Conscience is never fully formed, but always in the course of formation.'

As Whewell himself realised, there is an 'apparent inconsistency' in his conception of morality. It is our duty to obey its 'subordinate' rules embodied in the law of the land; but these rules stand under the judgement of the 'supreme' rule of morality. Duty requires us to recognise rights; but rights are subordinate to duty. Whewell resolved matters in this way,

... at any time, morality depends upon law; but in the long run, law must be regulated by morality. The morality of the individual depends on his not violating the law of his nation; but the national law must be framed according to the national view of morality. The moral offence of coveting my neighbour's goods, as well as the crime of stealing, extends to everything which the law determines to be his goods. But the law which gives him everything, and leaves me to starve, may be an unjust law; and if so, may be altered by the progress of time, and by the improved morality of the legislative body.

The problem, of course, is to think how morality can be conformity both to positive law and to a law which is above positive law. What we seem to need is some criterion—other than simply the supreme rule that we must do what is right and abstain from doing what is wrong—whereby we can test the morality of the rules which have hitherto determined what is right or wrong. Mill[13] scathingly criticised Whewell for not providing such a criterion. As we shall see, Mill himself took it to be utility; and he accused Whewell, with some justification, of covertly introducing that principle into his account of the elements of morality. What, asked Mill, is Whewell's remark that without some provision for the 'tranquil gratification' of desires society will become 'disturbed, unbalanced, painful', if not an appeal to utility? A palpable hit. But Whewell was simply nodding here. His definitive view is uncompromisingly that the rule of reason is not a means to any end, such as the general happiness, but an end in itself. Mill gave Whewell no credit for having perceived that there is no standard of morality—utility included—which might not conceivably be superseded. The question 'But is it right to do what produces the general happiness?' makes perfectly good sense. As we shall see, Whewell's refusal to tie the 'supreme' law of morality to any specific standard has seemed to many philosophers to be wellfounded.

*Utilitarianism*

Utilitarianism, very broadly speaking, is the view that acts are right in so far as they bring about an increase in human happiness and wrong when they produce misery. This view became a significant influence in British moral philosophy during the eighteenth century. In the early days its most prominent exponents were

7

theological writers, notably, William Paley (1743–1805), who believed that virtue is 'doing good to mankind in obedience to the will of God and for the sake of everlasting happiness'.[14] Paley tried to combine egoistic psychological hedonism and altruistic ethical hedonism by arguing that the motivating force of human action is both a desire for one's own happiness and the obligation, once we know that God will bestow eternal bliss only upon those who promote the general happiness, to seek that goal. However, the founder of utilitarianism is generally taken to have been Jeremy Bentham (1748–1832); and its most widely read exponent is un-doubtedly John Stuart Mill (1806–1873), whose *Utilitarianism* was first published in *Fraser's Magazine* during 1861.

When Bentham went up to Queen's College, Oxford, at the tender age of twelve, he was required to sign the Thirty Nine Articles. Before doing so he read them carefully. In some he could see no meaning and for others, find no rational or scriptural grounds. The fellow of the College, whose job it was to dispel undergraduate doubts, chided him for pitting his own puerile judgement against that of all the good and wise men who had given their assent to these articles of faith through the ages. Duly cowed, Jeremy signed. But not without misgivings. The whole business, so he tells us[15] had an effect upon him which lasted throughout his life. It made him abhor all self-styled authorities which demand assent without proof. Even when the authority was said to be conscience within, Bentham would have none of it. As a law student, he rapidly came to the conclusion that legal theory as embodied in Blackstone's *Commentaries*, and legal practice as he witnessed it in the courts, were both bedevilled by what he called 'ipsedixitism'. That is, by the view that some things just are in-trinsically right or wrong, good or evil. Certain principles of con-duct, such as the inherent wrongness of some forms of sexual beha-viour or the inherent rightness of promise-keeping, were assumed to be beyond question and applied in particular legal cases without any regard to the misery which might thereby be caused. Bentham came to the conclusion that belief in the intuition of moral truths occasions either despotism or anarchy. Despotism, if any man's intuitions are represented as binding upon others; anarchy, if they are deemed to be binding only upon the man himself. Bentham dismissed all intuitionist expressions for conscience or its deli-verances—such as 'moral sense', 'the understanding', 'eternal and immutable rules of right', 'a law of nature'—as empty phrases, mere contrivances for evading the obligation to provide a single, external, scientifically objective standard of morality.

Bentham's philosophy, which reduced all human motivation to self-love or sympathy, was, however, too simplistic for Mill.[16] In his essay *Bentham*, he said of his mentor, 'Nothing is more curious than the absence of recognition in any of his writings of the existence of conscience, as a thing distinct from philanthropy, from affection for God or man and from self-interest in this world or the next.' Mill loyally distinguished in his teacher between the writer and the man. Bentham the man was guided all his life by a conscientious love of justice. But Bentham the writer was 'one-eyed'. He took the only thing desirable for its own sake to be the general happiness and he equated all disinterested feelings which he found in himself with a desire for it. He knew little or nothing of moral anguish. Emotionally, he was 'a boy to the last', said Mill. And so he overlooked what Mill called 'the great fact in human nature' that man is 'a being capable ... of desiring, for its own sake, the conformity of his own character to his standard of excellence without hope of good or fear of evil from other source than his own inward consciousness'. Conscience, according to Mill's *Utilitarianism*[17] is a fact 'proved by experience'. He described it in these terms, 'A mass of feeling which must be broken through in order to do what violates our standard of right, and which, if we do nevertheless violate that standard, will probably have to be encountered afterwards in the form of remorse.' There is, of course, a most important difference between what Bentham denied and what Mill affirmed, concerning conscience. Bentham's denial was epistemological: we do not *know* moral truths by intuition. Mill's affirmation was psychological: we do have *feelings* of moral approbation or disapprobation. It should be borne in mind that intuitionism is an *epistemological* theory. Mill's acknowledgement of conscience as a psychological fact did not make him any more of an intuitionist than Bentham.[18]

The external, objective, scientific, standard of morality, which Bentham and Mill said that intuitionism lacked, they thought to supply in their principle of utility. Bentham defined it in these terms,

By the principle of utility is meant that principle which approves or disapproves of every action whatsoever, according to the tendency which it appears to have to augment or diminish the happiness of the party whose interest is in question: or, what is the same thing in other words, to promote or to oppose that happiness. I say of every action whatsoever; and therefore not only of every action of a private individual, but of every measure of government.[19]

And Mill, in these,

> The creed which accepts as the foundation of morals Utility, or the Greatest Happiness Principle, holds that actions are right in proportion as they tend to promote happiness, wrong as they tend to promote the reverse of happiness. By happiness is intended pleasure, and the absence of pain; by unhappiness, pain, and the privation of pleasure.[20]

They did not invent this principle. Bentham acknowledged that he got it from Helvétius[21] and Mill claimed that there had been utilitarians in all ages.[22] For both Bentham and Mill 'happiness' meant pleasure and the absence of pain. Their utility principle laid it down that, if an action brings about in sum more pleasure than pain, its moral value is positive; if more pain than pleasure, negative; and if an equal quantity of both, neutral.[23] Instead of consulting a mysterious faculty of intuition, therefore, all we have to do, in order to decide whether an action is right or wrong, is to observe its pleasurable and painful consequences and compare them with those of other possible actions. Bentham and Mill were at one in their hedonic consequentialism but they had somewhat differing ideas about the nature of pleasure and pain. Bentham said that pleasures (and pains) are homogeneous. They differ from one another only *quantitatively*, 'a quantity of pleasure being equal, pushpin is as good as poetry'. Mill, on the other hand, denies that either pleasures or pains are homogeneous. They differ from one another in *quality* as well as quantity, it is 'better to be Socrates dissatisfied than a fool satisfied'.[24]

Bentham's view was that pleasures and pains can be measured objectively against one another along certain 'dimensions of value'. He listed seven of these.[25] They were, (i) the *intensity* of the sensation; (ii) its *duration*; (iii) the *certainty* or otherwise that it will occur; (iv) its *propinquity*, or how soon it will occur. These four dimensions belong to pleasures or pains, considered by themselves. We must also take account of two more, (v) *fecundity*, i.e. the chances of a pleasure or pain being followed by other sensations of the same kind; and (vi) *purity*, i.e. the chances of it being followed by sensations of the opposite kind. Bentham said that the two latter are not, strictly speaking, dimensions of pleasures or pains themselves but of the actions which cause them. He added a final dimension, (vii) *extent*, i.e. the number of people who experience the sensation. The problem, which Bentham does not solve, is how these dimensions of value are to be broken down into common units so that they can be measured against each other. Spatial dimensions, of length, width, height, depth, can all be broken down into common units of measurement, viz. inches, centimetres or whatever, and so the sizes of two objects, which are respectively, say, $5'' \times 4'' \times 2''$ and $6'' \times 5'' \times 3''$ can be computed and compared. But, whilst each of Bentham's seven dimensions could no doubt be divided into its own appropriate units of measurement, there are no units which are common to all seven. If a pleasure has, say, 4 degrees of intensity, 3 of duration, 2 of certainty and 1 of propinquity, how can we tell whether it is quantitatively greater or less than another pleasure which has 1 degree of intensity, 2 of duration, 3 of certainty and 4 of propinquity? Some commentators think this criticism takes Bentham too literally and that all he intended by his talk of 'dimensions' was that our comparison of pleasures, or pains, will be more rational, if we take all these seven factors into account.[26]

Mill's[27] view was that it is 'quite compatible' with the utility principle to consider differences of quality, as well as quantity, between pleasures or pains. According to him, every utilitarian type of theory has, in fact, taken the pleasures of the intellect, the imagination and the conscience to be more valuable and more desirable than those of man's animal nature. How, then, are differences in quality to be measured against each other? Mill's reply is, by 'the feelings and judgement of the experienced'. More explicitly, 'Of two pleasures, if there be one to which all, or almost all, who have experience of both give a decided preference, irrespective of any feelings of moral obligation to prefer it, that is the more desirable pleasure.' He was not, however, handing all moral judgement over to an élite. He believed that there is 'a sense of dignity, which *all* human beings possess in one form or another' (italics mine). No one, he thinks, knowingly and calmly prefers the pleasures of the fool to those of the intelligent man, or of the base man to those of a man of conscience. But he adds that many people have broken down, trying to combine the two! We may have doubts about the factual truth of some of this; but the more important question for our purposes is whether the view that pleasures differ in quality is—as Mill believed—'quite compatible' with utilitarianism. Many critics have thought not.

G. E. Moore,[28] for example, contends that when Mill speaks of pleasures differing in quality, he must mean both, (i) that they all have something in common which makes it appropriate to call them 'pleasures', viz. the fact that they give pleasure; and (ii) that each of them has something individual to it, which entitles us to say that it differs from the rest, viz. the quality of the pleasure it gives. When, therefore, Mill goes on to say that some pleasures are more valuable and desirable than others because of their superior quality, there are only two ways in which this view can be sustained. One is by taking 'superior in quality' to mean having *more* of the property which is common to all pleasures. But this is a *quantitative* notion. It abandons Mill's view that pleasures differ in quality. The alternative is to dispense with the basic principle that having positive value means giving pleasure; and to recognise some things as intrinsically better than others, irrespective of the pleasure they may, or may not, give. But this is a denial of Mill's utilitarianism and, in effect, replaces the latter with a form of intuitionism. Mill[29] certainly tried to have it both ways. He wanted to admit that we desire some things—e.g. money, fame, power, virtue—for their own sakes and, at the same time, to stick to both his psychological (the only thing we *do* desire is pleasure) and ethical (the only thing we *ought* to desire is pleasure) hedonism. He tried to do this by arguing that things like money, fame, etc., from being merely a 'means to happiness' can come to be 'a principle ingredient in the individual's conception of happiness'. 'Part' of it, in fact. Such things are *both* a 'means' to the end and 'part' of that end itself! Moore dismisses this view as 'contemptible nonsense.' 'Does Mill mean to say,' asked Moore incredulously, 'that "money," these actual coins, which he admits to be desired in and for themselves, are part either of pleasure or of the absence of pain?'[30] I shall have more to say about Moore's criticism of Mill in chapter 4.

Bentham and Mill did not only think it our duty to increase happiness but to distribute it in certain ways. Mill [31] said quite clearly that we should try to distribute it as widely as possible, 'to all mankind; and not to them only, but, so far as the nature of things admits, to the whole sentient creation.' He realises, however, that in the great majority of cases what any individual does will affect only a limited number of people. Bentham's opinion is less clear. Three different views of his opinion about how we should distribute happiness have been taken, viz. the 'universalistic', 'parochial' and 'differential'.[32] According to the 'universalistic', he thought, like Mill, that we should take into account the pleasure or pain of all those affected by what we do, whether humans or animals. On the 'parochial' interpretation, he held that we ought to consider only members of our own political community. The 'differential' interpretation varies from the others in two respects. First, whereas they take the crucial thing in ethics to be the fact that people *can be affected* by what we do, this third interpretation takes the crux of the matter to be the fact that we *can direct* what people do. Bentham certainly talked of such direction in connection with ethics. He said that ethics 'at large' can be defined as 'the art of directing men's actions to the production of the greatest possible quantity of happiness, on the part of those whose interest is in view'.[33] The second difference explains why this interpretation is described as 'differential'. It differentiates two kinds of actions which we can direct, namely, our own and those of others; and two sorts of interests which we may have in view, again our own and those of others. So, on this third interpretation, there are two ways in either of which an action can be right: namely, because in it the agent directs his own activity to his own greatest happiness as a particular individual; or because by means of it he directs the actions of other people to their greatest happiness. David Lyons,[34] who proposes this third interpretation, holds that *au fond* both these ways of being right come to the same thing: namely, that government should serve the interests of the governed. Where it is ourselves that we are governing, the interests of the governed are our *own* interests; where it is others, *their* interests. The truth is probably that Bentham during his long and voluminous literary life adopted all three of these views about the distribution of happiness, at one time or another.

The question arises as to whether the views of Bentham and Mill about our duty to distribute happiness in certain ways are consistent with either their psychological or ethical hedonism. As psychological hedonists, they both believed that the motive from which each of us acts is, in the last analysis, a desire for his own pleasure. What sense, then, is there in saying that we should increase the pleasure of others? The only possible answer is: because by so doing we can increase our own. This condition is fulfilled according to Bentham and Mill through the operation of both external and internal 'sanctions'. Bentham[35] had it that there are four external ones, viz. the physical (natural forces), the political (legal rewards and punishments), the moral (the pleasure of favourable public opinion), and the religious (God's putative judgements). All these make it in anyone's own interest to consider the interests of others. Bentham did not deny that there is also an internal 'sanction' of sympathy; he says, for instance, that rulers can sometimes find their own happiness in seeking that of their subjects.[36] But it was left to Mill to develop this idea of internal sanctions further. He identified two such.[37] The first was conscience and we have already noted his opinions about that. Mill thought there is another internal sanction which is more fundamental to human nature. He called it 'the social feelings of mankind'. These feelings constitute the desire we all have to be in unity with our fellow-creatures; they make it impossible—for most people at any rate— to show a complete disregard for other people.

Given that there are such 'sanctions'—whether external or internal—psychological hedonism can be reconciled with the view that we ought to distribute happiness in specific ways. But can *ethical* hedonism? As ethical hedonists, Bentham and Mill would have said that happiness is the *sole* good. But the distribution of happiness in any specific way—widely, equally, or whatever—is not itself happiness. A given amount of happiness is not made greater simply by being divided between two (or more) persons instead of given to just one or by being divided equally instead of unequally. The views of Bentham and Mill, that it is better to distribute happiness in certain ways than in others, seem to be plainly inconsistent with their view that happiness is the sole good. Mill tried to dismiss this criticism in a footnote.[38] He equated the principle that 'everybody has an equal right to happiness' with the principle that 'equal amounts of happiness are equally desirable, whether felt by the same or by different persons'. The latter, as he rightly said, is consistent with the doctrine that happiness is the sole good. But, of course, the two principles do not mean the same thing. The latter is negative—it does not matter how happiness is distributed so long as there is as much of it as possible. The former principle is positive—it does matter, however much happiness there may be, that it should be distributed as widely and equitably as possible. Bentham and Mill never succeeded in reconciling their insistence that pleasure should be distributed in certain ways with their ethical hedonism.

Both of them took up the question whether utilitarianism can be proved and came to the conclusion that it cannot.[39] But this did not deter them. 'That which is used to prove everything else cannot itself be proved,' said Bentham, meaning that because the utility principle is the ultimate criterion within morality of right and wrong its own rightness or wrongness cannot be established within morality. A point, which Mill also seems to have been making when he said that the general happiness principle does not admit of 'ordinary' proof because it is a 'first principle' or 'ultimate end'. Although formal proof is impossible, Bentham[40] believed that there are 'steps' which 'reconcile' a reasonable man to the utility principle, and Mill[41] that there are 'considerations' which 'determine the intellect' to accept it. These are to quote Mill's own words, 'another kind of proof'.[42] One such step is the fact that even those who explicitly reject the utility principle accept it implicitly. In support of this contention Bentham[43] claimed that, when opponents of the utility principle say that it is 'dangerous', what they mean by 'dangerous' turns out on careful analysis to be, 'not consonant to utility'. In other words, they are saying that the trouble with aiming *directly* at the general happiness is that this is not the best way of attaining it. Mill[44] in his turn pointed out that even intuitionists like Kant, when called upon to deduce actual duties from their prime principles, do so by estimating the consequences of one course of action as against others.

Another 'step' or 'consideration', to which both Bentham and Mill pointed in support of their utilitarianism, is the fact that the motive from which people normally act is a desire for their own happiness. This is said to imply—albeit in an informal way—that the general happiness is not only psychologically possible but also ethically desirable. Bentham[45] made the point by challenging those who propose any alternative to the utility principle to say 'whether there is any such thing as a motive' which one can have for conforming to it. He is confident that there is not. Mill[46] in his turn declared that the fact that each of us desires his own happiness is 'not only all the proof which the case admits of, but all which it is possible to require' in support of the utility principle. Mill's

15

argument here has seemed to some philosophers to be absurd—how can he say that because we each *desire* our *own* happiness we each *ought to desire* the happiness of *all*? But others have been more sympathetic to Mill's view as we shall see (below pp. 81 ff.).

## Whewell versus Mill

In his *Lectures on the History of Moral Philosophy in England*, of which the first edition appeared in 1852 and the second in 1862, Whewell trenchantly attacked Bentham's utilitarianism. Mill responded just as forthrightly with criticism of Whewell's intuitionism in his 'Dr. Whewell on Moral Philosophy', first published in the *Westminster Review* in 1852 and subsequently in Mill's *Dissertations and Discussions*, vol. ii. in 1859. I will mention three main criticisms of utilitarianism, delivered by Whewell, to each of which Mill replied.

1. The first criticism[47] was that we can never know that we have taken *all* the consequences of an action into account when we are passing judgement upon it. It may have an infinite number of consequences of which we are completely ignorant; and so we cannot estimate with any certainty, or even probability, whether or not it will in the end cause a greater surplus of pleasure over pain than any alternative action which was open to the agent. Given the principle of utility, this means that we can never say with confidence whether an act is right or wrong.

Mill [48] replied in two ways. First, he claimed that no one, Bentham included, ever supposed that we can calculate all the consequences of an action; but that this does not mean that there is no point in considering the consequences which we can discern. Whewell's argument, according to Mill, commits the error of proving too much. It sets out to show that morality cannot be reduced to mere prudence and ends up by implying that there is no such thing as prudence. But we all know there is. Do we not have to decide in some way or other every day of our lives what it would be prudent to do? Secondly, Mill contends that, although the consequences of individual acts may be unpredictable, those of *classes of actions* can be calculated with assurance. Take murder for instance. We may not know whether an individual murder will cause more happiness than misery. But we know full well that, if murder became widespread, this would greatly

16

increase the wretchedness of mankind. Every case of murder is an infringement of the general moral rule which forbids it. A sufficient number of such infringements would undermine this rule and open the flood-gates to misery. Suppose $x$ number of infringements are necessary to destroy the hold which this rule has upon people. Then, when we are estimating the consequences of an individual act of murder, we have to balance any happiness it may cause in isolation against $1/x$th part of the misery which it would cause, as a contributory factor to the abrogation, or at least the jeopardising, of the general moral rule against murder. Mill has no doubt that this misery will 'generally far outweigh' any happiness caused by the isolated act. He says 'generally' to allow for exceptions such as the murder of the enemy in wartime. But he adds that the exception should itself be made a general rule so that it does not shake the hold upon us of the rule against murder, in cases to which the reason for the exception does not apply.

Mill's defence of Bentham against Whewell's first criticism is effective. The two points which he makes are perfectly legitimate as a defence of Bentham for they are implicit in the latter's principle of utility. That principle (see above p. 9 speaks of judging an action 'according to the *tendency* which it *appears* to have' (italics mine) to cause happiness or misery. The word 'tendency' here points us to a *class of actions*; for to say that an act, e.g. of murder, has a tendency to effect anything means that it does so in more cases than not. And 'appears' indicates that Bentham meant us to judge by the consequences *we can discern*, not by all there are or may be.

2. Whewell's second criticism[49] was that some happiness is derived from 'moral elements' and therefore we cannot say that all morality is derived from happiness, as utilitarians like Bentham want to do. What did he mean by some happiness being derived from moral elements? Quite simply, that sometimes at least when we do a virtuous action we gain happiness from the facts that we approve of ourselves for doing it and that other virtuous men approve of us as well. The points to take in order to understand Whewell's argument here are these. First, the two kinds of approval (our own and that of others) are the logical precondition of this happiness which we feel. Secondly that, where this happiness is concerned it cannot, therefore, be said that any action can

be thought virtuous if and only if it causes happiness, because, in order to cause this kind of happiness, the action must *first* be thought virtuous. If Bentham and his followers—Whewell is contending—try to include happiness which is derived from moral elements in their felicific calculations—and what grounds could they have simply as utilitarians, for leaving it out?—then they are trapped in a vicious circle. They are maintaining in effect both that happiness is the precondition of virtue and that virtue is the precondition of happiness. Whewell accused Bentham of trying to escape from this vicious circle by attributing the moral elements in happiness to education and public opinion—'he has recourse to the dimness of childhood and to the confusion of the crowd, to conceal his defect of logic.' But there is no such hiding place. What is moral education, if not instruction in the distinction between virtue and vice? What does public opinion considered as a source of morals consist of, if not judgements as to what is virtuous or vicious? Moral education and public opinion about morality presuppose that certain actions are thought virtuous, just as much as happiness derived from moral elements does. Bentham is caught again in the same vicious circle—presupposing what he purports to be deriving. There he must stay, argued Whewell, so long as he looks for 'a morality which does not depend on a moral basis' but merely on the natural fact that certain courses of action may cause happiness.

To this Mill's first[50] retaliatory salvo fell wide of the mark. He reproached Whewell for attributing to Bentham the view that the test of morality is the greatest happiness of the agent *himself*. But Whewell did not say that being approved (by oneself or others) is the *only* element in happiness. He merely pointed out that if happiness as such is being thought of, then this sort of happiness must not be forgotten. Mill is closer on target when he goes on to accuse Whewell of mistakenly thinking that education and public opinion were taken by Bentham to be the 'sources', i.e. tests or constituents, of morality. In reality, Bentham merely thought of them as means or 'sanctions' whereby the self-interest of the individual could be made to accord with the greatest happiness principle.

But the most interesting part of Mill's reply to Whewell's second criticism is, I think, that which concerns Bentham's own account of the origin of the moral elements in happiness. It was, said Mill, as follows. People desire their own happiness. Consequently, they like other people who promote it and dislike those who endanger it. In due course, each of us becomes aware of himself as liked or disliked by other people. It gives us satisfaction to be liked, and dissatisfaction to be disliked. Our specifically moral feelings of being worthy of moral approval or disapproval—feelings like guilt or remorse, integrity or virtuousness—'naturally arise' from these feelings of being liked or disliked by other people. But how? That is a question of metaphysics, not ethics, said Mill dismissively. Bentham, he tells us, was not interested in it. He recognised that there are moral feelings and prescribed that they should be trained to approve only of utility, but he did not trouble himself with the question of how they are related to our other feelings. And so, Whewell's doubts about how a Benthamite can account for the 'moral elements' in happiness are misconceived, said Mill; 'Dr. Whewell's attempt to find anything illogical or incoherent in this theory (i.e. Bentham's), only proves that he does not yet understand it.' But never was a short way with criticism less appropriately taken! So far from failing to understand Bentham, Whewell had put his finger on a problem about utilitarianism which has continued to trouble philosophers down to this day. How can utilitarians cope with the fact that *moral* feelings of satisfaction and dissatisfaction are on a different level logically from our other such feelings? Utilitarianism implies a difference of level. Other feelings of satisfaction have moral significance only *after* they have been taken into a felicific calculation of consequences; but these *moral* feelings must (logically) have moral significance *before* they are taken up into any such calculation. We shall find that a version of this problem was still troubling one of Whewell's successors in the chair of moral philosophy at Cambridge as recently as 1973 (see below p. 180.

3. Whewell's third criticism[51] is an attempt at *reductio ad absurdum*. As we saw above, Bentham and Mill extended the utility principle to include all sentient beings. Whewell is ready enough to agree that we should not be cruel to animals. They are 'objects of morality' in that sense. But any duties we may have to them are 'on a very different footing in morality' from those we have to our fellow men. He points out that if the utility principle is extended to animals as well as men, it could on occasion be 'our

duty to increase the pleasures of pigs or of geese rather than those of men, if we were sure that the pleasure we could give *them* were greater than the pleasures of men'. Bentham had indeed accepted this implication without demur and Whewell quotes him to that effect. But, as Whewell remarks contemptuously, most persons would consider it 'not a tolerable doctrine that we may sacrifice the happiness of men, provided we can in that way produce an overplus of pleasure to cats, dogs and hogs, not to say lice and fleas.' He holds that 'there is a tie which binds together all human beings, quite different from that which binds them to cats and dogs . . .' Morality must be conceived as an aspect of man's 'human capacity' not his 'mere animal condition'.

Mill[52] hit back hard. He describes as 'noble' Bentham's defence of the rights of animals to have their pleasures and pains compared on an equal footing with those of men. Contemptuous in turn, he accuses Whewell of extending to animals those 'superstitions of selfishness', which once made most people think that the happiness of white men is more important than that of slaves, or of feudal lords than that of serfs. Indignantly, he asserts that he is willing to stake his whole defence of utilitarianism against Whewell's intuitionist attack on this one issue, 'Granted that any practice causes more pain to animals than it gives pleasure to man, is that practice moral or immoral?' 'And,' he asseverates, 'if, exactly in proportion as human beings raise their heads out of the slough of selfishness, they do not with one voice answer "immoral", let the morality of the principle of utility be for ever condemned.' Mill, I suppose, would have taken it to be a necessary truth that if they do not answer as he supposes, this shows that they are still in the slough of selfishness. But was he entitled to?

Notice one highly significant difference between the words of Whewell and of Mill at this point. It is a difference, I think, which shows that Mill was mistaken in thinking that he had effectively disposed of Whewell's criticism. Whewell spoke of increasing the *pleasure* of animals rather than the *pleasure* of men; whereas Mill spoke of causing more *pain* to animals than *pleasure* to men. This being so, it is possible to agree with Mill without disagreeing with Whewell. Most people would agree, I think, that if bloodsports, circuses, etc. cause considerable *pain* to animals, it is wrong to hold them just in order to give human beings the *pleasure* of a day's hunting or an evening's entertainment. But they would surely also agree that if we have to choose between giving *pleasure* to animals and *pleasure* to human beings, the latter is the more important. Suppose, for instance, that there were just enough milk to save the lives of either a baby or of three puppies. Would anyone think it right to save the lives of the puppies rather than that of the baby, even if it could be known that, in sum, they would enjoy more pleasure during the rest of their lives than the baby would have done? If anyone does think so, I, like Whewell, would consider him morally blind.

---

1. For a fuller account of this controversy see my 'Ethical Intuitionism' in *New Studies in Ethics* volume 1, edited by W. D. Hudson, London, 1974; and also my *Reason and Right*, London, 1970, pp. 13–18.
2. *Dissertation upon the Nature of Virtue* in L. A. Selby-Bigge, *British Moralists*, 249, italics mine.
3. *Essays on the Powers of Man*, volume III, Essay iii, parts iii and iv.
4. Op. cit., III. iii, parts iii and viii.
5. *Sermons* II, Selby-Bigge, op. cit., 219.
6. *Elements of Morality, including Polity*, first edition, paras. 65–77.
7. *An Inquiry Concerning Moral Good and Evil*, III. viii, Selby-Bigge, op. cit., 121.
8. *Dissertation*, Selby-Bigge, op. cit., 249.
9. *A Discourse Concerning the Being and Attributes of God and Obligations of Natural Religion*, I. 4, Selby-Bigge, op. cit., 498–505.
10. *Review of the Principal Questions and Difficulties in Morals*, chapter VII. See my *Reason and Right*, pp. 102–16.
11. Op. cit., III, v. 1.
12. Op. cit., 1–24, 35–55, 65, 80, 82, 233, 366, 105. Cf. also Whewell's *Novum Organum Renovatum*, third edition, London, 1858, and *On the Philosophy of Discovery*, London, 1860.
13. See 'Dr. Whewell on Moral Philosophy' in *Dissertations and Discussions*, volume II, London, 1867, pp. 494ff.
14. *Moral and Political Philosophy*, I. vi.
15. Bowring, *Bentham's Works*, Edinburgh, 1843, volume X, p. 37.
16. Cf. Mill's essay *Bentham*, first published 1838 in the *Westminster Review*, reprinted with revisions in Mill's *Dissertations and Discussions*, volume I; and more recently in B. Parekh's collection, *Jeremy Bentham; Ten Critical Essays*, London, 1974, pp. 16–18.
17. Op. cit., Everyman edition, London, 1910, pp. 26–7.
18. Cf. Mill's *Autobiography*, edited by J. Stillinger, London, 1971, pp. 134–5.
19. *An Introduction to the Principles of Morals and Legislation*, (1789) I. ii,.
20. Op. cit., p. 6.

21. See his *A Fragment of Government*, I. xxxvi, note n.
22. Essay on *Bentham*, op. cit., p. 10.
23. Cf. G. E. Moore, *Ethics*, London, 1947, pp. 40–2 and A. J. Ayer, *Philosophical Essays*, London, 1954, p. 256.
24. See Bentham, *Introduction* VI. vi. note; and Mill, op. cit., pp. 9–10.
25. Op. cit., IV. ii.
26. Cf. A. Quinton, 'Utilitarian Ethics' in *New Studies in Ethics*, volume 2, edited by W. D. Hudson, London,, 1974, pp. 35–6.
27. Op. cit., pp. 7–10.
28. *Principia Ethica*, Cambridge, 1903, pp. 78–9.
29. Op. cit., pp. 33–5.
30. Op. cit., pp. 71–2. I think there is some ambiguity in the explanation which Mill gave of what he had in mind (see op. cit., p. 35). First he speaks in this way, 'things originally indifferent but conducive to, or otherwise associated with, the satisfaction of our primitive desires, become in themselves sources of pleasure more valuable than the primitive pleasures, both in permanency ... and even in intensity.' This would appear to mean (for example) that we desire money initially in order to buy food; that is, as a means at one remove to the primitive pleasure which eating gives us. But then money comes to be desired for its own sake because we find that we get more pleasure, measured by the dimensions of intensity and duration, from the possession of money than we do from eating food. This line of thought would be quite consistent with the views that pleasure is the only thing which we desire for its own sake and that pleasures can be quantitatively compared. A line or two lower down, however, we find Mill speaking in this way, 'Whatever is desired otherwise than as a means to some end beyond itself, and ultimately to happiness, is desired as itself a part of happiness and is not desired for itself until it has become so.' Here the line of thought is not simply that money may give us more pleasure than food, but that it is itself *part* of pleasure—'a principal ingredient in the individual's *conception* of happiness'. It was this latter line of thought which Moore described as 'contemptible nonsense'.
31. Op. cit., pp. 11 and 17.
32. D. Lyons, *In the Interest of the Governed*, Oxford, 1973.
33. Op. cit., XVII. ii.
34. Op. cit., p. 20.
35. Op. cit., III.
36. *Constitutional Code*, introduction.
37. Op. cit., pp. 26–32.
38. Op. cit., p. 58n.
39. Bentham, op. cit. I. xi; Mill, op. cit., p. 32.
40. Op. cit., I. xiv.
41. Op. cit., p. 4.
42. Ibid.
43. Op. cit., I. xiii.
44. Op. cit. p. 4.
45. Op. cit., I. xiv.

46. Op. cit., pp. 32–3.
47. Op. cit., pp. 210–14, reprinted in Parekh, op. cit., pp. 42–5.
48. Op. cit., pp. 473–8.
49. Op. cit., pp. 215–23, reprinted in Parekh, op. cit., pp. 45–50.
50. Op. cit., pp. 478–82.
51. Op. cit., pp. 223–30, reprinted in Parekh, op. cit., pp. 50–55.
52. Op. cit., pp. 482–85.

2

# An attempt at reconciliation

Henry Sidgwick (1838–1900), who became professor of moral philosophy at Cambridge in 1883, explored the possibility of a rapprochement between the two conflicting schools of thought to which I referred in the last chapter. He came to the conclusion that the antithesis, commonly supposed to exist between intuitionism and utilitarianism can be 'transcended', or 'discarded'.[1] Not only are these two schools of thought compatible with one another, but they need each other both logically and practically. Sidgwick's arguments to this effect are deployed in his book *The Methods of Ethics*, which was first published in 1874 and ran into seven editions during the next twenty years. It was described by C. D. Broad in 1930 as 'the best treatise on moral theory that has ever been written'.[2] No doubt that was exaggerated praise but there is no denying the book's significance. It served as, so to speak, a watershed between past and future moral philosophy. Sidgwick wanted to show how some of the main lines of thought which had been followed by writers on ethics during the previous two centuries were related to one another; and, in attempting to do this he raised many of the questions which were to preoccupy moral philosophers during the next hundred years.

*What is moral judgement?*

*The Methods of Ethics* begins with some discussion of the subject-matter which is common to intuitionism and utilitarianism. They both claimed to be correct theories of moral judgement. What, then, is moral judgement? I will refer briefly to three important preliminary points which Sidgwick made about it.

1. The first was that moral judgement is *sui generis*. We cannot reduce it to judgement of any other kind because morality is constituted by an unanalysable notion, i.e. one which is 'too elementary to admit of any formal definition'.[3] This is the notion which gives moral experience its unique tone and moral language its distinctive logic. The evidence which Sidgwick adduced for its indefinability was partly psychological, partly linguistic.

He claimed, on the one hand, that introspection discovers moral feelings to be quite different from those of any other kind. Take, for example, 'the sentiment of veracity'.[4] When people, who are normally convinced that they should tell the truth, decide that it is permissible to lie in unusual circumstances, they will probably still feel some repugnance towards doing so. But this aversion is 'a feeling quite different in kind and degree'[5] from that which they normally have towards telling lies. No doubt there is a psychological difference between the two sorts of aversion, as Sidgwick said. But this does not prove that morality is constituted by a *sui generis* notion. All it shows is that there are different sorts of aversion.

Sidgwick was on firmer ground when he turned from psychological to linguistic argument. What he had to say comes to this. Suppose 'ought' is defined as 'bound under penalties'. That may serve well enough as a definition of legal obligation, the penalties being fines, imprisonment, etc. But not of moral obligation. As Sidgwick put it, 'it is ... evident that what we mean when we say that a man is "morally though not legally bound" to do a thing is not merely that he "will be punished by public opinion if he does not".'[6] He backed up this claim in three ways. We can say that someone ought to be punished by public opinion if he fails to do something; but this is not tautological, as it would be if 'ought' meant 'will be punished by public opinion if he does not'. Again, we can say that someone ought to do something, even though we know that he will *not* be punished by public opinion if he fails to do it; but this is not self-contradictory, as it would be if the definition just referred to were correct. Yet again, we may ask whether the failure to do something, which we know will be punished by public opinion, ought to be so punished; but that is not a self-answering question, as it would be if the said definition were acceptable. On these grounds the words 'will be punished by public opinion if he does not' are obviously inadequate as a definition of the moral 'ought'. Are we then to conclude that we must look for a definition which is more suitable? No. Sidgwick's point was that *whatever* is proposed in non-moral terms as a definition of the moral 'ought', it will be open to exactly similar objections. We will always be able to say something which would be tautologous, self-contradictory, or self-answering, *if* the definition were correct, but which is, as a matter of linguistic usage, none of these things. Sidgwick made substantially the same point about 'good'. If it is defined as 'happiness', then the utilitarian doctrine that happiness is good becomes 'a mere tautology'.[7] But that doctrine is not so regarded, either by those who subscribe to it or those who do not. Obviously, then, the two expressions—'good' and 'happiness'—do not have the same meaning, however close their denotations.

It may be felt—as it was by Broad[8]—that this linguistic argument of Sidgwick's confuses analytical and tautological propositions. If the correct analysis of a term $T$ is $A$, and if people have used $T$ in the main correctly without knowing this, then to tell them that the correct analysis of $T$ is $A$ will be analytical, but not tautological. (E.g. 'The correct analysis of "good" is happiness,' would not in such circumstances be a tautology.) True. But if $A$ is the correct analysis of $T$, the proposition that whatever is $A$ is $T$ must mean that whatever is $A$ is $A$. And that *is* a tautology. (E.g. If the correct analysis of 'good' is happiness, then 'Happiness is good' means 'Happiness is happiness.') Now, I take Sidgwick's point to have been as follows. Whatever analysis, $A$, is proposed for a moral term, $MT$, the proposition 'Whatever is $A$ is $MT$', which should be tautologous, will turn out not to be and therefore this analysis will be incorrect. Broad's objection does not, I think, impugn that point. I return to this matter below (p. 77). At the moment it suffices to remark in passing that Sidgwick's linguistic arguments were to some extent anticipated by earlier intuitionists; and to note that they reappear in G. E. Moore (see chapter 4) with considerable effect upon the course of modern ethical theory.

2. Sidgwick contended that the faculty of moral judgement is

reason. Although he professed not to be greatly interested[9] in the controversy about the nature of the moral faculty which had divided philosophers for two centuries,[10] he came down firmly on the side of reason rather than sense. In support of this decision he made two points about moral judgements. One, that they are 'cognitions'[11] or 'propositions'.[12] The other, that they refer to objective reality, not simply subjective feeling. Once again he called both psychological experience and linguistic usage to witness.

Moral feelings, he said, are feelings that conduct is ' "really" right—i.e. that it cannot without error be disapproved by any other mind'.[13] His point was to this effect. Suppose you think sago pudding nice and I think it nasty. Neither of us will feel that it is *really* the one or the other. We shall simply feel what is between us as a difference of taste. But if I think that we ought to tell the truth, and you that we ought not, then we shall both feel that the other is *in error*. What is between us now will have the *feel* of an issue of truth or falsity, rather than a difference of taste. This was the kind of thing Sidgwick had in mind when he wrote, '... it is an essential characteristic of a moral feeling that it is bound up with an apparent cognition of something more than mere feeling.'[14]

Turning to linguistic usage, he pointed out that, in moral discourse, judgements are not normally taken to state subjective feelings. If someone says, 'The truth ought to be told,' and someone else replies, 'It ought not,' they will be taken to have contradicted one another. But this is not consistent with interpreting their judgements as statements of subjective feeling. If one person says that he has a subjective feeling of approval for truth speaking and another that he has not, they will not be contradicting one another. Both their statements could be true. We must therefore conclude that in ordinary use moral judgements are not merely statements of subjective feeling. This is what was evidently in Sidgwick's mind when he wrote, '... it is absurd to say that a mere statement of my approbation of truth-speaking is properly given in the proposition "Truth ought to be spoken"; otherwise the fact of another man's disapprobation might equally be expressed by "Truth ought not to be spoken"; and thus we should have two co-existent facts stated in two mutually contradictory propositions.'[15]

Here again, Sidgwick's arguments, psychological or logical,

echoed earlier ones which rational intuitionists had used. They also pointed forward to the controversy which was yet to come between emotivists and their critics, though Sidgwick did not draw the distinction as clearly as later philosophers between stating that one has a feeling and expressing it. However, he was aware that if moral judgements are conceived to be propositions, the question arises as to how they acquire their action-guiding character. To say that something *is the case*, whether truly or falsely, is different from recommending that anything *should be done*. And moral judgement is nothing if not practical in intention.

3. This then, was the third point which Sidgwick made about moral judgement—it is essentially practical. What he had to say on this subject is reminiscent of those classical philosophers who emphasised the magisterial or imperative nature of moral judgements, like Butler, Kant or Whewell,[16] and it foreshadows, in some degree, the imperativist and prescriptivist conceptions of morality, which are to be found in such later authors as R. Carnap or R. M. Hare.[17] Here, as elsewhere, Sidgwick is thinking at times of psychological processes, at others of linguistic usage.

On the former count, for instance, he said that by means of moral judgement reason controls the other two morally significant elements in human nature, namely sentience and activity.[18] Moral 'cognitions' give rational agents 'an impulse or motive to action',[19] though not always a predominant one. The relation of reason to the non-rational impulses and inclinations in human nature is a matter of 'imperatives', 'dictates', 'precepts'.[20] It is like that 'between the will of a superior and the wills of his subordinates.'[21] Psychological conflict is here in mind.

But turning more explicitly to linguistic considerations, Sidgwick spoke of 'good' as meaning what a completely rational being would *desire*[22] and of 'right' (and 'ought') as indicating what such a being would *do*.[23] He did not think that judgements in terms of 'good' and 'right' (or 'ought') entail imperatives with the same degree of definiteness as each other. To say that conduct is 'good' 'does not involve a definite precept to perform it'.[24] The reasons given for this are that when we judge conduct to be good, we leave open the question whether it is the greatest good we can obtain under the given circumstances; and we do not take it for granted that it is conduct which we can in fact perform. In the case of 'right' (and 'ought'), on the other hand, Sidgwick thought the implied imperative quite definite.[25] Presumably, he supposed that, whenever we judge an action to be 'right' (or such as 'ought' to be done) we express the conviction that it is the most complete performance of our duty of which we can conceive in the given situation, and the belief that in fact we are able to do it.

I can see that there is something in this distinction. If 'good' means 'such as a rational being would desire', then we must bear in mind that people cannot *desire* things at will as they can (often at any rate) *do* things at will. And this, no doubt, is why we say that supererogatory virtue is *good* but do not say that we *ought* to practise it. Nevertheless, I think Sidgwick overdid the distinction between 'good' and 'right' (or 'ought'). If we call something 'good' we (sometimes at least) imply an imperative to *seek* to desire it. Although desire itself cannot be produced at will, the means of quickening it sometimes can. Two questions will settle the matter. Would it not be just as logically odd to say, 'I think this is good but I don't intend to seek to desire it,' as to say, 'I think this is right (or such as ought to be done) but I don't intend to do it'? Conversely, when we are judging what it is our duty to do in a given situation, may we not speak of various courses of action as all *prima facie* right[26] (or such as *ought* to be done) whilst leaving open the question which of them in particular it is our duty to do? If the answer to both questions is yes, then Sidgwick does draw too sharp a distinction between 'good' and 'right' (or 'ought').

In the case of each of these three points about moral judgement, the 'watershed' character of *The Methods of Ethics* is apparent. Its author was drawing on the work of his predecessors, but he was also bringing into focus the problems which his successors in moral philosophy attempted to solve.

### Methods of Ethics

Sidgwick regarded scientific thinking as the paradigm of reasoning. He wished to find out whether moral thinking could be as precise and fruitful as scientific. The most important feature of scientific thinking seemed to him to be its generally agreed method of procedure and he wondered whether something of the same kind could exist in ethics. This explains his interest in what he called the methods of ethics. Such a method, he said, is, 'any rational procedure by which we determine what individual human beings "ought"—or what it is "right" for them—to do, or to seek to realise by voluntary action.'[27] The nearest thing to an agreed procedure in morals was the appeal to common sense morality. Sidgwick described such morality as 'a body of moral truth, warranted to be such by the *consensus* of mankind—or at least of that portion of mankind which combines adequate intellectual enlightenment with a serious concern for morality'.[28] British moral philosophers in his day, whatever their school of thought, tended to appeal to common sense morality in support of their opinions.[29] Here, then, was the obvious place to start. So Sidgwick set out to analyse and refine the morality of common sense.

Implicit within it, he found, not one method, but three. They were intuitionism, egoistic hedonism, and universalistic hedonism (or utilitarianism). At the beginning of *The Methods of Ethics* he describes his aim as that of expounding these three methods, pointing out their mutual relations and, where they seem to conflict, defining what is at issue between them as clearly as possible—all this, in the hope that the three methods 'may ultimately coincide[30] and provide an agreed procedure for ethical enquiry. Sidgwick came to the conclusion that intuitionism and utilitarianism are complementary to each other on both practical and logical grounds. But he found egoistic hedonism less easy to harmonise with either.

### Sidgwick on Intuitionism

There are, according to Sidgwick, three distinguishable conceptions, or 'phases', of intuitionism, namely, the 'perceptional', the 'dogmatic' and the 'philosophical'.[31] The first is that of 'simple immediate intuitions'. These are not always consistent with one another, as between man and man or even within the conscience of the same individual at different times. The content of 'dogmatic intuitionism' is by contrast, 'certain general rules'. These rules are what Sidgwick had in mind when he spoke of 'the morality of common sense'. Thirdly, there is 'philosophical intuitionism', which accepts common sense morality as 'in the main sound' but looks for 'some deeper explanation *why* it is so'. This explanation, said Sidgwick, will be provided when one or more 'absolutely and undeniably true and evident' principles of conduct are discovered, from which common sense morality can be deduced, if not just as it is, then with 'slight modifications and rectifications'.

So the important question is: what are the necessary conditions which a principle of conduct must fulfil in order to be clearly and distinctly self-evident? Sidgwick listed four.[32] First, the terms of the principle 'must be clear and precise': we must be sure that we know exactly what is meant by it. Then again, its self-evidence 'must be ascertained by careful reflection': we must be on our guard against mistaking merely long-standing or deeply-felt beliefs for intuitions. Yet again, it 'must be mutually consistent' with all other principles which we take to be self-evident: when two statements are contrary or contradictory they cannot both be self-evidently true. Lastly, a self-evident principle must gain ' "universal" or "general" consent': because truth is the same for all minds, it follows according to Sidgwick that if many people dissent from a principle, this creates a strong presumption (though not of course a proof) that it lacks self-evidence. Here, as so often, Sidgwick places psychological and logical considerations alongside each other indiscriminately. The first and third conditions are logical; the second, psychological, and the fourth, a mixture.

He examined the main principles of common sense morality exhaustively in order to discover whether any of them fulfil these four conditions.[33] Included in the list of duties through which he worked were: wise action, self-control, benevolence, justice, promise-keeping, veracity, sexual purity, liberality, courage and humility. His penetrating and painstaking discussion of all these elements in 'dogmatic intuitionism' was a considerable *tour de force*, but they all fell short of self-evidence when judged by his criteria. Even promise-keeping, which so many moralists have taken to be a paradigm case of self-evident moral obligation, does not meet any of the conditions of self-evidence completely. As an example of Sidgwick's exhaustive style of inquiry, take this passage,

If we ask (e.g.) how far our promise is binding if it was made in consequence of false statements, on which, however, it was not understood to be conditional; or if important circumstances were concealed, or we were in any way led to believe that the consequences of keeping the promise would be different from what they turn out to be; or if the promise was given under compulsion; or if circumstances have materially altered since it was given, and we find that the results of fulfilling it will be different from what we foresaw when we promised; or even if it be only our knowledge of consequences which has altered, and we now see that fulfilment will entail on us a sacrifice out of proportion to the benefit received by the promisee; or perhaps see that it will even be injurious to him though he may not think so;—different conscientious persons would answer these and other questions (both generally and in particular cases) in different ways: and though we could perhaps obtain a decided majority for some of these qualifications and against others, there would not in any case be a clear *consensus* either way.[34]

To recall the four conditions listed just now, these questions reveal the difficulties of, (i) saying precisely what promise-keeping means; (ii) being sure that we do think it self-evident; (iii) reconciling it with other seemingly self-evident duties such as benevolence; and (iv) finding instances of it which would be regarded by people in general as self-evident obligations.

A random sample of the questions which Sidgwick raised in his critique of common sense morality could include: Is it always right to act wisely?, How are family loyalties to be reconciled with wider social obligations?, When is it just to break the law?, Are there any natural rights?, Is there any unifying conception of sexual purity running through all the different ideas of it which have been held?, and so on. At the end of it all, he wrote, 'The morality of common sense may still be perfectly adequate to give practical guidance to common people in common circumstances: but the attempt to elevate it into a system of intuitional ethics brings its inevitable imperfections into prominence without helping us to remove them.'[35]

Must we leave things there? Sidgwick thought not. There is a level of intuitionism, deeper than the 'dogmatic', at which 'real ethical axioms—intuitive propositions of real clearness and certainty'[36] can be discovered. As a 'philosophical' intuitionist, Sidgwick looked for what he called 'those primary intuitions of reason, by the scientific application of which the common moral thought of mankind may be at once systematised and corrected'.[37] In the preface to the sixth and seventh editions of *The Methods of Ethics*, notes for a lecture, which Sidgwick evidently intended to give on the development of his thought, are published. He had been raised on Whewell's intuitionism but had soon rejected it in favour of Mill's utilitarianism. However, Mill's way of deciding between duty and self-interest, where they conflict, struck Sidgwick as too facile. It was not self-evident to him that the general happiness should always take precedence to one's own. So he had turned for enlightenment to Kant and found himself in sympathy with the latter's maxim that we should always act on the principle which we can will to be a universal law. It threw the Golden Rule of the Gospels into a form which commended itself to Sidgwick's reason. In the manner of Aristotle, he then set himself to study common sense morality in order to discover, as he says, 'whether I had or had not a system of moral intuitions.' He came to the conclusion that there are 'certain absolute practical principles' implicit in common sense morality, 'the truth of which, when they are explicitly stated, is manifest.' They are justice, prudence and rational benevolence. But he adds that they are 'of too abstract a nature, and too universal in their scope' to tell us what we ought to do in any particular situation.[38] More than one formulation of each of these principles was given by Sidgwick and it is not certain which he would have regarded as the most precise. But J. B. Schneewind[39] is probably correct in listing the following versions as the most fundamental,

*Justice:* 'it cannot be right for *A* to treat *B* in a manner in which it would be wrong for *B* to treat *A*, merely on the ground that they are two different individuals and without there being any difference between the natures or circumstances of the two which can be stated as a reasonable ground for difference of treatment.'

*Prudence:* 'the mere difference of priority and posteriority in time is not a reasonable ground for having more regard to the consciousness of one moment than to that of another' (or in the form in which it practically presents itself to most men: 'that a smaller present good is not to be preferred to a greater future good (allowing for difference of certainty).'

Benevolence then follows from two 'rational intuitions' (BI and BII) which embody justice and prudence respectively and from which 'we may deduce, as a necessary inference, the maxim of Benevolence in an abstract form'.

*(BI):* 'The good of any one individual is of no more importance from the point of view (if I may say so) of the Universe than the good of any other.'

*(BII):* 'As a rational being I am bound to aim at good generally—so far as it is attainable by my efforts—not merely at a particular part of it.'

From these we get benevolence,

'viz. that each one is morally bound to regard the good of any other individual as much as his own, except in so far as he judges it to be less, when impartially viewed, or less certainly knowable or attainable by him.'

The apprehension of these self-evident principles—justice, prudence and rational benevolence—is said to be, 'the permanent basis of the common conviction that the fundamental precepts of morality are essentially reasonable.' Sidgwick claimed that the difference between them and any other putatively self-evident moral principles can be discerned 'by merely reflecting upon them'. This sounds like an appeal to introspection; as does Sidgwick's claim 'to know by direct reflection' that propositions such as 'I ought to speak the truth' are 'not self-evident' to him, whereas the principles of justice, prudence and benevolence 'do present themselves as self-evident' in the same way as mathematical axioms.[40] However, his main argument is a logical one, the gist of which I take to be as follows.

We have already noted[41] that, because reason is the moral faculty, an act is right if it is what a reasonable man would do and an end, good, if it is of the kind a reasonable man would desire. Now, to describe a man as reasonable is to say that he has a valid reason for whatever he does or desires. And to call anything a valid reason is to say, in effect, that it is free from two kinds of particularity. These may be called respectively the particularities of person or time, of individuality or temporality. In his axiom of *justice* Sidgwick was recognising the need to exclude the former kind of particularity from moral judgements. The mere fact that it is the *individual* Smith, rather than Jones, whom we are considering can never make what is done right or wrong. In his axiom of *prudence* Sidgwick was excluding temporal particularity: the formulation of prudence in parenthesis above indicates that the mere *time* at which an end is attained cannot by itself be a reason why that end is good. The axiom of benevolence excludes both kinds of particularity. The premise BI above explicitly prohibits that of individuality; and in BII I take the phrase 'any particular part of it' (i.e. of good) to refer to temporal (and no doubt also to spatial) particularity.

Sidgwick's insistence upon the non-particularity of moral judgements owed much to Kant, as he himself acknowledged.[42]

His 'ultimate intuitions of reason', justice, prudence and benevolence, have a lot in common with Kant's formula, 'act from a maxim which thou canst will to be a universal law.' But Sidgwick did not agree with Kant's inference that a rational man is bound to aim only at the happiness of other men. Following Butler, he thought that we have a moral obligation to aim at our own happiness, independently of our relation to others.[43] We shall consider shortly (below pp. 40–3) the problem which this opinion created for Sidgwick. Meanwhile, notice that his principles of justice, prudence and benevolence do not only recall Kant but anticipate the point which R. M. Hare was to make in his universalisability thesis (see below pp. 135 ff.). What Hare means by judgements being 'U-type' is much the same as what Sidgwick meant by them conforming to the 'primary intuitions of reason'. It is significant that Sidgwick, the Victorian, thought in terms of a moral faculty and its intuitions, whereas Hare, our contemporary, simply analyses the language of morals in order to disclose its coventions. But, that apart, both writers make much the same basic points about the need for moral judgements to be given some rational justification and about what it means for this condition to be fulfilled. The criticisms, valid or otherwise, which have been made of Hare on universalisability, and the defence against them which might be offered (see below pp. 136–40), would be equally applicable—I think on all counts—in Sidgwick's case.

The axioms of justice, prudence and benevolence were not regarded by Sidgwick as premises from which substantive moral judgements may be deduced. Like Kant's categorical imperative, or Hare's universalisability test, they constituted a criterion which a judgement must meet in order to be moral. That is the sense in which, as Sidgwick said, they 'do not specially belong to Intuitionism';[44] his point being, presumably, that everyone, whether an intuitionist or not, would have to agree that these axioms lay down logical rules to which a judgement must conform in order to be moral. In another sense, of course, he did think of them as specially belonging to intuitionism because he supposed that the only way to discover them is to press the intuitionist question— what is self-evident in morals?—as far as it will go.

I come now, to the point about intuitionism which is of major interest to us in this chapter. Why did Sidgwick think that it requires utilitarianism for both its logical and practical completion?

So far as *logical* completion is concerned, his argument, as I understand it, was to this effect.[45] Two of the 'primary intuitions of reason', namely prudence and benevolence as stated above on pp. 33–4, contain a reference to the 'good'. In order to understand these intuitions, therefore, we must know what the 'good' means. Does it mean virtue? If we give it that meaning we involve ourselves in a logical circle. Within intuitionism many of the duties which constitute what is meant by virtue, are implicitly subordinate to prudence and benevolence. So, if we define the 'good' as virtue, we are in effect saying, Practising virtue is realising the good and realising the good is practising virtue. In order to escape from this vicious circle we must abandon the idea of virtue as the 'good' and conceive of the latter as an end to which virtue is simply the means. It may therefore be said that the question with which intuitionism leaves us in the end is, what is the 'good'? It requires us to have some rationally justified conception of the 'good' other than virtue. Now it is just this on which utilitarianism claims to be based. In a moment we shall see why. But here the point is simply that it is what utilitarianism claims to supply which intuitionism needs for its logical completion.

As for *practical* completion, intuitionism's need for utilitarianism is, according to Sidgwick, apparent in the 'unconscious' or 'latent' utilitarianism of common sense morality.[46] The 'dogmatic' intuitionism of common moral reasoning is frequently supplemented in practice by utilitarian calculations. Sidgwick offered numerous examples:[47] in working out the precise mutual duties of husbands and wives or the precise circumstances in which promises should be kept, the truth spoken, and so on. People normally decide such things by 'a forecast of the effects on human happiness' of various solutions. Although utilitarianism is not the 'germinal' method by which ordinary people decide moral questions, it is the 'adult' method to which the development of common sense morality has always been tending.[48] In practice, as in logic, intuitionism is incomplete without utilitarianism.

## Sidgwick on Utilitarianism

Although Sidgwick complained that there were 'several distinct theories', all called utilitarianism in his day, there is nothing unusual in his own definition of it, 'By Utilitarianism is here meant the ethical theory, that the conduct which, under any given circumstances is objectively right, is that which will produce the greatest amount of happiness on the whole; that is, taking into account all whose happiness is affected by the conduct.'[49]

Such a definition may, of course, be interpreted in different ways but Sidgwick gave it much the same meaning as Bentham would have done.[50] Like him, he took happiness to mean the greatest possible surplus of pleasure over pain. All pleasures or pains, he seemed to think, can—roughly at least—be quantitatively compared according to Bentham's 'dimensions'. By 'all whose happiness is affected' he meant, as Bentham did, all sentient creatures and not just all humans.

Sidgwick realised that two important questions can be asked. We may call them the questions of 'happiness distribution' and of 'the as yet unborn' respectively. Do all persons have an equal right to happiness? And, ought those as yet unborn to count equally with those who already exist when we are calculating felicific consequences? To both Sidgwick answered in the affirmative. He accepted Bentham's principle of equity as settling the former. And in reply to the latter, he pointed out that his definition of utilitarianism refers to 'happiness on the whole', not simply that of existing individuals. He realised that this latter reply does not settle the matter. The further question may be raised—with respect to 'happiness on the whole'—whether it means that of the whole constituted only by existing individuals or also by those who are as yet unborn. Does utilitarianism require us to increase the size of the population in ways which will decrease the happiness of each individual, if this results in a greater sum total of happiness? Sidgwick evidently thought not. But he did not take the view which is popular nowadays, that a utilitarian should simply maximise the happiness of those who are already alive. This is the view, for example, of parents who justify an abortion on the ground that it will enable them to give their existing children a better chance in life. Sidgwick's view was that, provided the average happiness of individuals is not diminished, utilitarianism requires us to increase the number of individuals in the world so as to make the sum of happiness greater.[51] If we ask what in Sidgwick's eyes justified the answers he gave to the questions of 'happiness distribution' and 'the as yet unborn', we are back with his principles of justice and prudence.[52] The former, it will be recalled, excludes the particularity of individuality and the latter, that of temporality. Here, then, the basic insights of intuitionism are required for the logical completion of utilitarianism. I will have more to say about this in a moment.

First, I want to point out why Sidgwick thought utilitarians are justified in their view that happiness is the good.[53] He thought it inconceivable that the ultimate end of rational action—and so of virtue—should be merely the preservation of physical life, rather than the production of a certain state, or states, of consciousness. But not just any such state or states! There are desirable ones and undesirable. By 'desirable' he meant such as a reasonable man would desire and by 'undesirable', such as he would not. Is pleasure, then, the only desirable state of consciousness? What of the cognition of truth, the contemplation of beauty, the will to freedom or virtue?—are not such states of consciousness desirable on grounds other than their mere pleasurableness? Sidgwick was prepared to concede that they may appear to be so; but he said that this was because they are valued for the pleasurableness of their future effects on consciousness or the relationships with other persons or things in which they involve us.[54] Such pleasurableness is different from immediate present pleasure, but it is pleasure none the less. He appealed for support to common sense morality. Roughly speaking it commends truth, beauty, freedom or virtue only in proportion as they produce pleasure. True, we also find in common sense morality 'an aversion to admit happiness ... to be the sole and ultimate end and standard of right conduct' but this is only because the word 'pleasure' in ordinary use suggests the coarser pleasures, because human beings in practice tend to experience less pleasure if they are preoccupied with a desire for it, and for other such reasons. There is no aversion to happiness in a rounded sense. It is—and is recognised by common sense morality to be—the ultimate good.

I return now to the question of why utilitarianism requires intuitionism for its logical completion. Sidgwick was no doubt familiar with the hostile criticism of utilitarianism which had proliferated in the years immediately following Mill's publication of his definitive views on the subject in *Fraser's Magazine* for 1861. W. E. H. Lecky's *History of European Morals* came out in 1861 and John Grote's *Examination of Utilitarian Philosophy* in the following year. The criticisms in these and other such works, which Sidgwick would know about, are usefully summarised by J. B. Schneewind.[55] They include condemnations of Mill for defining 'right' in naturalistic terms, for comitting the fallacies of equivocation and composition, for inconsistently introducing the idea of different qualities of pleasure, etc. We shall see below (pp. 85ff.) that in recent times Mill has been defended against these criticisms but Sidgwick evidently concurred in them. In *The Methods of Ethics* he echoed, in particular, the accusation that Mill committed the fallacy of composition. It was just here, thought Sidgwick, that Mill had revealed the logical 'gap' in utilitarianism, which only intuitionism can fill.[56] It is not enough to have seen that happiness is the only rational ultimate end for conscious agents. Utilitarianism's basic principle is that the *general* happiness is the good. Why this 'general'? How is the belief that we must aim at the happiness *of all* to be justified? Obviously not as Mill tried to justify it, thought Sidgwick. Mill had tried to prove that the general happiness is desirable (in the sense of '*ought* to be desired') from the fact that each person's happiness *is* desired by that person. This is inadmissible, of course, because 'ought' cannot be deduced from 'is'. But even if it could be, the so-called proof would not work because the fact that each man desires a part of the general happiness does not establish that anyone desires the general happiness.

Something better than Mill's so-called proof is needed to bridge the logical gap between the natural fact that we each desire our own happiness and the moral principle that we all ought to desire the general happiness. Until it is found, utilitarianism lacks justification. The 'gap', said Sidgwick, 'can, I think, only be filled by some such proposition as that which I have tried to exhibit as the intuition of Rational Benevolence.' This can supply the requisite logical justification of utilitarianism because, (i) being self-evident it requires no further justification itself and (ii) being a principle about what 'each one is morally bound to do', it leaves no gap between 'is' and 'ought'. Put this principle together with the fundamental doctrine that happiness is the good—the rational grounds for which we considered a moment or two ago—and utilitarianism can be validly deduced. Just as we saw that Sidgwick thought intuitionism requires utilitarianism in order to make clear what is *meant* by its primary intuitions of prudence and benevolence; so we see now that he thought utilitarianism needs intuitionism in order to *justify* its fundamental principle that the *general* happiness, and not simply happiness as such, is the good at which we ought to aim. When discussing the intuition of benevolence (see above p. 33) we saw that it rests on both justice and prudence. And a moment or two ago we noted that these intuitions are needed to decide the questions of 'happiness distribution' and of 'the as yet unborn', which eventually arise in connection with it. All three of the fundamental axioms of intuitionism are therefore needed for the logical completion of utilitarianism.

As for its *practical* completion Sidgwick evidently thought that utilitarianism needs to be embodied in the specific duties which make up 'dogmatic intuitionism', if it is to be a practical code of behaviour. His remark, 'such specialised affections as the present organisation of society normally produces afford the best means of developing in most persons a more extended benevolence to the degree that they are capable of feeling it,'[57] claims, in effect, that the ends of utilitarianism can best be achieved by fulfilling the duties, domestic and otherwise, which common sense morality enjoins. Utilitarianism as Mill remarked requires its 'secondary principles'.[58] The point is not simply that this reliance on common sense is possible but that it is necessary for utilitarians. In that sense, utilitarianism in practice needs the deposit of common sense morality which intuitionism has preserved.

## The Dualism of the Practical Reason

The three methods of ethics—intuitionism, utilitarianism and egoistic hedonism—are found more or less vaguely combined in the practical reasonings of ordinary men, according to Sidgwick.[59] In so far as the moral faculty is reason, we are entitled to expect that they will be consistent with one another. We have seen how Sidgwick showed, to his own satisfaction at least, that intuitionism and utilitarianism are complementary. But he had trouble with egoistic hedonism.

Sidgwick's mentors, Mill and Kant, both took the view that where an individual has to choose between his own and the general happiness he ought to aim at the latter. This Sidgwick could not accept. In the preface to his sixth edition he says, 'The rationality of self-regard seemed to me as undeniable as the rationality of self-sacrifice.' He tells us what a relief it was to discover that Butler had thought reasonable self-love an obligation. It was the latter's 'dualism of the governing faculty' which inspired Sidgwick to develop his own ideas about the dualism of the practical reason.

By egoistic hedonism he meant 'a system that fixes as the reasonable ultimate end of each individual's action his own greatest happiness'.[60] He said that there are at least three conceivable ways of deciding what will bring about one's own greatest happiness. The first he called the 'empirical reflective'.[61] This means deciding on the basis of one's own, or other people's past experience. We have already noted that Sidgwick thought pleasures and pains can be quantitatively measured (at least roughly) according to Bentham's 'dimensions'. But he also recognised that, because we change, our own past experience may not be a safe guide to what will give us pleasure now or in the future; and *a fortiori* because people are different they cannot rely on each others' past experience for guidance. Secondly, there is the method which Sidgwick called 'objective hedonism'.[62] Divergences in one's own, or others' experience are said to be 'neutralised', when we are guided by the 'continued experience of mankind from generation to generation'. This is what common sense morality represents. There are certain 'objects', such as health, wealth, social status, fame, power, which are approved by common sense as conditions or sources of happiness; and Sidgwick thought some account could be taken of these, though not without risk. At best, the estimates of the pleasure caused by these 'objects' will apply only to 'the average or typical human being'; and at worst, they will represent only the opinions of the 'rich and leisured'. Either way, they are likely to be misleading. Is there then, any third way? —any hope of a 'scientific hedonism'?[63] Sidgwick thinks there is very little. He considers Herbert Spencer's theory that 'pains are the correlatives of actions injurious to the organism, while pleasures are the correlatives of acts conducive to its welfare.' But this seems plainly false, if, as Spencer said, 'injurious' means destructive of one's life and 'conducive to its welfare' means life-preserving. Many very injurious activities can be pleasurable. There is no scientific short-cut to knowing what will give one the greatest happiness.

However difficult it may be to decide what will give one pleasure, Sidgwick has no doubt that it is rational for each of us to seek his own. Kant's view, that egoism cannot be willed as a universal law and is therefore irrational, he firmly rejects.[64] Provided the egoistic hedonist sticks to the opinion that his own happiness is more important *for him* than anyone else's, Sidgwick does not see how he can be refuted.[65] No principle of conduct, he says, is more widely accepted than the proposition 'that it is reasonable for a man to act in the manner most conducive to his own happiness.'[66] He notes that this proposition has been affirmed by moral philosophers as diverse in their views as Bentham, Clarke and Butler. Beyond all doubt it seems clear to him that, '"I" am concerned with the quality of my existence as an individual in a sense, fundamentally important, in which I am not concerned with the quality of the existence of other individuals.'[67] If, however, any egoistic hedonist says that his own happiness is good from the point of view of the universe—e.g. by saying that Nature has designed him to seek it—then we *can* refute him by appealing to the self-evident axiom of benevolence (cf. BI above). But so long as he simply sticks to the claim that his own happiness is the rational ultimate end *for him*, Sidgwick sees no way of refuting him. We shall have to consider whether he was right about this.

Being convinced that he was, he did not conceal the depressing dilemma in which he found himself. Reason, as the moral faculty, evidently prescribes *both* egoism and benevolence! One method of ethics shows that it is reasonable for each individual to regard his own good as more important than that of others; but another, that it is reasonable for him to regard it as of no more importance than that of others! There must, therefore, be 'an ultimate and fundamental contradiction in our apparent intuitions of what is reasonable in conduct.'[68] From which the grim conclusion follows that 'the apparently intuitive operation of the practical reason manifested in these contradictory judgements, is after all, illusory.'[69] There is no knowing what is right or wrong.

Grasping at straws, Sidgwick entertained the hypothesis that egoism and benevolence may be reconcilable because they coincide in what they demand of us.[70] As Bentham and Mill had pointed out,[71] various 'sanctions' may induce an egoist to seek the happiness of others because thereby he will maximise his own. External sanctions, like the fact that in any tolerable society ruthless self-seeking attracts legal penalties or social ostracism. Internal ones, like the fact that seeking the good of others can give us the pleasures of fellow-feeling and an easy conscience. But these sanctions do not operate rigorously. The external ones can be evaded simply by *appearing* to seek others' good. And there is ample evidence that many people derive more pleasure from self-indulgence than from sympathy with others or a sense of their own virtue.[72] A religious sanction is admittedly conceivable, but Sidgwick could not find in his own moral consciousness any clear and certain intuition that duty will be rewarded in the long run, and its dereliction punished, by God or any other agency.[73] But the important point to take in all this is that even if these 'sanctions' operated without exception, the most they could establish is a mere *contingent* fact—that egoistic and universalistic hedonism coincide in what they demand of us. They could go no way towards eliminating the *logical* incompatibility between these two forms of hedonism.

G. E. Moore,[74] Sidgwick's pupil, dismissed as 'absurd' his teacher's conclusion that an egoist—provided he sticks to the opinion that his own happiness is 'the rational, ultimate end *for himself*' (italics mine)[75]—cannot be refuted. Moore's grounds were these. In so far as *my* happiness is a rational, ultimate end it must be such for *all* rational beings. There are, therefore, only two logical possibilities. *Either* my happiness, rather than their own, is an ultimate end for all other rational beings as well as for me; *or* my happiness is part of a whole which is the ultimate end for all rational beings, myself included. Both these conclusions are inconsistent with egoism on Sidgwick's definition of it. Such is 'the fundamental contradiction of egoism' according to Moore. I shall return to Moore's moral philosophy in the next chapter but one. First, however, we must consider some other philosophers who differed from Sidgwick.

---

1. Cf. *The Methods of Ethics* preface to second edition: cf. also preface to sixth edition (both reprinted in seventh edition) and p. 496. The pagination throughout these notes is that of the seventh edition, 1907, unless otherwise stated.
2. *Five Types of Ethical Theory*, London, 1930, p. 143.
3. Op. cit., p. 32.
4. Op. cit., p. 27.
5. Op. cit., p. 28.
6. Op. cit., p. 29.

7. Op. cit., p. 109.
8. Op. cit., pp. 173–4.
9. See preface to his first edition.
10. Cf. chapter 1.
11. Op. cit., p. 34.
12. Op. cit., p. 26.
13. Op. cit., p. 27.
14. Op. cit., p. 77.
15. Op. cit., p. 27.
16. See above pp. 3, 5.
17. See below p. 126.
18. Op. cit., p. 78.
19. Op. cit., p. 34.
20. Ibid.
21. Op. cit., p. 35.
22. Op. cit., pp. 111–12.
23. Op. cit., p. 34.
24. Op. cit., p. 113.
25. Cf. op. cit., pp. 34–5
26. Below p. 97 (Ross etc.).
27. Op. cit., p. 1.
28. Op. cit., p. 215.
29. Cf. J. B. Schneewind, *Sidgwick's Ethics and Victorian Morality*, Oxford, 1977, p. 193.
30. Op. cit., p. 14.
31. Op. cit., pp. 100–2.
32. Op. cit., pp. 338–42.
33. Op. cit., pp. 199–361.
34. Op. cit., pp. 353–4.
35. Op. cit., p. 361.
36. Op. cit., p. 373.
37. Op. cit., pp. 373–4.
38. Op. cit., p. 379.
39. Op. cit., pp. 290–7: cf. *The Methods of Ethics*, pp. 380–2.
40. Op. cit., p. 383.
41. Cf. above p. 28.
42. Op. cit., pp. 389–90., and the preface to the sixth edition (in seventh edition, pp. xiv–xxi).
43. Op. cit., p. 386, and preface to sixth edition, op. cit.
44. Ibid.
45. Op. cit., pp. 391–407.
46. See op. cit., pp. 424, 435, 438.
47. See op. cit., pp. 436, 443–4, 448–9.
48. Op. cit., p. 457.
49. Op. cit., p. 411.
50. Op. cit., pp. 411–17.
51. But cf. Smart in J. J. C. Smart and B. Williams *Utilitarianism: For and Against*, Cambridge, 1973, pp. 27–8.

52. See above p. 33.
53. Op. cit., pp. 395–407.
54. Op. cit., pp. 399 and 128.
55. Op. cit., pp. 178–88.
56. Op. cit., p. 388.
57. Op. cit., p. 434.
58. *Utilitarianism*, Everyman edition, London, 1910, p. 22.
59. Op. cit., p. 496.
60. Op. cit., p. 120 in the fifth edition of *The Methods of Ethics*.
61. Op. cit., pp. 123–50.
62. Op. cit., pp. 151–61.
63. Op. cit., pp. 176–95. He calls it 'deductive' in the seventh edition but 'scientific' in some earlier editions.
64. Op. cit., pp. 386, 389–90n.
65. Op. cit., pp. 420–1.
66. Op. cit., p. 119. Cf. fifth edition, 1893, p. 119.
67. Op. cit., p. 498.
68. Op. cit., p. 508.
69. Ibid.
70. Op. cit., pp. 162–75, 496–507.
71. See above pp. 14.
72. Op. cit., pp. 52 and 175.
73. Op. cit., pp. 506–7.
74. *Principia Ethica*, pp. 99–102.
75. Op. cit., p. 497.

# 3

# Two proposed foundations for ethics

Two lines of thought, taken by some of Sidgwick's contemporaries, diverged from his views. They were hegelianism, represented by T. H. Green and others, and evolutionism, of which Herbert Spencer is the best known exponent. Both these schools of thought rejected Sidgwick's attempt to combine intuitionism and utilitarianism. As we shall see, Green roundly repudiated utilitarianism and Spencer had no time for intuitionism. Both these types of moral philosophy also denied Sidgwick's 'dualism of the practical reason'. We shall consider the different ways in which they claimed to have reconciled self-love and benevolence. Their most significant divergence from Sidgwick, however, was their view—as he put it—that ethics cannot stand alone. Sidgwick thought it can because *ought* 'must be independent' of *is*[1] ('ought' here standing for moral judgements in general). In the *Lectures* which he gave on Green and Spencer—published posthumously in 1903—he argued that the former was mistaken in basing ethics on metaphysics, and the latter, on science.

There can be no doubt that it was the intention of Green and Spencer to give ethics these respective foundations; but there is room for some uncertainty as to precisely *how* they intended to do so. Did they think that they could *define* moral terms metaphysically or scientifically—did Green think that 'good' *means* 'self-realising' and Spencer that it *means* 'more evolved'? Sometimes they write as if they did.[2] But moral judgement can be conceived as 'dependent', or 'based', on statements of metaphysical or scientific fact without being considered definable in terms of them. Did Green and Spencer intend then to make the connection in some other way? This much seems certain. Neither of them intended to say that other views than their own of what is good were simply mistaken. They intended to say that such views are not logically possible. As we shall see, they both seem to have regarded their move from *is* to *ought* as a matter of double necessity. Green thought that whatever constitutes the self-realisation of the eternal self-consciousness *must* be morally good: *and* that our self-realisation *must* be an aspect of the self-realisation of the eternal self consciousness; and so our self-realisation is morally good. Spencer, in his turn, seems to have thought that whatever gives pleasure *must* be good; *and* that whatever is more evolved *must* give pleasure; and so whatever is more evolved is good. We must now look at the arguments with which each of them tried to establish the premises which I have just attributed to him. Underlying their respective ethics is the assumption that it is possible to deduce what *ought* to be from what, metaphysically or scientifically, *is* (was or will be) the case.

## I. The Hegelians

The three authors whom I have in mind under this heading were all Oxford philosophers. T. H. Green (1836–82) became professor of moral philosophy in 1878 and was probably, in his day, the most influential of the three. It is with his *Prologomena to Ethics*, based on lectures given in the last few years of his life and posthumously published in 1883, that I shall be principally concerned. F. H. Bradley (1846–1924), a lifelong fellow of Merton College, was no doubt the ablest of the three and his *Ethical Studies*, published in 1876, is generally considered to be the most readable introduction to the hegelian type of ethics. Bernard Bosanquet (1848–1923) was perhaps the most thoroughly hegelian of them all. He published *The Philosophical Theory of the State* in 1899. It was through these three thinkers that the influence of Hegel entered into British moral philosophy but I must not give the impression that any of them followed Hegel slavishly. Green was certainly influenced as much by Kant as by Hegel; and in the work of all

47

three authors hegelian collectivism is considerably modified by the ideal of individual self-realisation.

## Green's Metaphysics

According to Green, there exists an eternal self-consciousness. He called it 'the mind which the world implies'.[3] His reasons for believing in it are, to say the least, not very convincing. From the indisputable fact that human beings could not perceive any order in nature if they lacked intelligence, Green inferred that 'some unifying principle analogous to that of our understanding'[4] is necessary in order to explain the uniformity of nature. And from the putative fact that this principle unifies the whole spatio-temporal order of things he drew the conclusion that it cannot itself be part of that order.[5] This is metaphysics at its worst. The former argument is obviously invalid: it confuses a necessary condition of something existing with a necessary condition of its being *perceived* to exist. And, as for the latter, why should it be thought inconceivable for one element in nature to hold the other elements together?

Green's two favourite adjectives to describe the eternal self-consciousness were 'self-distinguishing' and 'self-seeking'. We must not think of it, and the manifold which it unifies, dualistically, i.e. as existing independently of each other. They are like the two sides of a coin. The eternal self-consciousness must 'distinguish itself from the manifold' in order to unify it; but it is only by so doing that it 'gives itself its character, which ... but for the world it would not have.'[6]

Human consciousness can only be explained—Green went on to argue—as the reproduction of itself by the eternal consciousness 'in and upon'[7] our animal nature. But here again, he said, we must avoid false dualism. It is not that human beings have a double consciousness; only that 'the one indivisible reality of our consciousness' cannot be comprehended unless we think of it in terms of both the eternal consciousness and our animal nature.[8] As we would expect, this reproduction of itself in us by the eternal consciousness is self-distinguishing and self-seeking. It is also both speculative and practical. Speculatively, the eternal consciousness presents to itself our organic sensations as perceptions of the order which it gives to nature. Practically, it presents to itself our animal wants as objects of desire in which it seeks satisfaction.[9] Sidgwick was entitled to raise, as he did in his *Lectures*[10] the question of how the eternal consciousness could be conceived to reproduce itself *practically*, when Green had given us no reason to think of it as possessing *will*. A fair point, because Green expressly enjoins us to think of the eternal self-consciousness as the logical condition, rather than the antecedent cause, of the order of nature.[11] Would it not therefore be more appropriate to conceive of the eternal self-consciousness purely in terms of speculative cognition?

Untroubled by such thoughts, Green turned his mind to human action. Voluntary actions have motives. A motive is an object of the agent's desire. This object may be the performance of the action itself, or something which it is expected to achieve, or both. But it must not be thought of simply as the agent's strongest desire. It is rather the desire with which he identifies himself in the action. When, for instance, Esau sold his birthright for a mess of potage, it was not hunger as a natural force 'but his own conception of himself, as finding for the time his greatest good in the satisfaction of hunger'[12] which prompted him to act. A voluntary agent necessarily distinguishes himself from his objects of desire in so far as he selects one from among them as his motive; and he necessarily seeks himself in them in so far as he sees the one which he has selected as at the time his own greatest good.[13]

Does the agent make his selection freely? Green thought so, though he had two ideas which struck Sidgwick as inconsistent with that opinion.[14] He took it that an agent's choice of his own greatest good is conditioned both by his own moral disposition and by what he called the moralising influences of society.[15] 'Surely then,' said Sidgwick, 'determinism wins'! How can an agent be free at the point of action, if his choice is determined by his disposition, which is the outcome of his own past choices, or by social forms or institutions which are the outcome of other men's past choices? Sidgwick's criticism at this point strikes me as unfair. If Green's argument had been simply this—from the facts, (a) that an agent's disposition is the product of his own choices, and (b) that his true self is a social self (we shall see Green's reasons for thinking this in a moment), it follows that, in so far as the agent is determined by his disposition or his society, he is self-determined and that is no denial of freedom—then it would have been open to Sidgwick to object that there is no ground here for Green's view that the agent has 'a perpetual potentiality for self-reform, consisting in the perpetual discovery ... that he is not satisfied.'[16] It is quite conceivable on these premises, that he should have become so completely conditioned by his disposition and his society that he had lost any such potentiality. But, of course, at the heart of Green's conception of an agent there was the thought of him as self-distinguishing and self-seeking. *By definition* for Green, an agent *can* step back from his disposition and society—even though they *are* himself—and ask himself whether what they bid him choose is his own greatest good. However mistaken Green's metaphysic may be it does not seem to me to be inconsistent *with itself* at this point. And that was Sidgwick's accusation.

What is it, then, in Green's opinion, which makes some actions virtuous? It is the fact that they are done for the sake of moral good. And what is moral good? He defines it as, 'the realisation of the moral capability'.[17] The obvious objection to regarding moral good as the realisation of moral capability is that which Sidgwick put in a nutshell: surely the sinner realises moral capabilities just as much as the saint![18] Green's reply would no doubt have been that at least we know the difference between the sinner and the saint. Through the long dialectic of man's moral development, certain conceptions of virtue and vice have taken shape. These are our only guide in morality, but a safe one. 'We all recognise, and perhaps in some fragmentary way practise, virtues which both carry in themselves unfulfilled pos-sibilities, and at the same time plainly point out the direction in which their own further development is to be sought for ... No one is eager *enough* to know what is true or make what is beautiful; no one ready *enough* to endure pain and forego pleasure in the service of his fellows; no one impartial *enough* in treating the claims of another exactly as his own.'[19] And so on.

Three characteristics of the moral good, as Green conceived of it, should be noted. First, an agent's moral good is a *rational* good. Why? Because it consists in 'a possible state of himself better than the actual'.[20] The idea here seems to be the sound one that rationality is essentially self-critical. Second, the moral good is an *imperative* one. Categorically so, for it is 'a fulfilment of the capabilities of which a man is conscious in being conscious of himself'.[21] Here the underlying idea is that nothing could conceivably be as 'absolutely desirable' as self-fulfilment. If self-fulfilment is defined simply as that which fulfils an agent's desire, then this is true but trivial. If it means, as we shall see that it did for Green and his fellow hegelians, filling my station in society and doing its duties, then its desirability would seem to most people to depend on whether our society was a good one and what it expected of us was right.

Third, the moral good is a *permanent* one. Green wrote, 'For an agent merely capable of seeking the satisfaction of successive desires, without capacity for conceiving a satisfaction of himself as other than the satisfaction of any particular desire, and in consequence without capacity for conceiving anything as good permanently or on the whole, there could be no possibility of judging that any desire should or should not be gratified.'[22] It is obviously true that, in order to decide whether a particular desire should be gratified or not, some criterion is needed other than the satisfaction of that particular desire. But what Green is saying goes far beyond this. He is arguing that it lies in the very nature of moral judgement that this criterion must be a permanent one; and that it can only be such, if it is the development within each of us of the moral capabilities of the eternal self-consciousness. Metaphysical argument is often criticised on the ground that it draws ontological conclusions from purely linguistic premises and this looks like a case in point. It is certainly a feature of moral discourse that one is expected to have reasons for one's moral judgements. In that they are reasons, they will be universalisable. If for instance I comment that it was right of you to say what you did because it was the truth, it may properly be assumed that I should judge any other instance of truth-speaking *ceteris paribus* to be right. But to make this point by saying that I have a permanent self which conceives of a permanent good looks very like multiplying entities without necessity. Moral discourse has its conventions such as the need to have a reason for one's moral judgements. But it is a long jump from them to Green's kind of metaphysical conclusions.

More than enough has been said to show what is intended by saying that Green treated ethics as a subject which cannot stand alone. He thought that, in order to understand morality, we must see that it is based on metaphysics. Such a view leaves us with two kinds of question. One is whether Green's metaphysics will bear critical examination. I have already indicated some of its defects; but it is beyond our present purpose to pursue this question further. The other question is whether G. E. Moore was right in his opinion that, even if Green's metaphysics were entirely free from defect, they would not have any logical bearing whatever upon the fundamental ethical question, 'What is good in itself?'[23] We shall return to this criticism in the next chapter.

## Green on the Dualism of the Practical Reason

Green claimed that the distinction, commonly supposed to exist between benevolence and reasonable self-love, is 'a fiction of philosophers'.[24] He found no basis for Sidgwick's gloomy belief in the 'dualism of the practical reason' (see above pp. 40ff.). His idea of the moral good as permanent, to which I referred a moment ago, seemed to him to lead to the conclusion that it is also social. A man's thought of himself, and the good which he seeks, as permanent 'is inseparable from an identification of himself with others, in whose continued life he contemplates himself as living'.[25] From primitive notions of themselves as members of families or tribes, men gradually come to the Stoic conception of themselves as citizens of the world, or the Christian belief that they belong to a universal brotherhood.[26] Hostile as he was to utilitarianism, Green conceded that it had been beneficial in extending our ideas of the number of those whose good we must seek. However, he preferred Kant's 'Act so as to treat humanity, whether in your own person or in that of others, always as an end, never merely as a means', to Bentham's principle of equity, because the former escapes any possible suggestion that it is every pleasure, rather than every person, which must be taken into account.[27]

Green put forward two further arguments to support his rejection of Sidgwick's antithesis between private and public good. In the first place, he found it 'impossible' to conceive of the 'divine self-realising principle' coming to full expression in anything less than humanity as a whole.[28] In the second place he thought it a 'fallacy' to suppose that individuals can achieve their greatest good independently of each other. Sometimes he speaks as if he simply meant by this—and Sidgwick would not have dissented—that internal and external sanctions make it in an individual's interest to seek the good of others: no more than this might be meant, for instance, by his remark that an individual 'finds satisfaction for himself in procuring and witnessing the self-satisfaction of the other'.[29] But Green's view was in fact radically different from Sidgwick's. He closed a long discussion of the moral good with remarks to the effect that virtue is 'the only good in the pursuit of which there *can* be no competition of interests, the only good which is really common to all who may pursue it'.[30] The 'can' (my italics) is logical. As a kantian, he believed that virtue—the good will—is the highest good; but as a hegelian, he believed that it follows from the very nature of morality that, in seeking it for ourselves, we are seeking it for our society.[31] He took the thoroughly hegelian line that an individual can realise his moral capabilities only by fulfilling 'the duties of his station'.[32]

F. H. Bradley gave classical formulation to this view in one of his *Ethical Studies*.[33] He thought of our 'stations' as quite particular to us—I am the father of *this* family, the teacher of *this* class, etc.; and our duties within them, as laid down by the traditional morality of our time and place. His remark is often quoted, that 'to wish to be better than the world is to be already on the threshold of immorality'[34] (where the 'world' means 'the morality already existing ready to hand in laws, institutions, social usages, moral opinions and feelings'); but he also made his opinion clear, that 'there is no ... fixed code or rule of right ... the morality of one time is not that of another'.[35]

Sidgwick accused both Bradley and Green of failure to carry through their conception of the moral good consistently. In his review of the former's *Ethical Studies* for the first edition of *Mind* in 1876, he pointed out that Bradley, in *Essay VI* (called 'Ideal Morality'), immediately following the one to which I referred just now, had to concede that an aspirant after the ideal finds some modification of traditional morality 'unavoidable'; and that elsewhere he acknowledged the legitimacy of a 'cosmopolitan morality', which has a 'notion of goodness not of any particular time and country'.[36] These views are plainly at variance with others which we noted above to be Bradley's.

Against Green Sidgwick remarked in his *Lectures*[37] that, if there is assumed to be no difference between good for self and good for others, then this radically changes certain conceptions of virtue. Take justice for instance. Green himself can only define a just man as one who does not promote his own good at the cost of the good of others.[38] But this presupposes that the two goods are different and clearly contradicts his view that they are the same. Moreover, Green recognised that participation in the arts and sciences is an element in man's well-being. But the resources needed to cultivate them are limited and it is obvious that if some possess them, others cannot do so. Sidgwick was expressing a real dilemma for his well-to-do Victorian readers when he wrote, 'the hardest choice which Christian self-denial imposes is the preference of the work apparently most socially useful to the work apparently most conducive to the agent's own scientific and aesthetic enjoyment.'[39] They sometimes had to choose between private and public good, whatever Green might say.

### Against Hedonism

One of the most influential features of Green's *Prologomena* was its attack on hedonism. He subjected both psychological and ethical hedonism to criticism which many of his readers thought entirely triumphant.

Psychological hedonism—the view that we always *do* act for the sake of pleasure—owes its plausibility, in Green's submission, to two considerations. One is the fact that in all voluntary action the agent is seeking some object of desire; and the other, that in the attainment of this object he finds a satisfaction which is pleasurable.[40] Hence arises the notion that the object of desire is always pleasure. A notion, Green thought, the falsity of which can be established on both empirical and logical grounds. Would it not be absurd, he asks, to suppose, as an *empirical* fact, that the satisfaction of a saint or hero in the fulfilment of a mission which has demanded a lifetime of sacrifice, will—regarded as simply 'so much pleasure'—make up for all the pleasures foregone or pains endured?[41] Green's *logical* objection to psychological hedonism is that the very idea of satisfaction, or pleasure, in the attainment of an object of desire presupposes that this object is logically distinct from, and anterior to, the satisfaction of attaining it. The argument applies whether the object of desire is that of a voluptuary or a saint. Green's point is not that the object of desire is *never* pleasure; but simply that it cannot be shown to be *always and only* pleasure on the grounds indicated above. 'However much pleasure there may prove to be in the self-satisfaction ... which the attainment of his object brings with it ... it cannot be *this* pleasure that is the object which he desires ... any more than the pleasure of satisfying hunger can be the exciting cause of hunger ... A man may seek to satisfy himself with pleasure, but the pleasure of self-satisfaction can never be that with which he seeks to satisfy himself'[42] (italics mine).

In his *Lectures* Sidgwick said that he was almost entirely in accord with Green's criticism of psychological hedonism.[43] His only complaint was that Green evidently did not see that the analysis which shows that I do not always aim at my own pleasure also shows that I do not always aim at own self-satisfaction.[44] It too can only be the consequence of desiring an object, not that object itself. Green's reply would presumably have been that the concept of voluntary action implies an agent who selects an object of desire as his motive and who is necessarily satisfied when this object is attained. Just as the object is logically anterior to the satisfaction of attaining it, so the self which selects it is anterior to the selection of the object. Therefore, every object satisfied implies a self satisfied.

Turning to Green's attack on ethical hedonism, I think we find in it three main criticisms. First, that if happiness (in the sense of the greatest possible surplus of pleasure) is the end at which we ought to aim, then what Sidgwick called the 'dualism of the practical reason' is inevitable because a desire for the pleasure of others cannot (sanctions apart) be the same thing as a desire for one's own pleasure.[45] Sidgwick did not, of course, demur. In his *Lectures* he merely commented that Green himself had not escaped this dualism in his account of justice and other virtues (cf. above p. 54).

Green's second criticism was the familiar one which Whewell (above p. 16) advanced against Bentham, that although ethical hedonism seems to have a very clear and definite criterion of moral value, namely, pleasurable or painful consequences, it is in practice very difficult to calculate hedonistic consequences.[46] Again, Sidgwick, while agreeing, adds a *tu quoque*. It may be hard to calculate pleasures and pains but is it not very much harder to apply Green's own criterion and decide which of all possible actions will effect the fullest realisation of moral capabilities?[47] I am not sure that this *is* harder, when 'realising moral capabilities' simply

55

means—as it did for Green—acting in accordance with the prevailing moral beliefs of one's society.

The utilitarian doctrine that we ought to aim at the greatest possible *sum* of pleasures is the butt of Green's third criticism, which is derived in large part from Bradley's study, 'Pleasure for Pleasure's Sake'. Green has two main objections to the utilitarian doctrine. First, that there is a *non sequitur* at the heart of it. Much to Sidgwick's annoyance,[48] Green often talked as if all utilitarians were psychological, as well as ethical, hedonists; and this assumption lies embedded in this first objection. He takes the utilitarian view to be that because every good, i.e. every object of desire, is some pleasure, therefore the greatest good, i.e. the thing most desired, is the greatest sum of pleasures. Then his objection is that a sum of pleasures is not pleasure! The utilitarians 'argue from desire for a state of feeling to desire for something which is not a possible state of feeling . . .' Pleasures 'can be added together in thought, but not in enjoyment or in imagination of enjoyment'.[49]

As Bradley had put it, 'in order to have the sum of pleasures, I must have them all *now*, and that is impossible.' Pleasures are by nature transitory and mutually exclusive. When my attention is taken up by the pleasure of an outdoor game, it cannot at the same time be absorbed in the pleasures of the table, the study or the bed. What we experience is not a sum, but a series, of pleasures.

But surely, said Sidgwick in reply, if pleasures can be 'summed in thought', as Green admits, that will suffice. The utilitarian can make it his aim to gain for himself and others a succession of pleasures which is as rich, and as full as possible.[50]

Green's second objection fastens on this word *possible*. His criticism runs as follows. If the utilitarian standard is the greatest possible sum of pleasures, then it is logically impossible. Just as it makes no sense to speak of the greatest possible quantity of space or time because, whatever quantity we think of, there could always conceivably be more; so, however great the sum of pleasures which we imagine, it is always conceivable that there could be more. 'The sum of pleasures plainly admits of indefinite increase . . . it will never be complete while sentient beings exist . . . it is an end which for ever recedes . . . and such an end clearly cannot serve the purpose of a criterion by enabling us to distinguish actions which bring men nearer to it from those that do not.'[51] So much for the vaunted definiteness of utilitarianism. Better far to conceive of ultimate good as a state of society in which men fulfil the duties of their station along the paths of recognised virtue![52]

Sidgwick replied with an insistence that, just as we can conceive of the greatest possible amount of time or space which we think we can obtain for a particular purpose, so we can conceive of the greatest possible sum of pleasure, which we think we can foresee under certain conditions. And this is all that is assumed by the utilitarian's criterion. True, the greatest possible sum of pleasures is an end which for ever recedes, in the sense that it is always a state of affairs not actual, which we try to bring into existence. But what else can a criterion be, if it is an end at which men must for ever aim?[53]

## II. The Evolutionists

The view that the study of evolution provides the appropriate basis for ethics was held by a number of British philosophers at the turn of the century. The two best known by far are Herbert Spencer (1820–1903), who published *The Data of Ethics* in 1879 and the two remaining volumes of his *Principles of Ethics* in 1892 and 1893; and Leslie Stephen (1832–1904), whose *The Science of Ethics* came out in 1882.

Evolutionary ethics had some powerful opponents. The most forthright was T. H. Huxley, who hammered it in his *Romanes Lecture* of 1893. Sidgwick criticised Spencer at length in his *Lectures* and G. E. Moore devoted a chapter to the demolition of evolutionary ethics in his *Principia Ethica* (Cambridge 1903).

Spencer's declared aim in the preface to *The Data of Ethics* was to replace what he took to be the crumbling supernaturalistic and authoritarian foundations, on which morality had rested for so long, with a secure, rational alternative. He abjured the opinions that no such new foundations are either needed or possible. To his mind, evolutionary science provides exactly what is required. He conceived of his evolutionary ethics as the pinnacle and completion of his protracted labours to provide a complete synthesis of metaphysics, biology, psychology, sociology and ethics. I will confine my attention mainly to *The Data of Ethics* because it has been the most highly esteemed and influential of all statements of evolutionary ethics.

'Ethics has for its subject matter, that form which universal conduct assumes during the last stages of its evolution,'[54] wrote Spencer. Why so? Because only on this condition can ethics become a science. No science could exist without the first principles which all its theory and practice invoke.[55] Spencer illustrated the point from mechanics, in which he had been trained during his youth. We could predict the course of a projectile from mechanical laws which ignore air-resistance, and then subsequently take air-resistance into account, thereby bringing our calculations into closer correspondence with fact. This shows us that 'mechanical science fitted for dealing with the real can arise only after ideal mechanical science has arisen'. What ethics needs, according to Spencer, is similar first principles of moral science. That is, 'a system of ideal ethical truths, expressing the absolutely right, (which) will be applicable to the questions of our transitional state in such ways that, allowing for the friction of an incomplete life and the imperfection of existing natures, we may ascertain with approximate correctness what is relatively right.'

How, then, are we to arrive at these 'ideal ethical truths'? Spencer's reply was that we can only do so by studying the evolution of conduct. He defined conduct as 'the adjustment of acts to ends'.[56] Advance takes place in the evolution of conduct when the ends to which acts are adjusted constitute a greater 'quantity of life'.[57] Quantity of life was measured by Spencer as the product of length times breadth. What length of life means is obvious. By 'breadth' he meant the number and variety of 'the minor ends subserving major ends'. To take a trivial example, acts which provide food result in greater 'breadth' as the food they provide is 'more regular', 'higher in quality', 'free from dirt', 'greater in variety', 'better prepared'. Spencer summed up his conception of a greater quantity of life in these rather ponderous terms,

> Hence estimating life by multiplying its length into its breadth, we must say that the augmentation of it, which accompanies evolution of conduct, results from increase of both factors. The more multiplied and varied adjustments of acts to ends, by which the more developed creature from hour to hour fulfils more numerous requirements, severally add to the activities that are carried on abreast, and severally help to make greater the period through which such simultaneous

activities endure. Each further evolution of conduct widens the aggregate of actions while conducing to elongation of it.

He had in mind both 'self-maintaining' and 'race-maintaining' conduct; the former directed to one's own preservation, the latter, to that of one's offspring.[58] He thought they evolve hand-in-hand. But conduct is 'imperfectly-evolved' so long as a greater quantity of life is purchased for any one 'self' or 'race' at the cost of a less quantity for some other. Evolution only becomes 'the highest possible' when conduct achieves 'the greatest totality of life in self, in offspring, and in fellow-men'.[59]

What was Spencer's intention in all this? There are two possibilities. Was he intent on *defining* 'good' (or 'bad') as 'more (or less) evolved'; or was he simply proposing evolution as the correct *standard*, or criterion, of moral value? These are not, of course, the same. Even those who would most vehemently protest the indefinability of moral terms recognise that their use must be grounded in some standard or criterion of value. Which was Spencer taking evolution to be—the *meaning*, or the *measure*, of value? His remarks can be stretched to cover either interpretation. True, he explicitly invites us, at the beginning of his chapter on 'Good and Bad Conduct', to join him in ascertaining 'what good and bad *mean*'[60] (my italics). But his subsequent remarks—such as 'the conduct to which we apply the name good, is the relatively more evolved conduct'—are compatible with either interpretation. Not even G. E. Moore felt sure whether or not Spencer had committed the naturalistic fallacy.[61]

Either way, however, Spencer is making one clear assumption, namely that the more evolved conduct becomes, the morally better it is. He wants us to conceive of the ideal men, who will appear at the end of the ages, and judge ourselves and others by what they will be. He does not suggest that we can form a perfectly precise picture of these millenial paragons! But he expressly believes that there is a 'guidance which has established itself in the course of evolution';[62] and evidently supposes that we can get the picture sufficiently clear for all practical purposes. This picture provides us with an 'absolute ethic', which we can apply to our own day and age, as a scientist applies his first principles to the problems before him.

Sidgwick in his *Lectures*[63] described his own doubts about the value of this notion of an 'absolute ethic' as the main issue between Spencer and himself. He felt that Spencer's fully evolved society, in which—for reasons which we shall come to shortly (p. 63)—there is 'pleasure unalloyed with pain anywhere',[64] must necessarily be so unlike our own that, (a) we cannot conceive of it, and (b) even if we could its lifestyle would provide us with no practical moral guidance.[65] What, for instance, must the lives of men be like, who know nothing of pain—the pain of punishment, or remorse, or even love? Sidgwick had a point, of course. But I am inclined to think that he made rather too much of it. *If*, as Spencer supposed, evolution is proceeding in a certain direction, then it is surely conceivable that we might know enough about some trends, which have been evolving in conduct for a long time, to form some idea of what life will be like when these trends reach finality.

A much more telling criticism is that which challenges Spencer's basic assumption that the more evolved conduct becomes, the morally better it is. He is said to have coined the expression 'the survival of the fittest';[66] and he certainly took 'fittest' to mean 'best'. There is some evidence that Darwin did the same. He concluded in his *The Origin of Species* (1859) that 'as natural selection works solely by and for the good of each being, all corporeal and mental endowments will tend to progress towards perfection.'[67] But the only conclusion which Darwin's theory really supports is this, 'As many more individuals of each species are born than can possibly survive; and as, consequently, there is a frequently recurring struggle for existence, it follows that any being if it vary however slightly in any manner profitable to itself, under the complex and sometimes varying condition of life, will have a better chance of surviving, and thus be naturally selected.'[68] In other words, as T. H. Huxley pointed out forcefully towards the end of his famous *Romanes Lecture* of 1893, the 'survival of the fittest' does not mean, in cosmic nature, the survival of the best in any sense except 'the best adapted to the changed conditions.' If our atmosphere were to cool sufficiently, the fittest would be 'nothing but lichens, diatoms and such microscopic organisms as those which give red snow its colour;' and if it were to warm up sufficiently, no animated beings, 'save those that flourish in a tropical jungle'.

Sidgwick and Moore took up this line of criticism against Spencer. Sidgwick wanted to know why we should think biology able to prove an ethical end. He quoted Aristotle to the effect that in order to live well we must live somehow, but pointed out that this does not prove that living is identical with living well.[69] Moore could not understand how Spencer came to think that by proving certain kinds of conduct 'more evolved' he had proved them to be better. How could anyone, he asked, fail to see 'what a very different thing is being "more evolved" from being "higher" or "better"'.[70] Darwin, at least, seems to have seen it in the end—he pinned into his copy of R. Chambers' *Vestiges of the Natural History of Creation* the memo, 'Never use the words *higher* and *lower*.'[71] But not Spencer. The truth is that, for all his avowed intention of putting ethics on a scientific, instead of a supernaturalistic, basis, Spencer really grounded it in, to quote Antony Flew, 'a secular surrogate for Divine Providence.'[72]

### Evolutionist or Hedonist?

Spencer's moral philosophy is not, however, as simple and straightforward as I have so far made it appear. He complicated it by introducing the idea of conduct as 'more (or less) pleasure-giving' alongside that of it as 'more (or less) evolved'. Thereby he raised doubts as to whether he was, in the last analysis, an evolutionist or a hedonist. Was his basic argument as follows, Whatever gives more pleasure is more evolved; and whatever is more evolved is morally better; therefore, whatever gives more pleasure is morally better? In that case he was an evolutionist. Or was his basic argument, Whatever is more evolved gives more pleasure; and whatever gives more pleasure is morally better; therefore, whatever is more evolved is morally better? In which case he was a hedonist. The more carefully one reads him, the more certain it seems that the latter alternative is the correct one.

Spencer himself raised[73] the question, is any assumption made in calling acts good if they are conducive to life and bad if they are destructive of it? Yes—the assumption that life is worth living. And what does that mean? Spencer is quite explicit, 'there is no escape from the admission that in calling good the conduct which subserves life, and bad the conduct which hinders or destroys it, and in so implying that life is a blessing and not a curse, we are inevitably asserting that conduct is good or bad according as its total effects are pleasurable or painful.'[74] He thought we are entitled to assert this because it is 'self-evident'. The 'final justification for maintaining life, can only be the reception from it of a surplus of pleasurable feeling over painful feeling; and ... goodness and badness can be ascribed to acts which subserve life or hinder life, only on this supposition'. The repetition of these opinions puts it beyond doubt that Spencer was *au fond* a hedonist.

It is tempting to agree with Moore[75] that he simply took ethical hedonism for granted, but perhaps that is not quite fair. He attempted (very unsuccessfully) to support his contention that it is self-evident by showing that even intuitionists, when 'pushed home', have to admit as much.[76] Three questions, he thought, would suffice to push them home.

One is, what do virtues have in common? It seemed clear to him that because qualities such as courage, magnanimity, truth-speaking, etc. cannot be conceived to have anything intrinsic in common, the answer to his question must be, 'something extrinsic'. This something, he confidently opined, can only be 'the happiness which ... consists in the practice of them' (i.e. of the virtues). Once intuitionists admit as much, according to Spencer, they will have to surrender their view that conduct is *intrinsically* good or bad. But this argument of Spencer's is completely mis-conceived: it brings to mind Green's criticism of those who con-fuse an object of desire with the satisfaction of attaining it (see above p. 54). The phrase, 'the happiness which ... consists in the practice of virtue' can only mean, in the present context, the happiness of doing something which the agent thinks of as a virtue. This implies that the happiness of doing it *presupposes* thinking of it as a virtue. If an agent does not already think of what he is doing as a virtue, it is logically impossible for him to experience the happiness of doing it as something which he conceived to be a virtue. The mere fact that people who practise virtue are happy in so doing does not prove, as Spencer seemed to think, that this happiness must be conceived to constitute the virtue of their action. It proves the very opposite.

The second and third questions which Spencer, in effect, addressed to intuitionists can be taken together. They were, what would you say if the conduct which you think virtuous or vicious had the reverse effects?; and, how would you show that someone, whose intuitions differed from your own, was mistaken? What

Spencer wished to elicit by the former question was an admission from intuitionists that, if, for example, theft made its victims happy, they would think it right; and by the latter that, if they came, for example, on a Fijian, who thought murder honourable, they would refute him by showing that it causes misery. The point in each case being, of course that in reality they must then be hedonists at bottom. Again, Spencer's argument is by no means conclusive. Two matters of fact may be conceded to him. One, that intuitionists often disagree about what is right or wrong. The other, that they often decide this by considering felicific consequences. But from neither of these facts does it follow that they do not think conduct intrinsically good or evil. Just as an action's intrinsic characteristic of being the fulfilment of a promise entails, to the intuitionist's mind, the consequential characteristic of being morally right, so the intrinsic characteristic of being an act which causes—or is intended to cause—happiness may do so. Doing what will cause happiness can be conceived as a *prima facie* moral obligation, just as much as keeping promises can. Spencer has not refuted the intuitionists' doctrine that acts are *intrinsically* right or wrong, good or evil, simply by showing that intuitionists approve of benevolence.

Even if Spencer's attempts to convince intuitionists that they are really hedonists had been successful, they would not have proved that hedonism is a correct, only that it is a widely—perhaps universally—held view. It has to be acknowledged that he did take its correctness for granted.

But now, if he was in reality a hedonist, why did he bring evolution into his moral philosophy at all? The answer is that he took the fact that conduct is more evolved to be our surest guarantee that it will be more pleasure-giving. Why so? Because 'sentient existence can evolve only on condition that pleasure-giving acts are life-sustaining acts';[77] and therefore the more evolved conduct becomes, the nearer it must bring us to 'pleasure unalloyed with pain'.[78] And that is the end-state of evolution. This connection between 'continuance or increase of life' and 'pleasure-giving acts',[79] can, in Spencer's opinion, be verified from both empirical and logical considerations. As a matter of *empirical* fact, he contended, we see in the lowest forms of life that 'the beneficial act and the act which there is a tendency to perform are originally two sides of the same; and cannot be disconnected without fatal results'; and in the higher forms that 'each individual and species is from day to day kept alive by pursuit of the agreeable and avoidance of the disagreeable'. But there is said to be surer ground even than this. His 'can' is *logical* in the claim that 'those races of beings only *can* have survived in which, on the average, agreeable or desired feelings went along with activities conducive to the maintenance of life, while disagreeable and habitually avoided feelings went along with activities directly or indirectly destructive of life' (italics mine).

Sidgwick was sceptical on both counts and with good reason. It is, to say the least, not perfectly obvious that man in the nature of things must enjoy a greater surplus of pleasure than less evolved creatures. Ruminations like Walt Whitman's on the fact that the animals do not lie awake in the dark and weep for their sins put us in mind that there are pains men endure which humbler creatures do not. Nor again is it manifestly a logical impossibility that sentient beings should evolve in response to the stick rather than the carrot. Why could not natural selection work through penalties rather than rewards?

Such doubts do not, however, appear to have visited Spencer. In *The Data of Ethics* he quotes with undiminished assurance his own words in a letter to J. S. Mill, written some sixteen years earlier, 'I conceive it to be the business of moral science to deduce, from the laws of life and the conditions of existence, what kinds of action necessarily tend to produce happiness, and what kinds to produce unhappiness.'[80] The letter had been sent to repudiate the suggestion that he was an 'anti-utilitarian'. Not so. Now as then, all he wants to do is to put utilitarianism on a rational, scientific basis rather than a purely empirical one. This meant for him discerning from the scientific study of evolution what kinds of conduct will necessarily increase pleasure and diminish pain.

This 'guidance which has established itself in the course of evolution'[81] is to be discovered, according to Spencer, in physics, biology, psychology and sociology. Each of these lights up an aspect of ethics. The conduct with which ethics deals expends energy (physics), fulfils functions (biology), is prompted by feeling and guided by intelligence (psychology) and affects associated beings (sociology).[82]

Physical evolution is 'from an indefinite, incoherent, homogeneity to a definite, coherent, heterogeneity'.[83] Conduct as it rises to its higher forms is said to display a similar development. But how strange that Spencer should have thought, as he evidently did, that just because a businessman's conduct is more precise (definite), unified (coherent) and varied (heterogeneous) in its purposes, it is therefore morally better than that of less civilised men![84] For a hedonist of all people this seems a singularly odd conclusion.

Biological evolution, we are told, is towards the more complete fulfilment of functions. It follows for Spencer that 'the moral man is one whose functions ... are all discharged in degrees duly adjusted to the conditions of existence.'[85] But how exceedingly trivial some of the conclusions which he draws from these premises! For example, one must not sit in a cold wind and risk rheumatic fever with subsequent heart-disease; one must not over-work; and so on.[86]

Psychological evolution is towards an increasingly 'ideal' kind of sentience. It comes about through 'the subjection of immediate sensations to the ideas of sensations yet to come'.[87] One can see that taking the long view may result in 'the better preservation of life'.[88] But it is hard to see how Spencer deduces from psychological evolution that it is morally better to refrain from murder out of regard for the suffering one will cause others thereby, than from the fear of conviction and punishment. Or again, that it is better to discharge one's moral obligations from a love of virtue than from fear of the gods' ire.[89] These sentiments are in themselves unexceptionable, of course, but just how do we deduce them from the fact that it is more evolved to have regard to long-term sensations than to immediate ones?

Sociological evolution is towards 'those conditions under which alone associated activities can be so carried on, that the complete living of each consists with, and conduces to, the complete living of all'.[90] What moral deductions does Spencer draw from this? Among them, 'that ... completely evolved conduct ... excludes all acts of aggression—not only murder, assault, robbery and the major offences generally, but minor offences, such as libel, injury to property, and so forth.'[91] The immorality of such activities none would dispute. But all these scientific studies of evolution, sociology included, (it will be recalled) are commended by Spencer (see above p. 64) as ways of putting utilitarianism on a more *rational* basis. Sidgwick in his *Lectures*[92] raised the pertinent

65

question as to what difference they really make. It is not, so far as utilitarianism is concerned, a matter of putting morality on a scientific basis, which will replace the old supernaturalistic one; but of replacing the supposedly inadequate empirical calculations of the utilitarian with a foundation which will put the greatest happiness principle beyond all reasonable question. How is a study of evolution supposed to do that? Utilitarians already know that murder, etc., are wrong because experience teaches them that these things cause misery. Will they know it better simply because some sociologists have taught them that these activities break up group coherence? Sidgwick is surely correct in thinking not. If the standard of morality is happiness, then man's cumulative experience of what does, or does not, effect it is a safer guide to right and wrong than speculations about the course of sociological evolution.

## Egoism and Altruism

Sidgwick, as we saw (p. 42), made out that there is an 'ultimate and fundamental contradiction' at the heart of morality. Practical reason directs us to both self-love and benevolence, but they cannot be completely reconciled with each other, and so we are left at the last in some doubt about what is right or wrong. For his own reasons, Spencer, like Green (p. 52) thought otherwise. 'From the dawn of life,' he wrote, 'egoism has been dependent upon altruism as altruism has been dependent upon egoism; and in the course of evolution the reciprocal services of the two have been increasing.'[93]

He conceded a certain primacy to egoism. There is a 'law', whereby those who are superior—whether because of their ancestry or their self-produced modifications—must enjoy the benefits of their superiority and those who are inferior, suffer the penalties of their inferiority. This is the law under which life has evolved so far 'and it must continue to be the law however much further life may evolve'.[94] In so far as more evolved conduct is the moral faculty's guide, therefore, it will direct us to egoism. Spencer was quite happy with this implication. He argued that unless a person takes care of himself he will not be able to care for others, will reduce their happiness by his dullness, will encourage them to be selfish, and so on, all of which are morally deleterious effects.[95]

This is not so much an argument which shows that egoism is good as that altruism is good and egoism useful in so far as it enables us to be altruistic. Be that as it may, Spencer goes on to claim that altruism is as useful to egoism as *vice versa*. The prolongation and enjoyment of our own life can be increased by caring for others. If we co-operate with others for the protection of their lives or property as well as our own, we increase the security of our own thereby; if we keep others free from disease, we reduce the likelihood of infection ourselves; if we educate them, we raise the standard of the work they can do for us; and so on.[96] Such consequences all serve the ends of egoism

It may well be said that all Spencer's argument has shown so far is that some forms of egoism are means to the end of altruism and *vice versa*. The question is still open as to which of these ends it is our duty to pursue. For all Spencer has said so far, it may still be the case that they cannot both be our duty. However, he advances two further arguments, which seemed to him to dispose of that possibility.

The former is an attempt at *reductio ad absurdum*. If one of the alternatives, egoism or altruism, is taken to be the whole of morality to the exclusion of the other, then fatal absurdities result. Spencer thinks it harder to prove this in the case of altruism and so, in order to make his point as telling as possible, he chooses that alternative. His first moves are *ad homines*. Bentham and J. S. Mill he took to be 'if not absolutely altruistic, as nearly so as may be'.[97] The former's altruism was grounded in his equity principle, that everybody is to count for one and nobody for more than one; and the latter's in his view that as between our own happiness and that of others, utilitarianism requires us to be 'as strictly impartial as a disinterested and benevolent spectator'.[98] Well now, suppose there are four people, one of whom independently of the others makes a lot of money by his own efforts. Will it be his duty to distribute it equally among himself and the other three? Will equity or the impartial spectator so direct? Obviously not. This attempt at a *reductio* totally misrepresents the view of Mill and Bentham. Bentham certainly gave a place to egoism in his ethic (see above p. 13); and Mill took much fuller account of distributive justice than Spencer gives him credit for.[99]

The ground is firmer when Spencer goes on to expand his *reductio* in more general terms. There can be no altruistic pleasures unless there are first egoistic ones, from sympathy with which they arise; and so, if altruism eventually excludes egoism, it will destroy itself. There is progressively less room for altruism as other men become perfect and so, if altruism is taken for the whole of virtue, we land ourselves in the anomaly that virtue becomes less practicable as human nature improves![100] The ground is firmest of all when Spencer points out that it is logically impossible to universalise altruism. For everyone to become altruistic, it would have to be the case that some people at least were both egoistic and un-egoistic. They would have to be 'so unselfish as willingly to yield up the benefit for which (they have) laboured' and also 'so selfish as willingly to let others yield up to (them) the benefits they have laboured for'. And this is 'an inconceivable mental constitution'.[101]

Spencer thought that he had a final argument which was conclusive. He could prove that egoism and altruism are reconcilable from the fact that human beings have a capacity for sympathy. What he understood by sympathy is contained in these words,

> Now a pleasurable consciousness is aroused on witnessing pleasure; now a painful consciousness is aroused on witnessing pain. Hence, if beings around him habitually manifest pleasure and but rarely pain, sympathy yields to its possessor a surplus of pleasure; while contrariwise, if little pleasure is ordinarily witnessed and much pain, sympathy yields a surplus of pain to its possessor.[102]

Sympathy is the capacity to enter into the feelings of one's fellows. Spencer's argument is as follows. If, as conduct becomes more evolved, it becomes more universally pleasure-giving, then, in one sense, altruism must diminish. There will not be the same opportunity for the happy to take care of the miserable. But, in another sense, altruism will increase. This is the sense in which it means 'the achievement of gratification through sympathy with those gratifications of others which are mainly produced by their activities of all kinds successfully carried on—sympathetic gratification which costs the receiver nothing but is a gratis addition to his egoistic gratifications'.[103] This, in effect, brings to an end all opposition between egoism and altruism. Egoism must lead one to altruism because thereby one will extend one's own pleasure. Altruism must lead one to egoism for, if I deny myself pleasure, I will thereby deny to others the altruistic pleasure of sharing it sympathetically. In so far as evolution is towards conduct which gives ever-increasing pleasure, sympathy makes possible a degree of it which would otherwise be impossible. If we could, so to speak, only enjoy pleasures which fall within the frontiers of our own existence, we might soon reach a surfeit. But in so far as we can enter into the pleasures of others—including their pleasures in the pleasure of others—the ranges of pleasure open to us would seem to have no conceivable limit.

It is difficult to see how Spencer could have thought that his evolutionism would put utilitarianism on a more secure basis. The process of evolution, as he describes it, has two aspects, relevant here. One, those who are superior survive (see above p. 66 and his §69). The other, those who survive get happier (see above p. 63 and his §33). The end-point of the process is conceived to be a society of completely superior, completely happy, beings. Now, how is this evolutionary process supposed to guide the utilitarian in bringing about 'the greatest happiness of the greatest number'? Assuming that he can envisage the ideally evolved society, he could conceivably take it as a picture of what life is like when the greatest number enjoy the greatest happiness. But how is he to use this picture? As something to realise here and now? But that would surely defeat the ends of evolution because it would mean treating some inferior beings as superior. Should he then use the picture as a goal to aim at in the future? But that surely must mean offending against morality, by sweeping away the inferior to make way for the more rapid progress towards complete happiness of the superior. This is the antithesis which T. H. Huxley so eloquently exposed in evolutionism,

> ... the practice of that which is ethically best—what we call goodness or virtue—involves a course of conduct which, in all respects, is opposed to that which leads to success in the cosmic struggle for existence. In place of ruthless self-assertion it demands self-restraint; in place of thrusting aside, or treading down, all competitors, it requires that the individual shall not merely respect, but shall help his fellows; its influence is directed, not so much to the survival of the fittest, as to the fitting of as many as possible to survive ... Let us understand, once for all, that the ethical progress of society depends, not on imitating the cosmic process, still less on running away from it, but in combating it.[104]

Hegelianism and evolutionism did not find favour among British moral philosophers for very long. The discrediting of the former was due to two main factors. One was the punishing attack on metaphysics generally, launched by the analytical philo-sophers,[105] G. E. Moore and Bertrand Russell, and reinforced by the influence of the logical positivists. The other was the morally outrageous practices of some fascist and communist totalitarians, who drew their intellectual inspiriation in part at least from Hegel's philosophy. As for evolutionism, some attempts have been made from time to time to revive it, notably by J. S. Huxley and C. H. Waddington, but without much success. Huxley, in a *Romanes Lecture*[106] delivered exactly fifty years after his grand-father, T. H. Huxley's, argued that the old man's pessimism was misplaced and we can learn from evolution 'a direction of change' to guide us, now that human evolution has become conscious. This direction, he said, shows us that it is right to realise ever new possibilities, to respect individuality, and to construct a society which will further these ends as fully as possible. But the idea always underlying evolutionary ethics—that, to quote Wad-dington, 'we must accept the direction of evolution as good simply because it is good according to any realistic definition of that concept'[107]—has proved too scandalous for most British moral philosophers since Moore published his *Principia Ethica* in 1903. The main service rendered to moral philosophy by Green and Spencer is that their work drew the critical attention of philo-sophical intellects more acute than their own to the problems of the meaning of moral judgement and the logical connections between it and the kind of reasons which may be given for it.

---

1. *Lectures on the Ethics of T. H. Green, Herbert Spencer and J. Martineau*, London, 1902, p. 1.
2. Cf. T. H. Green, *Prologomena to Ethics*, 1883, fifth edition, p. 196: 'The question . . . what do we *mean* by calling ourselves moral agents? is one to which a final answer cannot be given without an answer to the question, What is moral good? For the moral good is the realisa-tion of the moral capability, and we cannot fully know what any capability is till we know its ultimate realization.' And H. Spencer, *The Data of Ethics*, 1879, §8: 'Thus recognising the *meanings* of good and bad as otherwise used, we shall understand better their *meanings* as used in characterising conduct under its ethical aspects. Here, too, observation shows that we apply them according as the adjustments of acts to ends are, or are not, efficient' (my italics).

3. Op. cit., p. 93 (The pagination is that of the fifth edition, Oxford, 1906).
4. Op. cit., p. 34.
5. Op. cit., p. 32.
6. Op. cit., pp. 86–7.
7. Op. cit., p. 283.
8. Op. cit., p. 78.
9. Op. cit., pp. 150–1.
10. Op. cit., p. 13.
11. Op. cit., p. 32.
12. Op. cit., p. 108.
13. Cf. op. cit., p. 110.
14. Op. cit., pp. 15–22.
15. Op. cit., p. 126.
16. Op. cit., p. 123.
17. Op. cit., p. 196.
18. Op. cit., p. 64.
19. Op. cit., pp. 433–4.
20. Op. cit., p. 203.
21. Op. cit., p. 222.
22. Op. cit., p. 256.
23. *Principia Ethica*, Cambridge, 1903, pp. 139–40.
24. Op. cit., p. 272.
25. Op. cit., p. 271.
26. Op. cit., p. 242.
27. Op. cit., pp. 247–8.
28. Op. cit., p. 209.
29. Op. cit., p. 218.
30. Op. cit., p. 288.
31. On Kant and Hegel see chapters 5 (by H. B. Acton) and 6 (by W. H. Walsh) in *New Studies in Ethics*, volume I, London, 1974, edited by W. D. Hudson.
32. See op. cit., pp. 209–11, 275, 456–7 etc.
33. *Ethical Studies*, second edition, Oxford, 1927, Essay V: 'My Station and its Duties.'
34. Ibid.
35. Ibid.
36. Op. cit., p. 548.
37. Op. cit., pp. 65–7.
38. Op. cit., p. 245.
39. *Lectures*, p. 70. Cf. Green, op. cit., p. 465.
40. Op. cit., p. 180.
41. Op. cit., p. 181.
42. Op. cit., p. 180–1.
43. Op. cit., p. 102.
44. Op. cit., p. 103.
45. Op. cit., p. 263.
46. Op. cit., p. 440.

47. Op. cit., p. 107.
48. Op. cit., pp. 105, 117–18.
49. Op. cit., p. 258.
50. Op. cit., p. 110.
51. Op. cit., p. 441.
52. Op. cit., p. 444.
53. Op. cit., pp. 111–12, 120–1.
54. Op. cit., §7.
55. Op. cit., §104, cf. §22a.
56. Op. cit., §2.
57. Op. cit., §4.
58. Op. cit., §5.
59. Op. cit., §8.
60. Ibid.
61. See his *Principia Ethica*, pp. 48–50.
62. Op. cit., §37.
63. Pp. 199–213.
64. Op. cit., §101.
65. Cf. Sidgwick, op. cit., p. 220.
66. Cf. A. G. N. Flew's chapter on 'Evolutionary Ethics' in *New Studies in Ethics*, vol. II, edited by W. D. Hudson, London, 1974. Flew refers to Spencer's claim to have been the first, made in the *Westminster Review*, 1852.
67. Quoted Flew, op. cit.: see his note 38.
68. Ibid. See his note 20.
69. Op. cit., p. 144.
70. Op. cit., p. 49.
71. Cf. Flew, op. cit., p. 236.
72. Op. cit., p. 231.
73. Op. cit., §9.
74. Op. cit., §10.
75. Op. cit., p. 53.
76. Op. cit., §§11–14.
77. Op. cit., §33.
78. Op. cit., §101.
79. Op. cit., §33.
80. Op. cit., §21.
81. Op. cit., §37.
82. Op. cit., §22a.
83. Op. cit., §24.
84. Op. cit., §26.
85. Op. cit., §30.
86. Op. cit., §37.
87. Op. cit., §42.
88. Op. cit., §43.
89. Op. cit., §§45–6.
90. Op. cit., §55.
91. Op. cit., §51.

92. Pp. 192–3.
93. Op. cit., §81.
94. Op. cit., §69.
95. Op. cit., §§70–3.
96. Op. cit., §§77–80.
97. Op. cit., §83.
98. Quoted op. cit., §85.
99. Cf. chapter V of his *Utilitarianism*.
100. Op. cit., §§86–8.
101. Op. cit., §89.
102. Op. cit., §93.
103. Op. cit., §97.
104. See his *Romanes Lecture*, 1893.
105. Cf. A. J. Ayer, *Russell and Moore: The Analytical Heritage*, London, 1971.
106. *Evolution and Ethics*, London, 1947.
107. *Science and Ethics*, London, 1942. See also his *The Ethical Animal*, London 1961.

# 4

## Can Ethics Stand Alone?

The view that ethics stands alone survived attempts, such as those which we were considering in the last chapter, to base it on metaphysical or evolutionist foundations. Indeed, the idea that morality is *sui generis*, rapidly became the pivot around which discussion in moral philosophy revolved. The one philosopher above all others who won general assent for the proposition that ethics stands alone, and thereby gave its direction to modern moral philosophy, was G. E. Moore (1873–1958), professor of philosophy at Cambridge from 1925 to 1939. Moore's *Principia Ethica* was published in 1903. It offers a teleological account of moral judgement. According to Moore, when a moral judgement is called for, two questions have to be answered, namely, 'What ought to exist?' and, 'What ought to be done?'[1] In reply to the former, we must say what things we consider to have *instrinsic* value in that they are the ultimate ends of human action; and in reply to the latter, we must say what actions we think have *instrumental* value in that they bring about the fullest possible realisation of these ultimate ends. To mark the distinction between the two kinds of question, Moore restricted his use of the word 'good' to ends which have this intrinsic value; and of the words 'right', 'ought' and 'duty', to actions which have this instrumental value. In the opening pages of *Principia Ethica* he develops his view that 'good' so used is indefinable. He does not think the same is true of the other words mentioned; indeed he explicitly defines them to mean that the actions to which they refer are the cause of the greatest possible amount of good. But he is quite certain that 'good' itself cannot be defined. His reasons for thinking that it cannot, and for considering it very important to recognise that it cannot, have been most influential in modern moral philosophy and so I will begin by trying to make them clear.

## The Naturalistic Fallacy

Moore coined the expression 'the naturalistic fallacy' for all attempts to define 'good'. It is a slightly misleading expression because he did not restrict his condemnation to definitions of 'good' in terms of natural fact (e.g. 'pleasant', 'conducive to evolution', etc.) but extended it also to those in supernatural, metaphysical or religious terms (e.g. 'realising the eternal self-consciousness', 'fulfilling the will of God', etc.). All these are, to Moore's way of thinking, 'instances of the naturalistic fallacy'. What then, is wrong with them?

Besides lexical and stipulative definition, there is, according to Moore, a sense of the word in which a 'definition' 'states what are the parts which invariably compose a certain whole.'[2] A horse, for example, can be defined by enumerating its parts—legs, tail, head, etc. These parts can, in turn, be defined by enumerating their parts. And so on until in the last analysis we come to 'objects of thought which are themselves incapable of definition, because they are the ultimate terms by reference to which whatever is capable of definition must be defined'.[3] The word 'yellow' stands for one such simple, indefinable object of thought. And, said Moore, the word 'good' for another. Just as you cannot verbally define 'yellow', so you cannot put what 'good' means into other words. You can, of course, say that whatever is yellow is also something else—e.g. productive of certain light vibrations; and similarly, you might wish to say that what is good is also something else—e.g. pleasant. But 'yellow' does not *mean* 'productive of such-and-such light vibrations', nor does 'good' *mean* 'pleasant', or whatever is proposed as the additional property which all good things have in common. At this point Moore sharply differentiated 'good' from '*the* good'. '*The* good' *can* be defined. A hedonist will say that it means pleasure; an evolutionist, evolution; a religious moralist, God's will; and so on. These proposals are not compatible with each other of course, but they are all significant. The thing to notice, said Moore, is that they are meaningful, only because 'good' (as distinct from 'the good') is *not* defined as 'pleasant' or whatever. For, there would be no point in saying that whatever is pleasant is good unless 'good' meant something different from 'pleasant'.[4]

What grounds did Moore offer for his view that 'good' is indefinable? They appear to have been partly psychological and partly linguistic. He appealed first to introspection and claimed that whoever attends with sufficient care to what is 'before his mind' when he asks himself whether something is 'good' 'may become expert enough to recognise that in every case he has before his mind a unique object.'[5] But Moore's main grounds are linguistic. Whatever definition of 'good' is proposed—call it D—the question, 'Is what is D good?' is an open one. That is to say, it is one to which the answer 'No' may be given without self-contradiction. Now, if for example I were to answer the question, 'Is a bachelor unmarried?' in the negative, I would have contradicted myself because, in conceding that he is a bachelor, I would have implied that he is unmarried by definition. Moore's point is that *nothing* similar can be said about 'good'. It is always logically possible to deny that anything is good (whether it is pleasant, conducive to evolution, or whatever).

Moore thought it important to recognise that 'good' is indefinable because, if we fail to recognise this, we may be deceived into thinking that certain moralists have proved their point when they have not. The premise, for example, that whatever is pleasant is good—from which a moralist might deduce that an act which gives pleasure ought to be done—may be conceived as one of a number of things, namely, (a) a definition; (b) a proposition which is true by definition; (c) a moral proposition which is known by intuition; (d) a decision of principle; etc. Moore was concerned with cases where it is thought of as either (a) or (b). He noted that moralists sometimes try to persuade us that the basis of their ethic is true by definition and it seemed clear to him that it cannot be so. Hedonists, idealists, evolutionists—in Moore's opinion they were all guilty of this illegitimate move and he had them in his sights when he attacked 'the naturalistic fallacy'.[6]

The skill in Moore's linguistic argument is that it turns the tables on all moralists who make this move. If for example, a hedonist is allowed to get away with the argument that hedonism is true because 'good' really means 'pleasant', then he will have put those who reject hedonism in an impossible position. They will now have to admit that, in disagreeing with his moral belief, they are contradicting themselves. For if it is admitted that 'good' means 'pleasant', then to deny hedonism (i.e. to deny that what is pleasant is good) will be like denying that every bachelor is unmarried! It is understandable that many moralists have tried this trick of making their beliefs true by definition. If they could have brought it off, it would have been a knock-down argument against all comers. But it was Moore's achievement to have shown the self-defeating nature of any such manoeuvre. If 'good' means 'pleasant' then the hedonist's *own* moral belief—that whatever is pleasant is good—must simply mean that whatever is pleasant is pleasant. This is not a moral principle at all but a trivial tautology: there is no point in affirming it because it would be so obviously false to deny it. Moore showed that moralists who commit what he called 'the naturalistic fallacy'—i.e. who treat 'good' as definable in naturalistic or supernaturalistic terms—purchase invincibility for their moral beliefs at the price of insignificance.

## Broad's Criticism

C. D. Broad (1887–1971), professor of moral philosophy at Cambridge from 1933 to 1953, subjected Moore's view that 'good' is indefinable to careful criticism in a paper[7] which he read to the Aristotelian Society in June 1934. He considered one by one certain features which Moore had predicated of goodness in its primary sense.

1. Moore held that 'good' stands for a certain *characteristic* which some acts or states of affairs may have. Broad doubts whether the word stands for a characteristic at all. With due acknowledgement to A. E. Duncan-Jones, he suggests that 'good' has emotive, rather than descriptive, meaning. This criticism foreshadows an important development in moral philosophy and I will defer what I have to say about it until we can consider it at length in the next chapter. We shall see that Moore himself was eventually tempted to yield to it (cf. p. 117).

2. Moore held that the characteristic, to which he thought

'good' refers, is *unanalysable*. Broad contends that, so far as he can see, there is no means of proving this with regard to any characteristic. The most we can ever hope to show is that no analysis so far proposed is generally regarded as satisfactory. He has two lines of thought to this end.

His first appears to be that it is impossible to say what it would be like for a term to be analysable; and so we cannot say how any term which is *un*analysable differs from those terms which are analysable. Let *T* be a term standing for some characteristic such as circularity, goodness, or whatever, and *A* stand for a set of characteristics proposed as its correct analysis. If *A* is the correct analysis of *T*, then *T* and *A* are necessarily coextensive: there can be nothing which is *T* and not *A*, or *A* and not *T*. Now, Broad points out that more than one proposed analysis may fulfil this condition, 'The property of being circular, e.g. is necessarily coextensive with an enormous number of other complicated sets of characteristics ... there are enormous numbers of complicated properties which we can prove *must* belong to all circles and *cannot* belong to anything but circles.'[8] So, (i) if *only one A* is known to us, which also do so?; (ii) if *more than one A*, which fulfils the *T*, how can we ever be sure that there are not others, unknown to us, which also do so?; (ii) is *more than one A*, which fulfils the condition, is known to us, how can we ever say which of these is the correct analysis of *T* and which are simply sets of characteristics synthetically connected with *T*? As Broad puts this second question, 'Suppose e.g. that it seemed evident that anything that was good would necessarily be a fitting object of desire, and that anything which was a fitting object of desire would necessarily be good. How can we tell whether being a fitting object of desire is the *analysis* of being good, or whether it is just a complex characteristic which is necessarily and reciprocally but *synthetically* connected with goodness?'[9] It seems that neither question is answerable. There is no way of knowing what constitutes the analysis of a term.

Broad's second line of thought to this effect starts with the concession that most people do consider any proposed analyses of 'good' in purely non-ethical terms to be unsatisfactory. Is this because these analyses contain too much or too little? Moore seems to think, too much. He presents goodness as a simple quality of which non-ethical analyses give too complex a definition. But

Broad does not think that this is why people doubt them. It is, rather, because they contain too little; they 'omit some logical constituent of the characteristic'. He suggests that it is the emotive force of 'good' which is lacking in such non-ethical or 'naturalistic' definitions of 'good'.

3. Moore spoke of goodness as a *quality*. Broad cannot see why we should necessarily so regard it. Moore evidently thought that if goodness is unanalysable, then it must be simple; and if simple, then either a pure quality or a pure relation. Broad agrees that it is not a pure relation. But he is not convinced that it is a quality. Why should it not be a relational property? He ventures the opinion that 'better than' is simple and unanalysable; and 'good' complex and definable in terms of 'better than'. Why should not 'good' be conceived as an abbreviation for 'good of its kind' and thus mean 'better than the average member of its proximate series'?

4. Moore said that goodness is *non-natural*. Broad doubts whether this is compatible with Moore's view that it is an un-analysable, or simple, property. He has some difficulty getting clear just what Moore meant by a 'non-natural' property. In *Principia Ethica* (pp. 40–1), Moore said that, whereas a natural property *can*, a non-natural property *cannot*, be conceived as existing in time all by itself. But Broad rejects this distinction on the ground that characteristics such as brownness or pleasantness (which are certainly natural) can no more be conceived to exist all by themselves in time than goodness can. In his *Philosophical Studies* (London, 1922, pp. 253–75) Moore offered another definition of the distinction between natural and non-natural properties, which Broad thinks comes to this: ethical properties such as goodness are always dependent for their existence on the presence of some non-ethical ones, such as pleasantness. Broad calls the ethical (or non-natural) ones 'derivative', and the non-ethical (or natural) ones 'ultimate'. This, as we shall see (p. 97) is the distinction which W. D. Ross drew between 'consequential' and 'constitutive' characteristics. But Broad thinks it a distinction without a difference because pleasantness is no less derivative than goodness; it is just as reasonable to ask 'Why is this pleasant?' as 'Why is this good?'

Finding it impossible to get a satisfactory picture of what Moore meant by 'natural' and 'non-natural' properties, Broad offers his own account of the distinction between them in epistemological terms. He says that a *natural* property is one which '(a) we become aware of by sensing sensa which manifest it or by introspecting experiences which manifest it; or (b) is definable wholly in terms of such characteristics and the notions of cause and substance'.[10] A *non-natural* property lacks both these characteristics. We do not apprehend it either by sense perception or introspection. It is obvious that goodness is non-natural.

But what then of its simplicity? It seems equally obvious to Broad that if goodness were simple we should apprehend it by sense-perception or introspection. Moore had maintained that we are aware of it by intuition. Broad does not say dogmatically that his own empiricism is self-evident; he expressly refrains from doing so. But he makes two comments: (i) if anyone has an intrinsic idea of goodness, it will have to be *a priori*, or contain *a priori* notions as elements, 'for an *a priori* notion just is an intuitive idea of a characteristic which is not manifested in sensation or introspection and is not definable wholly in terms of such characteristics';[11] and (ii) if goodness is taken to be a 'derivative' characteristic, necessarily coexisting with some good-making characteristics, such as pleasantness, then these must be synthetically necessary facts, because a non-natural characteristic (goodness) cannot be analytically related to a natural one (pleasantness). Given the fulfilment of these two conditions—that goodness is *a priori* and that it is 'derivative'—moral judgements must be synthetic *a priori* judgements.[12] Whether such judgements are possible is one of the great continuing debates in philosophy. Broad does not think it impossible. His purpose is only to bring out what we let ourselves in for, if we embrace Moore's idea that 'good' stands for a non-natural property.

Before we leave Broad's discussion of Moore, note a criticism of the latter's 'open-question' argument, which is implicit in Broad's second criticism above and which he had in fact spelt out against Sidgwick in his *Five Types of Ethical Theory*,[13] published some four years earlier. He points out in his 1934 paper, that for any term *T* to be analysable, two conditions need to be fulfilled: (a) a person who is considering whether any proposed analysis, *A*, is the correct analysis of *T*, will have to know already in some sense what $T$ means; and (b) his knowing this will have to be different from his knowing the correct analysis of $T$. If either of these conditions is not fulfilled, the question 'Is $A$ the correct analysis of $T$?' cannot arise for him. As for the former condition, if he does not know what $T$ means then he will not know what the question is about. As for the latter condition, if knowing what $T$ means is the same as knowing the correct analysis of $T$, then our questioner will have to know—at least implicity—the answer to his question before he can know what it is he is asking. But now, if these conditions were fulfilled in the case of 'good', it would be perfectly possible to conceive of people using 'good' without explicitly knowing its correct analysis. And if they could do that, then it would be possible to conceive of someone telling them that some proposed analysis $A$ is the correct analysis of 'good' and this statement would not be an insignificant tautology for them. It would be analytic but informative.

This was a fair point to make against Moore, assuming that the meaning of 'good' can in some sense be known even where its correct analysis is unknown. But, of course, once people *did* know that $A$ was the correct analysis of 'good', the proposition 'Whatever is $A$ is good' *would* be an insignificant tautology for them. Moore's point that moralists who make their theories true by definition, thereby destroy them as ethical theories, still stands. If 'pleasant' *were* the correct analysis of 'good', then, in telling people this, hedonists would have trivialised hedonism. The theory that whatever is pleasant is good would now be for these hearers a mere tautology.

### Moore on Mill

Moore deployed his exposure of 'the naturalistic fallacy' to good effect. He denounced the moral philosophy of evolutionists like Spencer and metaphysicians like Green, as paradigm cases of this fallacy. These criticisms were widely accepted and are, no doubt, largely responsible for the demise of those types of ethical theory since Moore's day. The case has been rather different, however, so far as hedonism is concerned and particularly in respect of Moore's strictures upon Mill. For some time after the publication of *Principia Ethica* the feeling was widespread that Moore had discredited Mill's *Utilitarianism* once for all. But, recently, the opinion has gained ground that his criticism of Mill was unfair and misleading. I will first detail the criticism and then show why it is thought by some contemporary philosophers to have been misconceived.

Mill defined the utilitarian doctrine, of which he proposed to offer proof of a sort, in these terms, 'happiness is desirable, and the only thing desirable, as an end; all other things being only desirable as means to that end.'[14] By 'happiness' (as Mill had already said) he meant 'pleasure and the absence of pain';[15] and Moore adds that by 'desirable', or 'desirable as an end', Mill meant what is ordinarily meant by 'good as an end'.[16] So, Mill's utilitarian doctrine is that happiness (or pleasure) is the one and only thing which is desirable (or good) as an ultimate end. Moore[17] takes note of Mill's disclaimer that questions of ultimate ends do not admit of direct or ordinary proof; and quite rightly attributes to him the intention of simply showing what conditions are necessary and sufficient in order to make his utilitarian doctrine believable. But Mill's latter-day defenders would say that Moore seemed to forget this in the course of his criticism.

Moore quotes as central to Mill's argument the whole of the paragraph from which the following extracts are taken,

> The only proof capable of being given that an object is visible, is that people actually see it. The only proof that a sound is audible, is that people hear it: and so of the other sources of our experience. In like manner, I apprehend, the sole evidence it is possible to produce that anything is desirable is that people do actually desire it ... No reason can be given why the general happiness is desirable, except that each person, so far as he believes it to be attainable, desires his own happiness. This, however, being the fact, we have not only all the proof which the case admits of, but all which it is possible to require, that happiness is a good: that each person's happiness is a good to that person, and the general happiness, therefore, a good to the aggregate of all persons ...[18]

The first defect in this argument which Moore detects is that of equivocation.[19] He takes Mill to be saying, in the opening sentences quoted above, that, just as the proof of anything being visible is the fact that people actually see it—or audible, that they hear it—so the only proof we can have that anything is desirable is the fact that people actually desire it. The objection to this is obvious. 'Visible' and 'audible', as Moore points out, simply mean '*able* to be seen' or '*able* to be heard' respectively; but 'desirable' is ambiguous as between '*able* to be desired' and '*ought* to be desired'. Mill's argument from the analogy with 'visible' and 'audible' really comes to this: since the fact that anything is desired proves it to be desirable in the sense of '*able* to be desired', it must also prove it to be 'desirable' in the sense of '*ought* to be desired'. The argument only works by equivocation on the two meanings of 'desirable'.

Having shown—to his own satisfaction at least—that the fact that people desire something proves it to be desirable, Moore's Mill naturally went on to ask what it is which people desire and, of course, came up with the answer that it is happiness. This is the meaning which Moore finds in Mill's remark, quoted above, that 'each person, so far as he believes it to be attainable, desires his own happiness'. A page or so later,[20] Mill made it clear that he was not simply saying that pleasure is one of the things which people desire, but the *one and only* thing. He conflated two grounds for this opinion, one empirical and one linguistic. His empirical ground was that introspection and the observation of others will show pleasure to be the only thing which people desire for its own sake; and his linguistic ground, that desiring a thing and finding it pleasant are, 'in strictness of language', two different ways of saying the same thing. If we separate these two lines of argument from one another, we shall the better understand Moore's criticism.

Along the empirical line, Mill, according to Moore,[21] committed the fallacies of confusing 'a pleasant thought' with 'the thought of pleasure' and, in consequence, of equating a means to happiness with happiness as an end in itself. Moore's Mill would have said that the cause of desire is always 'a thought of pleasure'. What he meant by each person desiring his own happiness was, for example, that my desire for a glass of port is caused by 'the thought of (the) pleasure' which I shall get when I drink it. Now, says Moore, the idea of drinking a glass of port may indeed occur to me and give me pleasure; and this feeling of pleasure may well be among the causes of that incipient activity which is called desire. In such case the idea of a glass of port is 'a pleasant thought'. But notice that its pleasantness is actual. I feel it now, *before* I get my glass of port. This means, of course, that it is logically quite different from 'the thought of (the) pleasure' which I shall feel only *after* I have got my glass of port. Moore contends that Mill managed to hold on to his opinion that the cause of desire is always 'the thought of pleasure' only by confusing this with 'a pleasant thought'.

But why was such confusion the only way of holding on to his opinion that what we desire is always pleasure? Because, says Moore, it is perfectly obvious that 'the thought of (the) pleasure' which we shall feel when we attain an object of desire is *not* always the cause of our desire. Sometimes we desire things for their own sakes and not simply as a means to the pleasure we shall feel when we have obtained them. Mill himself, as we have seen (p. 12) recognised this, so far as money, fame, power and virtue are concerned. He was, therefore, in a dilemma. He wished to retain both his views—that the cause of desire is always 'the thought of pleasure' and that some things are desired for their own sakes. According to Moore, it is only by assuming Mill to have confused 'a thought of pleasure' with 'a pleasant thought'—i.e. a pleasure which can only come *after* we have attained the object of desire with one which comes *before*—that we can explain how he slipped into the 'contemptible nonsense' of talking about things like money as *both* means to, and a part of, happiness. This was blatantly confusing means with ends.

Along his linguistic line of argument, Mill according to Moore, strayed into the naturalistic fallacy. The relevant passage reads as follows, '... desiring a thing and finding it pleasant, ... are ... in strictness of language, two modes of naming the same psychological fact: ... to think of an object as desirable (unless for the sake of its consequences), and to think of it as pleasant, are one and the same thing.' If 'desiring a thing' and 'finding it pleasant' mean the same, as Mill is saying here, then, the view that each person desires his own happiness is true by definition. That was evidently Mill's line of argument. But how precisely did it land him in the naturalistic fallacy, as Moore contends?

I never feel absolutely sure where Moore intended to locate Mill's naturalistic fallacy. On page 66 of *Principia* he attributes to Mill the opinion that 'good' (which is synonymous with 'desirable') means 'desired'; and calls in evidence Mill's argument from the analogy between 'desirable' and 'audible'. The naturalistic fallacy, then, is evidently that of defining 'desirable' as 'desired'.

But on page 72, Moore points to the words just quoted above—'to think of an object as desirable ... and to think of it as pleasant, are one and the same thing' as a case of the naturalistic fallacy. Here it is the fallacy of defining 'desirable' as 'pleasant'. One can only assume that Moore thought that Mill's argument for hedonism proceeded by definition in some such way as this,

*Whatever is pleasant is desired* ('in strictness of language' they mean the same).
*Whatever is desired is desirable* (on the analogy of, whatever is seen is visible—from the meaning of 'visible').
*Therefore, whatever is pleasant is desirable.*

Moore called it 'as naïve and artless a use of the naturalistic fallacy as anybody could desire'.[22]

Such then was his case against Mill. To complete the picture we may add that Mill has been thought by many to be vulnerable to a further criticism. The last words quoted from his paragraph on p. 82 are said to involve the fallacy of composition. Mill's point was in effect, that because each person desires his own happiness and it is therefore desirable, or a good, to him, we may conclude that the general happiness is desirable, or a good, to the aggregate of all persons. He can hardly be uttering the trivial tautology that if each person's happiness is a good to that person, each person's happiness is a good to that person. So, say his critics, he must be claiming that because our own happiness is a good to each of us, everybody's happiness is a good to all of us. This is like saying that because every man finds his own car useful, he must find everybody else's car useful as well.

Moore was not the first by any means to criticise Mill's *Utilitarianism*. Each of the criticisms which I have just listed can, as J. B. Schneewind[23] points out, be found in one or other of several publications which appeared in the eighteen sixties and seventies. But for most of the twentieth-century Moore has been regarded as Mill's most incisive critic. Why have doubts about the validity of his criticisms now come to the fore? I think there are two main reasons. One, the feeling that, despite Moore's professed recognition that Mill was not offering a formal proof, he criticises him as though he were. The other, that the fallacies of which Moore finds Mill guilty are such as a first year undergraduate would be ashamed to commit and so it seems most unlikely that Mill was really guilty of them. For these reasons, if any interpretation of Mill's words which delivers them from Moore's criticisms can be found, it must have a *prima facie* plausibility.

Is any such saving interpretation in fact possible? Let me attempt one, which brings together a number of considerations put forward on Mill's behalf by those who think Moore's criticism misconceived.[24]

Even when formal proof is impossible there may be considerations which make a belief more (or less) credible to the minds of reasonable men. It was, as we have seen, (p. 15) just such 'considerations' which Mill said he wished to advance in order to 'determine the intellect' of his readers towards utilitarianism.

We should, therefore, in the first place, treat his comparison of 'desirable' to 'visible' or 'audible', not as equivocation but simply as an attempt to make the point that it would be as futile to have a morality which took things to be good or desirable when nobody in fact desired them, as it would to have an epistemology which postulated visible or audible things which nobody sees or hears. The first 'consideration' in favour of utilitarianism is that it is not futile in this way.

Mill went on to say that 'each person, so far as he believes·it to be attainable, desires his own happiness'. This is a second 'consideration' in favour of utilitarianism. It recognises the truth of the proposition that we would not desire things unless we believed that they would give us pleasure. That proposition can scarcely be disputed. Perhaps some people—masochists, saints, heroes?— desire things which they think will *not* give them pleasure; but if so that is simply the measure of what rare birds they are. People in general do not desire things unless they think they will give them pleasure. Utilitarianism, to its credit, recognises as much. Not only does it avoid the futility of telling people that what nobody desires is desirable; it is realistic enough to set before them an ideal which fits in with their actual desires.

Both these 'considerations' seem reasonable ones to put forward in support of utilitarianism. But Mill's most ardent defenders could not deny that, in what he went on to say about them, he landed himself in confusion. It is important to see why.

The root of the matter seems to be the fact that he thought of pleasure (and, of course, happiness also) as a sensation (or set of sensations) logically distinct from objects of desire which give rise to it—just as, for example, the thought of the fire in my study is logically distinct from the thought of the warmth which it makes me feel. The fire could exist apart from the sensation of warmth and *vice versa*. So pleasure, if it is a sensation, could exist without the object which causes it and *vice versa*. It is not surprising that Mill thought of pleasure as a sensation in this way because so did everyone else. But this, I think, is where things began to go wrong.

Mill wanted to say both that we desire things for the sake of the pleasure which their attainment will give us *and* for their own sakes. Moore was entitled to point out that this is, in effect, taking the cause of desire to be something which is *both* 'the thought of pleasure' *and* 'a pleasant thought'. We desire things, that is to say, for the sake of a sensation which is *both* the pleasure which we will experience when they are attained *and* the pleasure which the thought of them gives us here and now. But this is impossible because the pleasure in the one case is a *future* sensation and in the other a *present* one. As we saw above (p. 12) Mill tried to cut the knot by talk of desiring a thing *both* as a 'means' to pleasure *and* as 'part' of pleasure itself; and this Moore rightly called nonsense. It confuses means and ends.

Some philosophers in recent years have come to regard as a mistake the view that pleasure is a sensation, logically distinct from that which causes it. Why so? We can certainly conceive of pain in that way. If I described what happened when I caught my foot in a gin by saying that for a few moments I was so taken up with the pain in my foot that I did not observe what was causing it, this would make perfectly good sense. The pain can be conceived apart from the gin. But now suppose I were to say something like this, 'I was so taken up with my pleasure in a game of tennis that I did not observe the game.' Would that make sense? Gilbert Ryle[25] was surely right to think not. He concluded that pleasure is not a sensation.

What, then, is it? Ryle's answer was that it is a form of attention. Just as we cannot logically conceive of pleasure without having before our mind something which we are taking pleasure in, so attention cannot be conceived apart from some object to which it is directed. According to Ryle, doing something with attention should not be thought of as two things—viz. doing it and attending to the doing of it. It should be conceived as one thing done in a particular way—viz. with attention rather than absent-mindedly. What is meant by doing it with attention has to be spelt out in terms of hypotheticals; and so has what is meant by taking pleasure in something. The correct analysis, for instance, of 'I played tennis with pleasure' is not that I played the game and felt a certain sensation before, during, or after it. It is, rather, something like this, 'I played tennis and if anyone had interrupted the game I should have been annoyed; if the game had made me late for dinner, I would not have minded; if anyone had suggested another game tomorrow, I would have agreed, and so on.'[26] The particular type of attention which constitutes pleasure may be hard to define precisely. Ryle said that it is the kind which is *absorbed* in its object, rather than merely given to it; and G. B. Gallie[27] suggested that it is *appraisive* or *evaluative* attention rather than merely inquisitive or practical.

We need not go further into such matters. Enough has been said to make the point that if pleasure is conceived as a kind of attention, rather than some sort of sensation, then desiring an object for the sake of the pleasure it will give and desiring it for its own sake come to much the same thing. For instance, would not the analysis of 'I played tennis with pleasure', which I offered a moment ago, fit equally well the view that I played the game for its own sake or for the sake of the pleasure it would give? The kind of attention which constitutes the one state of affairs seems to be much the same as that which constitutes the other.

The point of these somewhat protracted remarks about pleasure, so far as the defence of Mill is concerned, is to show that he confused 'the thought of pleasure' and 'a pleasant thought', not because he was contemptibly stupid, but because he was trapped in a generally held misconception about pleasure, from which it took a good deal of later philosophical analysis to free us all Mill, by his outrageous talk of that which is both a means to, and a part of, pleasure, can, at least, be credited with some sense of the confusion in the concept of pleasure as a sensation.

I referred above (p. 84) to the linguistic ground for Mill's view that 'each person ... desires his own happiness', and to Moore's accusation that it landed Mill in the naturalistic fallacy. In Mill's defence at least two things have been said. One, that Mill was not much interested in the question, What does moral language *mean*? At the beginning of *Utilitarianism* he says simply that he is concerned to discover 'the criterion of right and wrong'. Later on he dismisses the question, whether talk of moral obligation is about an objective reality or a subjective feeling, as a 'point of Ontology'—to quote from J. O. Urmson, 'as though the analysis of ethical terms was not part of ethical philosophy at all as he conceived it.'[28] This opinion seems to be even more explicit in his defence of Bentham against Whewell, where he says that the question of how natural feelings are related to moral ones is metaphysical rather than ethical. If the point of this defence is that, since Mill was not interested in the analysis of ethical terms, he can be excused the mistake of defining 'desirable' naturalistically, I find it unconvincing. The mere fact that a philosopher is not interested in a subject does not excuse any mistakes which he makes about it.

However, the other defence of Mill is more impressive. In the light of his writings as a whole, it is said, we cannot believe that he would ever have equated the meaning of an evaluative judgement with that of a statement of natural fact. He insisted so frequently and so clearly on the difference between the two kinds of utterance. In later editions of his *Logic*, at VI.12.6., he himself quite explicitly draws the logical distinction between 'ought' and 'is'. In *Utilitarianism* itself he often warns against confusing factual with normative expressions—'can' with 'should',[29] 'motive of action' with 'rule of action',[30] 'origin of moral sentiments' with 'binding force of moral sentiments'.[31]

If the idea of Mill committing the naturalistic fallacy is deemed incredible then his remarks quoted above on p. 84, to the effect that desiring a thing and finding it pleasant name the same psychological fact—and that to be thought desirable is the same thing as to be thought pleasant—will have to be regarded as simply summing up what we learn from introspection and empirical observation. He certainly begins the paragraph[32] in which they occur with the simple remark that it concerns 'a question of fact and experience'. But, at the end he says that to desire anything except in proportion as it is pleasant is not simply a 'physical', but also a 'metaphysical', impossibility. The indications are that by 'metaphysical' he meant here what we would mean by 'logical'. So it is not easy to think that he only had empirical considerations in mind. But he may have had.

Such, then, is a conceivable defence of Mill against Moore's criticisms that he committed the fallacy of equivocation, the confusion of means with ends and the naturalistic fallacy. As for the fallacy of composition, of which many have accused him, we have Mill's[33] own word for it that this is not what he intended. He said in a letter, 'I simply meant . . . that since A's happiness is a good, B's is a good and C's is a good, the sum of all these goods must be a good.' That may be wrong; but it is not the fallacy of composition.

On Moore's behalf it can, I think, be said that many of Mill's readers must have taken him to mean the mass of fallacies and contradictions, which Moore accuses him of meaning. True, there is strength in the argument that it is not easy to believe that Mill could have been so muddled. But even if he is exonerated on that ground from the charge of fallacious reasoning, he seems to be guilty at least on the charge of not making his meaning as clear as, in the popular presentation of his views, he should have done.

## Moore on Sidgwick

Moore,[34] though he says that he found Sidgwick's style of lecturing 'too formal to be very interesting' records that he gained 'a good deal' from the latter's published work. Sidgwick's 'clarity and belief in common sense' were 'very sympathetic' to him. Moore said[35] in the *Principia* that so far as he knew, Sidgwick was the only philosopher who had clearly anticipated him in recognising and stating the indefinability of 'good'. He calls in evidence a passage[36] where Sidgwick criticises Bentham for defining 'right' (not 'good') when it is used of an ultimate end. The fact that the word here is 'right' and not 'good' is not, in itself, significant because Moore's fundamental distinction is not between the *signs* 'good' and 'right', but between any such word used to signify an ultimate end and one used to signify a means thereto. It is the former use which he considers indefinable, whether the sign in question be 'good', 'right', or whatever. There can be no doubt that Sidgwick shared the opinion that 'good' is indefinable. However, we noticed above (p. 25) that he anticipated Moore's 'open question' argument most remarkably in discussing the definition of 'ought' as 'bound under penalties'. He said that '"ought", "right" and other terms expressing the same fundamental notion' are indefinable.[37] Sidgwick, unlike Moore in the

*Principia* but like some other intuitionists (cf. below pp. 92ff.), thought of all moral terms as indefinable.

Sidgwick took the view that pleasure is the sole good. He was well aware, (cf. above p. 38) that there are some who think such things as the cognition of truth, the contemplation of beauty, free or virtuous action, more valuable than pleasure. But he invited his readers to apply a two-fold test. Let them consult, first, their own intuitive judgements and, next, the ordinary judgements of mankind.[38] What will they find? Sidgwick is quite sure that their own intuition will tell them that the cognition of truth, etc., are only valuable in so far as they give pleasure; and the ordinary judgements of mankind will show that common sense morality commends these things roughly in proportion as they do so.

Moore replied[39] that even if these things do give pleasure, this does not prove that pleasure is the sole good. Here he introduces his notion of 'organic relations' or 'organic wholes'. An experience such as the contemplation of beauty is a whole in which a number of elements are related to one another, e.g. the scrutiny of the object, our judgement about it, the pleasure we find in it, etc. Suppose we isolate each of these from the others in our imagination, with the question in mind, Which of them do we think good? We may find that we value none in isolation. Or some but not others. Or just one. Even if we value none of the elements in isolation, we may still value the whole which they constitute. And even if we do value one or some of the elements by themselves, it may well be that the value we place on them does not equal that which we place on the whole of which they are parts. Even if pleasure is the only element which we value in wholes such as the contemplation of beauty, this does not prove that it is the sole good.

We noted above (p. 43) Moore's attack on Sidgwick's egoistic hedonism. So far as Sidgwick's views on universal hedonism are concerned, Moore[40] finds two logical flaws in them. First, such utilitarianism tends to regard everything as a mere means. Present pleasure is valued only as a means to future pleasure. Such thorough-going consequentialism leads to an infinite regress. What is here and now does not have value in itself but is only to be judged by its consequences. And so *ad infinitum*. Something which has value in itself is never attained. The second flaw is that if happiness or pleasure is the only good (as hedonism of all forms lays down) how can it also be important (as universalistic hedonism takes it to be) that the greatest number of people should enjoy it? This is to forsake hedonism whilst proclaiming it.

## Moore and other contemporary Intuitionists

Moore, as we saw, was a teleologist. Morality, to his mind, has to be understood in terms of ends and means. It is a matter of deciding what will be the most effective way of attaining certain goals. These ends or goals have intrinsic value; the ways and means to them, instrumental value. The characteristic which gives the ends their place within morality Moore referred to as 'good'; and that which gives the means their place was what he had in mind when he spoke of actions in terms of 'right', 'ought' and 'duty'. We have seen that he thought of the former characteristic as indefinable. We cannot put what 'good' means into other words. But we saw that this is not how he thought of the latter characteristic. He defined the words which refer to it in the following ways, 'What I wish ... to point out is that "right" does and can mean nothing but "cause of a good result" and is thus identical with "useful"; whence it follows that ... no action which is not justified by its results can be right ... Our "duty" ... can only be defined as that action which will cause more good to exist in the universe than any possible alternative. And what is "right" or "morally permissible" only differs from this as what will *not* cause *less* good than any possible alternative.'[41]

Such was Moore's view in the *Principia*. But by 1912 when he published *Ethics* he had modified it considerably. In the *Principia* he had said, 'If I ask whether an action is *really* my duty or *really* expedient, the predicate of which I question the applicability to the action in question is precisely the same.'[42] This is in line with the idea, which we noted a moment ago, that 'right' is identical with 'useful'. But contrast it with what Moore says in *Ethics*. He there gives a negative answer to the question whether there is 'any characteristic, over and above the mere fact that they *are* right, which belongs to absolutely *all* voluntary actions which are right, and which at the same time does not belong to any except those which are right'.[43] With reference to the words 'duty' and 'expediency', he says that although whatever is our duty may also be expedient 'it is ... quite plain, I think, that the meaning

92

of the two words is *not* the same; for, if it were, then it would be a mere tautology to say that it is always our duty to do what will have the best possible consequences'.[44] This is precisely the same linguistic argument as that with which he supported the view that 'good' is indefinable, in the *Principia*.

Some of Moore's contemporaries felt that he had been misled by his teleology in the earlier work and were confirmed in that opinion by what they took to be a *volte-face* in the direction of deontology in *Ethics*. The philosophers I have in mind were H. A. Prichard (1871–1947), professor of moral philosophy at Oxford from 1928 to 1937, whose papers are gathered together in *Moral Obligation* (Oxford, 1949) and in *Moral Obligation and Duty and Interest* (Oxford, 1968); and W. D. Ross (1877–1971), Provost of Oriel College from 1929 to 1947, whose *The Right and the Good* was published in Oxford in 1930, to be followed in 1939 by *Foundations of Ethics*. These writers contended that *actions*, as well as their consequences, can have intrinsic value. They can be *in themselves* right or wrong, obligatory or otherwise, such as it is our duty to do, or to refrain from doing.

They said that Moore had been absolutely right to insist that there is a *sui generis* element in morality, something logically distinctive about its judgements. But this distinctive element is not exclusively the goodness of certain ends which our actions can achieve. There is a peculiar kind of appropriateness which certain actions have in certain situations. Moore's empirical and linguistic arguments against 'the naturalistic fallacy' (see above pp. 76) can be deployed, not only against definitions which violate the simplicity of 'good', but equally against all attempts to put words such as 'right', 'ought' or 'duty' into naturalistic terms. When we use 'right', it is no less clear than when we use 'good', that we have before our minds 'a unique object'. And again, if any naturalistic definition, such as, for instance 'maximising happiness', is proposed for 'right', the 'open question' argument can be applied against it. 'Is what maximises happiness right?' is no more self-answering, in ordinary linguistic usage, than 'Is what is pleasant good?'

In thus extending Moore's case for the indefinability of 'good' to all terms which express the distinctively moral evaluation of actions, Prichard and Ross revived a conception of morality as *sui generis* to which many of their intuitionist predecessors had held.[45]

Prichard published a paper in 1912 entitled 'Does Moral Philosophy Rest on a Mistake?' The mistake which he had in mind was to suppose that a reason can be given why we should act in the ways in which we ought to act. Moral philosophers have often set out to *prove* that such-and-such is our duty. But this has been a mistake, said Prichard.

He compared moral thinking to mathematical. Suppose we have to solve a problem in geometry. We shall need to find a number of things out in order to do so—the size of these angles, the length of those lines, etc. But when we have done so, how shall we solve our problem? In the last analysis, by invoking certain relevant axioms—e.g. things which are equal to the same thing are equal to one another, etc. We proceed similarly, said Prichard, in solving a moral problem. He wrote that the rightness of an action 'consists in its being the origination of something of a certain kind A in a situation of a certain kind, a situation consisting in a certain relation B of the agent to others or to his own nature'.[46] Well, suppose the situation is this. I come by chance on some discarded sheets of paper. After glancing at them I realise that they are pages from a sort of letter or report and I am fairly sure that they are about a friend of mine. The contents are derogatory; and if about my friend, I know them to be untrue. The handwriting looks familiar and I am fairly sure that they have been written by another friend of mine. Now, what ought I to do? Before I can answer that question, I shall have to do a good deal of what Prichard calls 'general thinking'. Are these sheets of paper from a responsible report or a malicious correspondence? Are they really about my friend or not? Are they in my other friend's handwriting or not? What is likely to happen, if I tell either of my friends what I know, or suspect? And so on. I must try to get the facts as clear as possible. Having done so, I shall have to ask myself whether I ought to interfere, whether I owe it to the one friend to warn him or to the other to keep silent, until my duty becomes clear. According to Prichard the awareness of my duty will be, in the last analysis, 'immediate, in precisely the sense in which a mathematical apprehension is immediate.' That is to say, it will be like seeing that, if a triangle has two sides equal, it must have two angles equal. This immediate apprehension of duty is what Prichard means by 'moral thinking' as distinct from 'general'. It is the intuitive awareness of a certain course of action as self-evidently the right thing to do.

The moral situation we supposed a moment ago was complicated, as indeed moral situations usually are in real life. It is all very well to say that one should always protect one's friends' best interests: but which friend's, if they conflict? Prichard was, of course, alive to this kind of complexity. He realised that two questions arise, if it is true that we apprehend what is right immediately: (i) Why is it that two or more individuals may differ between themselves as to what is right?; and (ii) Why is it that any one individual may find himself, in the last analysis, confronted by two incompatible courses of action, both of which seem to him 'immediately' to be his duty? Prichard had an answer to the former question. Just as people may differ about the solution of a mathematical problem, so they may about that of a moral one. Some have more moral insight than others, just as some have more mathematical acumen. And even the brightest can sometimes be foxed in morals as in maths. So the mere facts that moral opinions differ, or moral problems may prove too difficult to solve, do not dispose of the view that 'moral thinking' is immediate. The second question, however, Prichard did not answer. He realised that each of us may sometimes have to decide for himself which of two seemingly immediate obligations is the greater. But he does not seem to have realised that there is nothing like this in mathematics. A choice may sometimes be called for between two alternative systems; but within any given system the situation does not arise where axioms conflict and one is called upon to take some and leave others.

Prichard's conception of the immediate apprehension of moral, as of mathematical, truths was Cartesian in character. He believed that these truths are self-evident and that we have a capacity of intuition whereby we become aware of them. There are considerable difficulties in any such conception, as we shall see in a moment or two. However, the parallel between morals and mathematics which Prichard drew was not without value. It enabled him to bring out, perhaps somewhat more clearly than any previous moral philosopher had done, the fact that two elements, the 'moral' and the 'general', enter into the thinking which constitutes moral judgement.

W. D. Ross attempted to tidy up and substantiate Prichard's

basic ideas. He drew certain important distinctions more precisely than Prichard had done; and, in particular, he tried to solve the problem of how it comes about that the immediate apprehensions of a single individual's moral intuition may conflict.

Like Prichard, Ross believed that all distinctly moral terms denote characteristics which are indefinable, non-natural and intuitively apprehended. But he differentiated the meanings of 'right', 'ought' (or 'duty') and 'morally good' from one another.

One overriding distinction, which applies to all of them, is that between the objective and subjective forms of the characteristic in question. If anything is said to have 'objective rightness', for example, this means that it *really is* right; if it is said to have 'subjective rightness', that means it is *thought to be* right. And similarly with the other terms.

This distinction between the objective and the subjective is important when we are considering what it is our duty to do. Ought I to do what is *really right* or simply what I *think* right? One is inclined to say, the former, as Ross himself was until Prichard persuaded him to the contrary.[47] Ross took 'right' to have much the same meaning as Prichard had done. It 'means' he said, "suitable in a unique and indefinable way ... to the situation in which an agent finds himself." [48] If that is so, then there are two respects in which an agent must avoid error—he must not mistake either what the situation is or what it is right to do in such a situation. But how can he ever *know* that he is not mistaken? In virtually every situation there are some morally relevant factors about which any agent may conceivably be mistaken. Even if his moral insight is unerring he may be wrong about the facts of the situation and that will make him wrong about his duty in it. The best we can ever do is what we think is right in the circumstances as we sincerely believe them to be. That, said Ross, is what it *really is* our duty to do, as distinct from anything else which may be *thought* to be our duty.

The terms 'right' and 'wrong' denote properties of actions but, said Ross, following Prichard again, we must not suppose that there are any such characteristics as 'ought-to-be-doneness', attaching to actions. 'Ought' and 'duty' apply to *agents*, not actions—'*we* ought', 'it is *our* duty to' and so on. We might well say that an act would be right, *if it were done*. But we do not say that an act would be our duty, *if it were done*. The existence of the duty does not depend, as the existence of the rightness does, upon the act's existence. Our duty to do it exists before it is done.

'Morally good'[49] means something different again from either 'right' or 'ought'. We see this when we realise that it is possible to do what is right, or what we ought, from a bad motive as well as a good; but it is not possible to do what is 'morally good' from a bad motive or *vice versa*. I may give all I can afford to support an aged parent, hoping that I shall thereby embarrass a poorer brother or sister, who is not able to contribute anything. I shall have done what I ought, but my action will be a malicious one nonetheless. Equally, a kind action may be a dereliction of duty. Moral goodness always has to do with motives. I can control my intentions; and that is why it makes sense to say that 'ought' implies 'can'. But I cannot control my motives—in so far as they are the expression simply of what I feel or desire—and so the fact that it would be morally good for me to do certain things does not imply that I ought to do them, although it may imply that I ought to try to become the sort of person who would be inspired by the relevant motives.

What now had Ross to say about the conflict of obligations, which is so common an experience and which Prichard failed to explain satisfactorily? He began by attempting to list what he called 'the *prima facie* obligations'. These are the kinds of action which Ross believed all men of fully developed moral consciousness intuit to be their duty. Ross's[50] list included: promise-keeping, fidelity (i.e. not lying), reparation, gratitude, justice, beneficence, self-improvement, non-maleficence. In each case a certain natural property, or as Ross called it a 'constitutive characteristic' of actions—e.g. being the fulfilment of a promise, an instance of reparation, etc.—is taken to entail the ethical property or 'consequential characteristic' of rightness. This entailment we intuit. Ross compared his *prima facie* obligations to mathematical axioms.[51] 'If anything is the keeping of a promise, it is *prima facie* right,' is taken to resemble, 'If a triangle is equilateral, it is equiangular', though Ross did realise that the former is not reversible as the latter is.[52]

In most situations which call for moral judgement, more than one *prima facie* obligation is instantiated. Recall the illustration of the discarded pages, which I used a moment or two ago. As the facts became clear—as I discovered, for example, that those derogatory remarks were indeed about my friend and that the pages were from a report or letter, written by another friend— would not the *prima facie* obligations under which I found myself begin to multiply? Would not friendship (the obligations of which may be classified under Ross's 'gratitude') have required me to tell the one who had been reviled? And since I knew what was written to be untrue, would not fidelity have required me to correct it? But what of my obligations to my other friend? Do I owe him nothing just because he has lied about somebody else? And what of non-maleficence—surely one way of not causing embarrassment or trouble would be to keep my mouth shut! But then there is justice to consider. And beneficence no less. And what of self-improvement? Surely I have to consider the effect upon my own character which what I do will have—I must be careful that it does not reinforce either my priggishness or my cowardice! Frequently, we find ourselves sinking in this way into a positive morass of obligations in the midst of life's changes or chances.

Ross's analysis of such instances was as follows. Each *prima facie* obligation which is instantiated gives the relevant course of action a 'tendency'[53] to be right. Letting my friend know that untruths have been told about him, for example, would have such a 'tendency' to be right; but it would have a 'tendency' to be wrong in so far as it did my other friend harm or caused trouble. What I would have to do, according to Ross, in order to discover my duty is to 'weigh' possible courses of action against one another until I thought of the action which 'of all acts possible for the agent in the circumstances ... is that whose *prima facie* rightness (or obligatoriness) in the respects in which it is *prima facie* right (or obligatory) most outweighs its *prima facie* wrongness (or disobligatoriness) in any respects in which it is *prima facie* wrong (or disobligatory)'.[54]

There are two obvious philosophical defects in this analysis. One is Ross's talk of a 'tendency' to be right as if that were a characteristic which *all* members of a class of acts—e.g. those of gratitude—could have. To say that acts of gratitude (or of any other kind) *have a tendency* to be right is simply to say that they are right more often than not. Most of them are but some are not. So 'tendency to be right' obviously cannot be taken to mean, as Ross takes it to mean, a positive property which all the acts in question have.[55] The other defect is, of course, that Ross does not tell us of any 'balance' in which we can 'weigh' *prima facie* obligations against one another. The really worrying thing is that he seems to have thought that the same one can weigh more heavily against certain others in one situation, though less heavily in another situation, where exactly the same *prima facie* obligations are instantiated.[56] He does not grade *prima facie* obligations, so that we know, for instance, that beneficence always outweighs promise-keeping or *vice versa*. In one situation, where both are instantiated, we might be right to act on the one; in another such situation upon the other. But why? If there is no answer to that, beyond the leadings of our own intuition, it is hard to avoid the conclusion that moral judgement is not a reasonable exercise at all. How can it be, if it makes no overriding demands upon consistency?

### Can we know by Intuition?

The philosophers whom I have been discussing in this chapter were all intuitionists. They believed that there are certain moral truths which we know because they are self-evident. But they did not agree as to what these truths are. Moore of the *Principia* thought that they are truths about the intrinsic value of certain ends. He said, for instance, 'By far the most valuable things, which we know or can imagine, are certain states of consciousness, which may be roughly described as the pleasures of human intercourse and the enjoyment of beautiful objects. No one, probably, who has asked himself the question, has ever doubted that personal affection and the appreciation of what is beautiful in Art and Nature, are good in themselves; nor, if we consider strictly what things are worth having *purely for their own sakes*, does it appear probable that any one will think that anything else has *nearly* so great a value as the things which are included under these two heads.'[57] Prichard and Ross, by contrast, thought that what we intuit are truths about the intrinsic value of certain kinds of action, namely those which Ross defined as *prima facie* obligations.

Moore was anxious not to be mistaken for the same kind of intuitionist as the other two. 'I am not an "Intuitionist" in the ordinary sense of the term,' he writes in the Preface to *Principia Ethica*; and he goes on to explain that all he means by calling certain propositions intuitions is that they are incapable of proof, not that they are true. He even adds, 'I hold, on the contrary, that in every way in which it is possible to cognize a true proposition, it is also possible to cognize a false one'—which seems to imply, not simply that our powers of intuition may be limited or defective, but that intuition itself may be mistaken. However, that is hard to reconcile with his assurance at the end of the book, which we noted a moment ago, that 'by far the most valuable things we *know* or can imagine' are aesthetic enjoyments and personal affections. When he describes this as 'a simple truth', which is both 'universally recognised' and 'generally overlooked', it seems most natural to take his meaning to be that intuition apprehends it unerringly, though we ourselves are not guided by this intuition as exclusively as we should be. Whether he thought that intuition can err or not, Moore certainly believed that sometimes it apprehends the truth. He believed no less firmly than Prichard or Ross that there are some moral truths which we *do* know by intuition.

Is this belief viable? It has certainly come in for much hostile criticism.

One line of attack upon it has been as follows. Knowledge is justified true belief. The necessary and sufficient conditions of $A$ knowing that $X$ are, (i) It is true that $X$. I cannot know, for instance, that anyone is the king of France. (ii) $A$ believes that $X$. It would be self-contradictory to say 'I know that there is no king of France but I do not believe it.' (iii) $A$ must be able to offer some justification for his belief—some acceptable answer to the question 'How do you know that $X$?' The kind of answer which is acceptable will vary with the nature of $X$. Evidence which justifies a mathematical or logical proposition is not of the same kind, for example, as that which justifies a statement in empirical science or moral evaluation. There are different routes, so to speak, to knowledge. But it is necessary to follow one or other of them. It is not enough for the proposition that $X$ to be believed and true. If, in the ordinary meaning of the word 'know', $A$ is to be said to know that $X$, then $A$ must be able to offer grounds of an acceptable kind for his belief that $X$. Now, why will 'by intuition' not serve as an answer to 'How do you know?' The reason given is that there is no discernible difference in meaning between the claim '*A knows that X by intuition*' and '*A believes very firmly that X*'. 'By intuition' does not really take us beyond the second of the three necessary and sufficient conditions of knowledge. The above analysis of knowledge as justified true belief[58] has not gone unchallenged[59] but let us assume that it is correct as far as it goes. The point to take is that it applies to *inferential* knowledge, the kind where what is known is inferred from evidence of the appropriate kind. So far as knowledge of this kind is concerned, it is no use appealing to intuition because intuition is simply conviction, not evidence.

However, not all knowledge is inferential. Some is *immediate*. To borrow an illustration,[60] suppose I am on a train going to Basingstoke. I ask my travelling companions, who have recently boarded the train, how far we are from Basingstoke and whether this train was on time at the station where they joined it. I keep looking at my watch. I ask if the train usually runs to time. And so on. For their part, they may well infer from my behaviour that I am wondering whether we will be in Basingstoke on time. For my part, if I am wondering this, then I will know that I am. But not because I infer it from my behaviour. I will not need to say, 'Here I am asking these questions, looking at my watch, etc. I must be wondering whether I will be in Basingstoke on time!' I will know it immediately, not inferentially. Immediate knowledge does not only apply to that of my own states of mind. I may know, for instance, that there are people living in number 10 because I see or hear them; and this is different from knowing that they are there because I have inferred their presence from toys on the lawn, smoke pouring out of the chimney, etc. Again, I may know that I was in Birmingham last month because I remember being there; and this is not to say that I have deduced as much from the testimony of my diary, a railway ticket in my pocket, or any other such evidence. Well, then, why should not moral truths be known immediately by some sort of intuition which shares the immediacy of sense-perception or memory?

One thing which casts doubt on that as a possibility is the great diversity of opinion which exists about moral issues. People do not differ in their sense-perceptions to anything like the extent to which they differ in their moral judgements. It is logically possible, of course, that we all have a 'moral sense', analogous to physical sense, but much more variously defective. Moreover, it may be that the order which the 'moral sense' apprehends is much harder to be clear about than the physical world. That is the sort

101

of explanation which intuitionists always offer for the diversity of moral codes. But it takes some believing.

If moral intuition is compared, not to sense-perception, but to reason's awareness of self-evident truths, like the axioms of mathematics, then, whatever may be the correct account of such truths, there is the difference of which Prichard and Ross tried unsuccessfully to dispose, that the moral intuitions, even of a single individual, may conflict in a way to which there is no parallel in the case of the self-evident truths of any other axiomatic system.

The main objection to the view that ethical intuition gives us immediate knowledge of moral truths, however, is the lack of any independent check upon it. There are ways in which we can test our perceptions or memories for objective truth. The information they give us is immediate but not infallible. Perhaps I am deceived when I think that I see or hear people in number 10. Perhaps my memory is playing tricks and I was not in Birmingham last month. There are generally accepted ways of settling such matters. No one would claim that the way any individual sees the world is necessarily the way it is; or the way I remember the past is necessarily the way it was. But is it not something like that, which intuitionists claim for their moral judgements? There is, of course, the consensus of opinion to which appeal may be made; but, as I have already said, what confronts us in morality tends to be diversity rather than consensus. And even if there were a consensus, there is nothing in morality which is comparable to those predictions of future events, by which we can test whether or not things really are, or were, the way we have perceived or remembered them. Have I really seen people in number 10? We will knock and wait for them to come to the door. Have I correctly remembered that I was in Birmingham last month? I will phone my friends there and say 'When I came to see you last month ...' in order to see how they react. No such checks can be applied to moral intuitions. If they constitute immediate knowledge of an objective reality, then it is of a kind which is self-authenticating as other forms of immediate knowledge are not. We are back with the old question of how such knowledge is different from mere belief.

---

1. Op. cit., p. viii.
2. Op. cit., p. 9.

3. Op. cit., p. 10.
4. Op. cit., p. 14.
5. Op. cit., p. 16.
6. See op. cit., chapters ii, iii and iv.
7. 'Is "Goodness" a Name of a Simple Non-Natural Quality?', *Proceedings of the Aristotelian Society*, 1933–4.
8. Op. cit., pp. 256–7.
9. Op. cit., p. 257.
10. Op. cit., p. 264.
11. Op. cit., p. 267.
12. For Moore's views on moral judgements as intuitive and synthetic cf. *Principia Ethica* pp. 142–4.
13. Op. cit., pp. 173–4; cf. above p. 26.
14. *Utilitarianism*, Everyman edition, London, 1910, p. 32.
15. Op. cit., p. 6.
16. Op. cit., p. 65.
17. Op. cit., p. 65: cf. Mill, op. cit., pp. 4, 32.
18. Op. cit., pp. 32–3; cf. Moore, op. cit., p. 66.
19. Op. cit., pp. 67–8.
20. Op. cit., p. 36.
21. Op. cit., pp. 68–72, with due acknowledgement to F. H. Bradley's *Ethical Studies*.
22. Op. cit., p. 66.
23. *Sidgwick's Ethics and Victorian Morality*, Oxford, 1977, pp. 178–88.
24. Cf. Papers by E. W. Hall, J. O. Urmson, J. B. Mabbott, Mary Warnock and M. Mandelbaum in J. B. Schneewind (editor) *Mill: A Collection of Essays*, London, 1968.
25. See his *Dilemmas*, London, 1954, Lecture IV and the Symposium 'Pleasure' with G. B. Gallie in *Proceedings of the Aristotelian Society*, supplementary vol. 1954.
26. There are some difficulties in Ryle's view. For instance, if what is meant by the fact that someone is enjoying a game of tennis has to be spelt out in terms of hypotheticals describing his disposition to behave in certain ways, it seems to follow that his own awareness that he is enjoying himself will necessarily be an inference from the observation of his own behaviour—'Here I am, going on playing even though it's dinner time! I must be enjoying myself!'—which seems absurd. Some (e.g. T. Penelhum, 'The Logic of Pleasure', *Philosophy and Phenomenological Research*, 1956–7) would say that this shows enjoyment to be an episode in mental life, logically distinct from what causes it, even though it is a form of attention. They propose to call it a 'response episode' in order to take both points.
27. See Symposium 'Pleasure' op. cit.
28. 'The Interpretation of the Moral Philosophy of J. S. Mill' in J. B. Schneewind (editor) op. cit., p. 181.
29. Op. cit., p. 15.
30. Op. cit., p. 17.
31. Op. cit., p. 38.

32. Op. cit., p. 36.
33. H. S. R. Elliott, *The Letters of John Stuart Mill* (1910) II.116, quoted by E. W. Hall, op. cit., p. 162.
34. 'An Autobiography' in *The Philosophy of G. E. Moore*, edited by L. A. Schlipp, pp. 16–17.
35. Op. cit., p. 17.
36. *The Method of Ethics*, fifth edition, p. 33.
37. Op. cit., (seventh edition), p. 32.
38. Op. cit., pp. 400–2.
39. Op. cit., pp. 87–96.
40. Op. cit., pp. 106–7.
41. Op. cit., pp. 147–8.
42. Op. cit., p. 169.
43. Op. cit., p. 13.
44. Op. cit., p. 107.
45. Cf. A. N. Prior, *Logic and the Basic of Ethics*, Oxford, 1949.
46. Op. cit., *Mind* (1912) reprinted in *Moral Obligation*, p. 7.
47. *Foundations of Ethics*, chapter VII. It was Prichard's 'Duty and Ignorance of Fact' (1932) reprinted in *Moral Obligation* which changed his mind.
48. Op. cit., p. 146.
49. Op. cit., chapter XII.
50. *The Right and the Good*, chapter II.
51. Op. cit., pp. 29–30.
52. Op. cit., p. 121.
53. Cf. op. cit., p. 28.
54. Op. cit., p. 46: cf. *Foundations of Ethics*, p. 85.
55. Cf. P. F. Strawson, 'Ethical Intuitionism', *Philosophy*, 1949.
56. Cf. *Foundations of Ethics*, pp. 320–1.
57. *Principia Ethica*, pp. 188–9.
58. Cf. A. J. Ayer, *The Problem of Knowledge*, London, 1956, pp. 31ff.
59. Cf. E. L. Gettier, 'Is Justified True Belief Knowledge?', *Analysis*, vol. 23. (1963).
60. See H. H. Price, *Belief*, London, 1969, pp. 86–91.

# 5

# The Emotive Theory

Ethics stands alone in the sense that moral judgements have a distinctive meaning. Moore can be credited with having persuaded his contemporaries and successors that this conclusion is beyond doubt. The question which now arose within moral philosophy was, What account are we to give of this distinctive meaning which moral discourse has?

The account of it which Moore and his fellow-intuitionists gave was rooted in the referential theory of meaning.[1] This is the theory that language means whatever it is about. The word 'pen', for instance, means an implement of the kind with which I am writing; 'light' means the physical phenomenon without which I could not see to write; and so on. Given this theory, the meaning of the word 'red' in a sentence such as, 'This apple is red,' must be the natural property of redness, which we apprehend by means of sense-perception. And similarly, the meaning of the words 'good' or 'right' in the moral judgements, 'This end is good' and 'This act is right,' must be the properties to which they respectively refer. But these properties are obviously not natural ones like redness, nor do we perceive them by any physical sense such as sight, hearing, etc. They were, therefore, thought of as 'non-natural' properties; and the faculty which apprehends them was taken to be a kind of extrasensory perception. These two conceptions—non-natural, moral properties and a faculty of moral intuition—were the inevitable offspring of the marriage, which the intuitionists arranged, between the idea of the distinctive meaning of moral discourse and the general theory that the meaning of language is that to which it refers. One of these parent notions remained respectable, but it was not long before the other went down in the world.

The referential theory of meaning has a certain *prima facie* plausibility. If words are not about things, then what are they about? If what we say does not stand for what exists, then how can it have any meaning? True, some things are more complicated than others. That is why, for instance, it is more difficult to say what 'light' means than what 'pen' means. But if, in the last analysis, both words do not refer to realities which exist independently of language, what meaning can they have? These questions seem at first blush obviously rhetorical, but reflection raises doubts. What about words like 'and', 'but', 'if', 'then'? They contribute to the meaning of so many sentences and yet we cannot point to anything in the world to which they refer. Again, how does it come about that language sometimes has the same referent but not the same meaning? For example, the two expressions 'The Prime Minister of Great Britain' and 'Mr Denis Thatcher's wife' refer to the same lady; but they certainly do not have the same meaning because, if they did, the sentence 'Mr Denis Thatcher's wife is the Prime Minister of Great Britain' would be a trivial tautology. And it is not. Yet again, how can the meaning of language always be its referent, when it is quite obvious that, not only *what* we are talking about, but *how* we are talking about it, can make a difference to the meaning of the things we say. We can, for example, say something as simple as 'Jimmy Carter' in tones of either admiration or contempt. The referent is identical in the two cases but the meaning is worlds apart. I have, of course, presented the referential theory in its most simplistic light; and its more sophisticated proponents have manoeuvred skilfully in face of the kind of objections which I have just been illustrating. One need only think of Wittgenstein's 'picture theory' in the *Tractatus* to realise how far removed from naiveté some versions of the referential theory have been. Nevertheless, that theory has fallen into disrepute and the philosophical progeny which once lived off it in favoured security, like the intuitionist theory of ethics, have lost caste in consequence.

There were two particular features of intuitionism, as propounded by Moore, Prichard and Ross, to which a growing number of moral philosophers took exception. One may be described as its mysteriousness. The philosophical climate in the nineteen twenties and thirties became prevailingly empiricist. Philosophers tended to esteem natural science ever more highly and to regard metaphysics, and everything which savoured of it, with increasing distaste. The most intense expression of this tendency was, of course, logical positivism, the influence of which had become very pervasive among British philosophers by the end of the thirties. Notions such as those of 'non-natural properties' and 'extrasensory intuition' were exceedingly uncongenial to these empirically-minded philosophers, whose star was in the ascendant.

The second feature of intuitionism, which counted against it, was its failure to offer any explanation of the action-guiding character which moral judgements have. If we say that an apple is red we do not imply that anyone should eat it. But in saying that an act is right, or an end good, we are normally taken to be recommending that it should be pursued or performed. Intuitionists, in taking moral judgements to be simply a peculiar kind of factual statement—concerned with the non-natural and confirmed by the extrasensory—left this aspect of moral discourse unexplained. If such discourse concerns only what *is* the case (however mysterious) how can anything follow from it about what should be done? This, it was felt, is not a question which can be passed over in silence as it was by the intuitionists.

When the referential theory began to lose favour, intuitionism became more exposed to hostile criticism on both these counts. The best known exponent of the former kind of criticism is probably A. J. Ayer, whose *Language, Truth and Logic*, published in London in 1936, soon became the *vade mecum* of empirically-minded philosophy students. The second kind of criticism is most impressively represented by C. L. Stevenson. He published 'The Emotive Meaning of Ethical Terms' in *Mind* in 1937 and 'Persuasive Definitions' in the same journal in 1938. His *Ethics and Language* came out in 1944. In these writings he made a sustained effort to replace intuitionism by an ethical theory which would take full account of the action-guiding character which moral discourse has.

The type of ethical theory, which Ayer and Stevenson espoused is known as emotivism.[2] Although they are perhaps its most widely read exponents, they should not be thought of as its inventors. It had been in the philosophical air for some time. As early as 1923, C. K. Ogden and I. A. Richards, adumbrated it in their book *The Meaning of Meaning*[3] (parts of which are said in the preface to have been written as early as 1910 and most of which appeared in periodicals in 1920–22). They rejected Moore's view that 'good' refers to a common characteristic of things which are good and thought its use 'purely emotive'. It 'stands', they said, 'for nothing whatever.' If we say, 'This is good,' that 'serves only as an emotive sign expressing our attitude to *this*, and perhaps evoking similar attitudes in other persons, or inciting them to actions of one kind or another.'

W. H. F. Barnes put forward a similar theory in a paper which he read to the Jowett Society at Oxford in November, 1933, the relevant part of which was subsequently published in *Analysis* 1933–4 under the title 'A Suggestion about Value'.[4] He said that we must seek for the origin of our value judgements in the expressions of approval, delight and affection which children utter when confronted with certain experiences. Moore's view that the sentence '*A* is good' predicates a non-natural property of *A* is expressly rejected; and also the subjectivist view that it describes the speaker's approval of *A*. It is simply, said Barnes, a 'form of words *expressive* of ... approval' (italics mine). He compares it to a shout of 'Oh!', which does not describe, but rather expresses, the occurrence of certain feelings in the speaker. In words which—as we shall see—anticipate to a remarkable degree the views of Ayer and Stevenson on moral argument, Barnes said that if anyone does not agree with me that '*A* is good', what I can do is 'point out details in *A* which are the object of my approval' in the hope that my opponent 'when he becomes aware of these will approve of *A*: and so be ready to say "*A* is good"'. This is 'not really to gain his assent to a proposition'; it is simply 'to change his attitude from one of disapproval to one of approval towards *A*'.

A few months later, in June 1934, C. D. Broad read to the Aristotelian Society the paper to which I referred above (p. 77).[5] He attributed to A. E. Duncan-Jones the opinion that 'This is good' may be equivalent in meaning to something like, 'This is an act of self-sacrifice. Hurrah!' Broad thought Duncan-Jones' opinion 'quite plausible enough to deserve very serious consideration'. A sentence which is grammatically in the indicative mood, he pointed out, 'may really be in part interjectional or rhetorical or imperative.' It 'may be in part the expression of an emotion which the speaker is feeling,' or alternatively it 'may be used partly to evoke a certain kind of emotion in the hearer'. Yet again, it 'may be used to command or forbid certain actions' and 'be equivalent on a certain occasion to: "That's an act of self-sacrifice. Imitate it!"' Broad, like Barnes, believed that this theory gets some support from the study of children. For them, he said, 'good' acts are co-extensive with those which a child's parents name with a smile or command it to do; bad ones, with those they name with a frown or forbid it to do. Very soon, these ethical words acquire the same rhetorical or imperative force as the smile or the frown, the commanding or the forbidding. This force, Broad saw, is distinguishable from their descriptive meaning. He noted that moral judgements may be 'amphibious': 'That's a lie', for example, means, 'That's a statement made with the intention of producing a false belief'; but it also expresses or stimulates an emotion of aversion towards the making of such a statement. It was, we shall see, this same distinction between the emotive and descriptive meanings of a word which Stevenson drew and on which he based his important account of 'persuasive definitions'.[6]

## A. J. Ayer

In the nineteen-thirties, Ayer attended the meetings of the Vienna Circle, that influential group of scientists and philosophers which propagated logical positivism. They propounded a criterion of meaning which became known as the Verification Principle. In order to discover what any statement means, they contended, we must ask, not simply what it refers to, but how it can be verified. Their commitment to empiricism was as complete as David Hume's had been and, like him, they thought that there are two and only two ways in which anything which is said can conceivably be verified. In Ayer's words, 'A statement is held to be literally meaningful if and only if it is either analytic or empirically verifiable.'[7] By 'literally meaningful' he intended 'capable of being shown to be true or false'. What he had in mind, of course, was cognitive meaning, the kind statements need to have if they are to convey information and contribute to knowledge. Analytic statements are those of mathematics or formal logic, which can be true or false simply from the definitions of the terms used in them. If true, they are tautologies; if false, contradictions. 'Two plus two equals four' is the former, 'Two plus two equals three,' the latter. Empirical verification, by contrast, is a matter of appealing to the evidence of our physical senses. At its most accurate and decisive it is the kind of verification effected by scientific experiment; but ordinary common sense statements admit of it in their degree. Any statements which cannot be verified in either of these two ways— analytically or empirically—are cognitively meaningless. Those who take Ayer's view echo approvingly Hume's oft-quoted dictum, 'If we take in our hand any volume; of divinity or school metaphysics, for instance: let us ask, *Does it contain any abstract reasoning concerning quantity or number?* No. *Does it contain any experimental reasoning concerning matter of fact and existence?* No. Commit it then to the flames: for it can contain nothing but sophistry and illusion.'[8]

Moral judgements cannot be verified in either of the approved ways. Mistaken as they may have thought Moore to be on some counts, the logical positivists would have agreed with him that nothing can be shown to be right or good simply by definition; and that rightness and goodness are not natural properties which can be observed by sense perception. Ayer expressed what he took to be the conclusion of the matter in this way, 'The fundamental ethical concepts ... are pseudo-concepts. The presence of an ethical symbol in a proposition adds nothing to its factual content. Thus if I say to someone, "You acted wrongly in stealing that money," I am not stating anything more than if I had simply said, "You stole that money." In adding that this action is wrong I am not making any further statement about it.'[9] What, then, am I doing? Ayer's reply was that 'it is as if I had said, "You stole that money" in a peculiar tone of horror or written it with the addition of some special exclamation marks. The tone, or the exclamation marks, adds nothing to the literal meaning of the sentence. It merely serves to show that the expression of it is attended by certain feelings in the speaker.'[10]

As is well-known, the theory of meaning which the logical positivists propounded has come in for devastating criticism. Those who subscribed to it admired science and detested metaphysics. But it was eventually pointed out to them that their criterion of meaning excludes the former and admits the latter. In so far as scientific hypotheses are universal propositions of the form 'All As are B', they can be falsified but not verified. The discovery of one A which is not B will disprove any such hypothesis; but no amount of As which are B will put it beyond doubt because there may always be an A, as yet undiscovered, which is not B. So, if verifiability is the test of meaningfulness, scientific hypotheses are meaningless. The principle could be revised to read that statements, other than analytic ones, have literal meaning only if they can be *falsified* empirically, but even then problems would remain. Common sense statements of the form 'Some As are B' would then be meaningless, because they cannot be falsified. However many As we find which are not B there may still be some which are. Moreover, as Ayer himself points out, both verification and falsification in so far as they are empirical depend upon certain observations and it is always logically possible that those who make them are decieved for some reason. In the face of such difficulties, the Verification Principle was revised to read that a statement is meaningful if any empirical observations would be 'relevant' to its verification. And 'relevance' was taken to mean that an observation statement (i.e. one which records an actual or possible empirical observation) can be deduced from the statement under consideration in conjunction with certain other premises, without being deducible from those other premises alone. But then it became apparent that a metaphysical statement can fulfil this condition. 'The Absolute is pure spirit,' conjoined to, 'If the Absolute is pure spirit, then this rose is red,' yields, 'This rose is red' and that conclusion is an observation statement. So now by the revised principle, metaphysical statements are meaningful! Further attempts have been made to reformulate the Verification Principle, the intricacies of which I have described elsewhere.[11] Here it will suffice to notice that even Ayer himself is ready to concede that they have not been successful.[12]

What mainly concerns us are the implications of Ayer's view that moral judgements are emotive in meaning. He was careful to point out the difference between emotivism and subjectivism. A subjectivist is someone who thinks that moral judgements express *propositions* about the speaker's feelings. 'This is wrong,' for instance, is taken to be equivalent in meaning to 'I disapprove of this'. But Ayer makes it clear that this is not what he means when he says that moral judgements 'express certain feelings in

111

the speaker'. Here 'express' does not mean that anything is said to be the case. It is used in the sense in which to groan or to cheer is to express one's feelings. Ayer believed that moral judgements are precisely comparable to such ejaculations. His theory of ethics had indeed sometimes been called the 'Boo-Hurrah' theory. Ethical terms such as 'right' or 'good' and their opposites, he said, are 'used to express feelings about certain objects *but not to make any assertion about them*'[13] (italics mine).

What follows from this theory of the meaning of moral judgements? Where nothing is asserted, nothing can be denied. And so, said Ayer, 'it would be impossible to argue'[14] about questions of right or wrong, good or evil. This seems a paradoxical conclusion because, to all appearance, people do, and always have, argued most persistently about these very questions. Surely, if one man says 'This is right,' and another, 'It is wrong', they are arguing about moral value! It may be remembered that both Sidgwick and Moore attempted a *reductio ad absurdum* of subjectivism on this very ground. If the former speaker meant simply, 'I approve of this,' and the latter, 'I don't', they would not be contradicting one another. But that is manifestly absurd because they so obviously are! But not about moral value, insisted Ayer.[15] If we carefully analyse any moral argument, we shall find that the disputants are *agreed* as to the *value* of certain kinds of actions or states of affairs—equal pay for equal work, what will make most people happy, or whatever—and what they are arguing about is whether in *fact* some action or state of affairs is of the relevant kind—Is this really equal work? Will that make most people happy? etc. Since most of us have been conditioned by our upbringing and education to have the same moral values, argument is possible. But we must not suppose that it is about questions of value. 'When someone disagrees with us about the moral value of a certain action or type of action, we do admittedly resort to argument in order to win him over to our way of thinking. But we do not attempt to show by our arguments that he has the "wrong" ethical feeling towards a situation whose nature he has correctly apprehended. What we attempt to show is that he is mistaken about the facts of the case ... if our opponent ... acknowledges all the facts (but) still disagrees with us about the moral value of the actions under discussion, then we abandon the attempt to convince him by argument.'[16] Judgements of value are incapable of being true or false. And so it is logically impossible to convince anyone that he is deceived in his value judgements or that he was illogical in adopting them. Without truth or falsity there cannot be validity or invalidity.

Ayer's *Language, Truth and Logic* had a great *succés de scandale* and the most outrageous part of it has been deemed by some readers to be its ethical theory. If moral values cannot be argued about, then they must be beyond reason. Moral convictions must be indistinguishable from blind prejudice; and moral persuasion, nothing more than propaganda. A moral theory which arrived at such conclusions was considered by many to be unworthy of the name.

We shall see that there are elements in Stevenson's account of morality which seem to regard it as nothing more than prejudice or propaganda. But I think it would be unfair to say that this is what Ayer did. He was obviously intent upon pointing out in the most arresting terms at his command that, whatever moral thinking may be, it is not the same thing as scientific discovery or logical deduction. But the only alternatives to these forms of ratiocination are not prejudice or propaganda. Ayer challenges his readers to refute his emotivism by constructing an imaginary argument about a question of value 'which does not reduce itself to an argument about a question of logic or about an empirical matter of fact'.[17] He is confident that they will not be able to do so. His point was that the argument will never lead to the discovery or deduction of *values*; it will always be about what it is logically possible to *say* or what fits in with empirical *facts*. But even if one's value judgements are in the last analysis decisions rather than discoveries, commitments and not conclusions, there are different ways in which logical or empirical considerations can be deployed in support of them. A politician, for instance, who counters every attack upon his party with skilful rationalisation, is not doing exactly the same kind of thing as a fairminded magistrate, who tries to be clear about the facts of the case, and to work out what penalty it would be consistent with the law to impose. Nothing Ayer says implies that there is no difference between two such cases.

As I have already suggested, the notion of morality as prejudice or propaganda is more at home in Stevenson's account of emotivism than in Ayer's. The fundamental difference between them lies in their respective theories of meaning. Stevenson's theory had the virtue of recognising that the meaning of language in general is not simply *what* it is about but *how* it is about whatever it is about. He saw that we must ask, not simply what language refers to, but what use is made of it, what job it does. That said, however, his theory is vitiated by other features which are seriously misconceived.

It is usually described as the 'causal' or 'psychological' theory of meaning. Summarily put, what it comes to is this: the meaning of language is its disposition to cause, or to be caused by, certain psychological processes in the hearer or the speaker respectively.[18] It is easy enough to travesty a psychological theory of meaning by pointing out that the causes and effects of a word or sentence may vary from person to person and it is manifestly absurd to suggest that its meaning can vary accordingly. The cognitive meaning of the sentence, 'The successful applicant is Mr. Brown,' is surely the same for Mr. Brown and the unsuccessful candidates, even though it causes him delight and them despair. Because Stevenson is alive to this point, he introduces the notion of language's 'disposition'. When he says that a sign (i.e. a word or sentence) may acquire a 'disposition to be used', he means that it may become the thing to say (among certain people in such-and-such a situation) when one is in some specific mental state. And when he says that it can have 'a disposition to affect a hearer' he is pointing out that it may be such that it usually produces certain psychological effects in those to whom it is addressed. But this does not redeem his theory from absurdity. In so far as the meaning of language is its disposition to cause psychological effects, the meaning of a command will be the activity which it generates; the meaning of a statement, the belief which it causes; the meaning of a judgement, the assent which it gains; and so on. In the absence of such responses, therefore, the relevant utterances will be meaningless. A command will lose its meaning, if disobeyed; a statement, if not believed; etc. And that surely is absurd!

There is a grain of truth buried in Stevenson's theory, of course. For example, the words, 'I found your essay boring,' written by a tutor on his pupil's essay, are unlikely to be uttered with approval or heard with pleasure. There is a sense of 'mean' in which it can with significance be said that the disapproval of the tutor, or the displeasure of the pupil, are what this sentence means. Suppose, for instance, that two other pupils read this comment at the foot of the essay. One may say to the other with reference to the tutor who marked the essay, 'That means he was in a bad mood'; or, of their fellow-pupil, who wrote the essay, 'This means he will be disappointed.' This 'causal' sense of 'meaning' is, however, quite distinct from what is usually called the 'logical' or 'normative' sense of the word. The difference becomes clear, if we contrast two possible answers to the question, 'Why did the tutor say, "I found your essay boring"?' One—the *causal* explanation—would be, 'Because he felt bored with the essay and wanted to chastise its author.' The other—the *logical* or *normative* explanation—would be, 'Because he wanted to state the opinion that the essay was boring and *this was how to do so.*' The former reply finds the explanation in putative empirical facts about the speaker, which are thought to *cause* this remark. The latter reply appeals to certain linguistic *rules* or *norms* (those for expressing opinions) which provide the *reason* for the remark in question. The meaning which philosophers try to explain is of the latter 'logical' or 'normative', kind. Stevenson's mistake was to confuse it with the former kind.

He represented moral discourse as having two kinds of psychological meaning, viz, descriptive and emotive. The *descriptive* meaning of a sign is its disposition to affect cognition—by which he meant such mental activities as believing, thinking, supposing, presuming, etc. *Emotive* meaning he defined in these terms: 'The emotive meaning of a word is the power that the word acquires on account of its history in emotional situations, to evoke or directly express attitudes, as distinct from describing or designating them.'[19] There are possibilities of precision in descriptive meaning which do not exist in the case of emotive. Dictionary definitions fix descriptive meanings very precisely by means of linguistic rules which relate signs to one another. But emotive meaning is just 'a flexible mechanism of *suggestion*'.[20] The distinction between what a sign means and what it suggests is illustrated from a word like 'pig'. Applied to a certain kind of animal, it has a descriptive meaning which can be precisely defined in terms of rules for its use. Applied to human beings, it has a derogatory emotive meaning, which does not admit of precise definition. Emotive meaning can only be 'characterised', to use Stevenson's term,[21] as, for example, derogatory. But I am not sure that the meaning of 'pig' when applied to a man, really is *vaguer* than when applied to an animal. It may be simpler but that is different. Stevenson is certainly mistaken if he is suggesting that, in their emotive meanings, signs are not used according to rules. Even monosyllabic ejaculations such as 'Ugh!' are intelligible in some contexts but not in others. However, the main point which Stevenson wished to make was that a word's descriptive meaning may change whilst its emotive meaning remains constant. This would not be impugned by the recognition that both meanings demand conformity to rules.

Stevenson offered what he called two 'patterns of analysis' to show that moral judgements have *both* descriptive *and* emotive meaning. He said that both patterns are necessary in order to bring out the 'flexibility' of moral discourse.[22] He happens to give analyses of judgements using 'good' but says explicitly that *mutatis mutandis* they apply to all moral terms.

According to the first pattern, 'This is good' means 'I approve of this; do so as well.'[23] The descriptive element is: 'I approve of this'; the emotive: '... do so as well.'

The second pattern of analysis was expressed in these terms: ' "This is good" has the meaning of "This has qualities or relations X, Y, Z ...," ' except that "good" has as well a laudatory emotive meaning which permits it to express the speaker's approval, and tends to evoke the approval of the hearer.'[24] The variables X, Y, Z ... must be replaced by words which represent the accepted criteria of goodness in the society to which the speaker belongs. These provide the descriptive element. And, of course, the laudatory force of the word 'good' supplies the emotive element.

G. E. Moore in his 'A Reply to My Critics' (written in response to the papers, including one from Stevenson, in L. A. Schilpp's collection *The Philosophy of G. E. Moore*, Evanston Ill. 1942) dealt with Stevenson's first pattern of analysis. He rejected the first part of it out of hand. 'This is good' does not assert 'I approve of X.' It may be said to 'imply' it, though not in the sense that the one follows from the other but rather in the sense that we have all learnt by experience that a man who says that something is good does, in the great majority of cases, approve of it.[25]

The second part of Stevenson's first pattern '... do so as well' strikes Moore as more plausible. He is prepared to face the consequences of accepting this second part whilst rejecting the first. 'This is good' will then not be an assertion at all but simply an imperative. It will have no descriptive meaning but only an emotive one, as Stevenson here defines the latter. Well, why not? Moore now thinks that this may 'very possibly'[26] be true. He admits that it 'simply had not occurred' to him before reading Stevenson. He recalls that in his book *Ethics* he had insisted that if one man says 'This is right' and another 'It is not', they must be contradicting each other (cf. above p. 112); but he is now ready to concede that this may be the same kind of disagreement as that between a man who says 'Let's play poker' and one who says 'No, let's listen to a record'. That is to say, a disagreement in attitudes, rather than in logically incompatible opinions.

Stevenson's second pattern of analysis led him to the idea of 'persuasive definitions'.[27] which even his strongest opponents would agree is an illuminating conception. Terms with both descriptive and emotive meaning can be changed in the former respect whilst left unchanged in the latter. This device is frequently used in the attempt to change people's attitudes. A laudatory term like 'freedom', for example, can be used to commend some practice by redefining the descriptive meaning of the term so as to include this practice; a derogatory word like 'tyranny' can be used to discredit some practice in the same way. True freedom, people say, is such and such; real tyranny is this or that. Such moves are constantly made by preachers and politicians. I take two examples from recent newspapers. Mr Ian Paisley is reported to have said from his pulpit that the sympathetic coverage on television of the Pope's visit to Ireland shows the B.B.C. to be 'agents of the Jesuits'. 'Agent' is a sinister word and 'Jesuits' more so. Neither of them is intended literally. Mr Paisley does not wish to say that the B.B.C. has been paid an agent's fee from the coffers of the Society of Jesus. All he wants to do is to attach to what has actually happened—the fact that the B.B.C. has put out programmes showing the Pope in a sympathetic light—the opprobrium contained in words like 'agent' and 'Jesuit'.

Mr Neil Kinnock at the Labour party conference in Brighton described the Tory government's proposed cuts in education expenditure as 'an act of educational genocide'. Of course, Mr Kinnock did not mean that they have killed anybody. He just wished to give 'genocide' a new descriptive meaning—namely, reducing the amount of money spent on teachers, equipment, school meals, etc.—whilst retaining the horror in the word.

I said earlier that it was to Stevenson's credit that he recognised the action-guiding character of moral judgements (above p. 114). Quite explicitly he said that, 'a person who recognises X to be "good" must *ipso facto* acquire a stronger tendency to act in its favour than he otherwise would have had.'[28] The word 'tendency' used here is important because it indicates the psychological (rather than the logical) nature of the connection which Stevenson wishes to make out between moral judgements and action. Remember that he sees language's 'dispositional property' to have certain psychological causes or effects as the essence of its meaning. Here he is applying that theory to moral judgements. Their 'tendency' to move us to action is at the core of their meaning. As he puts it, their 'primary use' is to 'create an influence'.[29]

Moral judgements express attitudes, corresponding to their emotive meaning; and beliefs, which correspond to their descriptive meaning. An 'attitude' is defined by Stevenson as 'a *disposition* to act in certain ways and to experience certain feelings'.[30] Stevenson sees the purpose of moral thinking and argument to lie in the manufacture of attitudes through the manipulation of beliefs.

Consider how he thinks this is done in accordance with his first pattern of analysis, viz. by predicating 'good'. How do we get people to think that something is good? We 'describe' it in such a way that 'a preponderance of (their) desires' will move towards it.[31] If, for example, we want them to think of fidelity to one's spouse within marriage as good, we may try to get them to believe that it is the necessary condition of a peaceful mind, or the happiness of their children, or their financial security, etc. Their attitude of approval may thus be redirected through a change in their beliefs. That is how 'good' is attached to something new.

Beliefs may also be manipulated in accordance with Stevenson's second pattern of analysis. Here the change of attitude may be conceived as brought about by attaching something new to 'good' rather than vice versa. We can take a word with both a descriptive and an emotive meaning, such as 'freedom' and, whilst its emotive meaning (i.e. the goodness of freedom) stays put, get people to believe that what it really describes is not being able to do as you please but, for example, not having to pay school bills, or pay for medical treatment, etc.

Stevenson sees his first pattern analysis as the more fundamental. What is going on basically in the second, as in the first, is that something is being judged to be good. As Stevenson put it, words like 'freedom' are 'prizes which each man seeks to bestow on the qualities of his own choice.'[32]

The important point to take is that, according to Stevenson, what goes on fundamentally in moral judgement is not reasoning as normally understood but causation. Not proof, but 'a substitute for a proof'.[33] The nature of this 'substitute' comes out clearly in what he had to say about the methodology of moral judgement.[34] He finds in it both a 'rational' and a 'non-rational' (or 'persuasive') element. The rational element consists of 'reasons which change beliefs'; the non-rational, of 'the sheer, direct emotional impact of words'.[35] But *both* of them have their place in moral judgement only in so far as they are effective in 'creating an influence', in *causing* people to change their attitudes.

Examples of the 'rational' method would be instances where we point out to someone that his factual beliefs about something, which he considers good or bad, are false or take account only of certain aspects of the thing in question. We try to get him to abjure falsehoods or to consider every aspect of the thing, in order that we may change his attitude to it. Examples of the 'non-rational' method would be, 'rhetorical cadence, apt metaphor, stentorian, stimulating, or pleading tones of voice, dramatic gestures,'[36] etc. and persuasive definition, of course. Stevenson says that in many cases of moral argument there is 'so close a wedding of persuasive and rational methods'[37] that it takes much skill to differentiate them. Both these kinds of method are such as prejudice and propaganda may thrive on; this is true, not only of the persuasive, but of the rational no less. (When it suits the design of the 'hidden persuaders' of the commercial or political worlds, they are not slow to question the truth or comprehensiveness of the beliefs on which our attitudes are based.) Stevenson does not deny the comparison between morality and propaganda. He thinks the words 'moralist' and 'propagandist' are themselves persuasive.

'When the terms are *completely* neutralised, (*sc.* in emotive meaning) one may say with tranquillity that all moralists are propagandists and that all propagandists are moralists.'[38]

'Good' and other such words, used in a non-moral sense, are analysable in exactly the same way as 'good' etc. in a moral sense, according to Stevenson. What makes, say, war, want, abortion, pornography, crime, financial dishonesty in private and public life, etc., *moral* issues—as distinct from the preferences and aversions which we feel on such matters as films, food, sports, holiday resorts, etc., which are *non-moral*—is, the fact that we feel a special seriousness or urgency[39] where the former issues are concerned. There is nothing radically different in what we mean when we say that abortion is not a good practice from what we mean when we say that Aberdeen is not a good place to go to in the winter. It is just that we are more concerned to cause ourselves or others to have an attitude of aversion to abortion than to Aberdeen.

## *The Inadequacy of Emotivism*

Emotivism's most obvious inadequacy lies in its insistence that the 'primary use' of moral discourse is 'to create an influence.' This is certainly not a sufficient condition of such discourse. An influence on human conduct can be created by many other uses of language—plays, laws, advertisements, endearments, abuse, etc. The mere fact that discourse 'creates an influence' does not make it moral.

But neither is this a necessary condition of such discourse. G. J. Warnock in his discussion of 'Contemporary Moral Philosophy'[40] says that if we set out to create an influence by uttering a moral judgement, then three conditions will need to be fulfilled in order to give point to what we are doing: (i) we must be of the opinion that our audience does not already have the attitude we are trying to produce in it; (ii) we must want our audience to have it; (iii) we must think it possible that by uttering this moral judgement we will be able to induce our audience to have it. But moral judgements are frequently uttered when none of these conditions is fulfilled. I am writing in the season of party political conferences and the newspapers for days past have reported speeches full of moral indignation, made by Liberals, Socialists and Tories, on occasions when it is possible that none of the above three conditions was fulfilled: (i) the audience already agreed with the speaker; (ii) it can hardly be said that he wanted them to do so, since they already did; (iii) and in so far as he was addressing through the media a wider audience, it is quite possible that he did not think his speech would change anyone's opinions, but simply increase his popularity with his own party's supporters and his reputation, as a man to be reckoned with, among those of other persuasions. Discourse can be moral when it does not 'create an influence'.

A second inadequacy in Stevenson's emotivism is that it treats moral judgement as if it were entirely a matter of standard-setting. J. O. Urmson develops this criticism in his *The Emotive Theory of Ethics* (London, 1968).[41] Standard-setting is distinct from standard-using. When examiners meet to decide what merits a paper must have to gain a first-class mark, they are standard-*setting*. They can use 'good' and related words to pick out their criteria and debate about them. 'I think erudition should be regarded as a sign of excellence.' 'Yes, but clear-thinking is better.' And so on. Having set the standards, they must then proceed to use them. When they put Smith in the first class and Jones in the second they are standard-*using*. Urmson justifiably criticises Stevenson for treating moral judgement, in both his patterns of analysis, as though it were exclusively a matter of standard-setting —of expressing our own enthusiasm for something and attempting to arouse a matching enthusiasm in others. This is inadequate as an account of moral discourse for two reasons. First, because moral judgements are *normally* standard-using. Secondly, because there is *no point* in setting up a standard unless it is a preliminary to using it and so an account of moral judgment which treats only of the former has at best told only half the story.

Stevenson's emotivism is inadequate, thirdly, in the account which it gives of the distinction between morality and propaganda. I expressed the opinion earlier that he virtually eliminates the distinction between them (cf. above p.119). Stevenson obviously resents this line of criticism, and devotes the whole of chapter XI of *Ethics and Language* to its rebuttal. When, however, we examine the distinction between them, as he has it, we find that it is drawn entirely in terms of the *motives* from which morality and propaganda respectively may proceed. The motive of propaganda is exclusively to influence people's attitudes in the way which the propagandist desires. The motive of moral argument, he says, may be wider than that. Bearing in mind that moral judgements, according to Stevenson, express the speaker's attitudes or stimulate the hearer's attitudes, and that the reasons given for them may be either 'rational' or 'non-rational', we can understand how he conceives of two ways, in either of which moral argument may produce a desirable result. If our hearer is a man who has thought so much about some moral issue that his feelings on the subject are devitalised, we may decide that 'persuasion will assist, whereas rational methods will actually hinder, any quickening of his practical attitudes.'[42] Then we will use 'non-rational' methods of argument. If, on the other hand, our own feelings on a moral issue are so strong that we think it possible that they are overriding our better judgement, we may adopt 'rational', rather than 'non-rational', or 'persuasive', methods of argument in order 'to open the way to a counter-use of them'[43] by our opponents. That is to say we will provoke our opponents into giving reasons which will present us with the other side of the argument and counterbalance any unwarrantable excess in our own feelings on the subject. The point of all this on Stevenson's part is to bring out that 'it would be a gross distortion of people's motivation to say that this factor (*sc.* simply getting others to adopt certain attitudes whatever the method) is always the decisive one' in morality, as it is in propaganda. In moral argument, says Stevenson in effect, our motive may be to ensure that feeling is neither too strong nor too weak. Presumably, he thinks that this is a desirable end. He is entitled to do so, of course, and to say a good word for morality, if he thinks that it achieves this end. But if he supposes that he is indicating thereby some logical distinction between morality and propaganda he is plainly mistaken. It is not part of the meaning of 'morality', as distinct from 'propaganda', that it should cause feeling on so-called moral issues to be neither too strong nor too weak. Indeed, Stevenson himself said that the characteristic of moral issues is that they are marked by a special urgency (see above p. 120).

---

1. On this see my *Modern Moral Philosophy*, London, 1970, pp. 21–32.
2. See my op. cit., pp. 107–54.

3. Op. cit., eighth edition, p. 125.
4. Op. cit., pp. 45–6.
5. *Proceedings of the Aristotelean Society* 1933–4, pp. 249–54.
6. See below p. 117.
7. *Language, Truth and Logic*, second edition, London, 1946, p. 9. For a brief account of the Vienna Circle see A. J. Ayer *et al.*, *The Revolution in Philosophy*, London, 1956, pp. 70–87.
8. *Enquiry Concerning Human Understanding*, quoted by A. J. Ayer in his Editorial Introduction to *Logical Positivism*, Glencoe, III, 1959, p. 10.
9. *Language, Truth and Logic*, p. 107.
10. Ibid.
11. Cf. my *Wittgenstein and Religious Belief*, London, 1975, chapter 4 on 'Verificationism'.
12. Cf. *Logical Positivism*, p. 14; *Central Questions in Philosophy*, London, 1973, p. 27.
13. *Language, Truth and Logic*, p. 108.
14. Op. cit., p. 110.
15. Op. cit., pp. 110–12 cf. above p. 27 (Sidgwick) and below p. 117 (Moore).
16. Op. cit., pp. 110–11.
17. Op. cit., p. 112.
18. Cf. C. L. Stevenson, *Ethics and Language*, London, 1944, p. 54. On this theory see my *Modern Moral Philosophy*, pp. 37–44.
19. Op. cit., p. 33.
20. Ibid.
21. Op. cit., p. 82.
22. Op. cit., p. 89.
23. Op. cit., p. 81.
24. Op. cit., p. 207.
25. Op. cit., p. 542.
26. Ibid. This idea of moral judgements as imperatives was embraced by some of the logical positivists.
27. *Ethics and Language*, chapter IX; Cf. 'Persuasive Definitions', op. cit.
28. 'The Emotive Meaning of Ethical Terms' reprinted in C. L. Stevenson, *Fact and Value*, Yale, 1963, p. 13.
29. Op. cit., p. 16.
30. *Ethics and Language*, p. 90; on the distinction between attitudes and feelings see my *Modern Moral Philosophy*, pp. 123–4 and below pp. 130–31.
31. Stevenson, op. cit., p. 27.
32. 'Persuasive Definitions', op. cit., reprinted in *Facts and Values*, p. 35.
33. *Ethics and Language*, p. 27.
34. Op. cit., chapters V and VI, IX, X, XI.
35. Op. cit., p. 139.
36. Ibid.
37. Op. cit., p. 140.
38. Op. cit., p. 252.
39. Op. cit., p. 90.

40. Chapter 6 in my *New Studies in Ethics*, vol. ii., pp. 446–51.
41. Op. cit., pp. 64–71, 77–80. Cf. my *Modern Moral Philosophy*, pp. 150–1 where I attempt some defence of Stevenson at this point.
42. *Ethics and Language*, p. 157.
43. Ibid.

# 6

# A rationalist kind of Non-descriptivism

*Emotivism and Prescriptivism*

Emotivism had a considerable vogue in the nineteen thirties and forties, at any rate in academic philosophical circles. But even its most committed adherents occasionally had their doubts. In his *Human Society in Ethics and Politics* (London, 1954), Bertrand Russell sets down at the beginning of his first chapter the thoroughly emotivist view that ethical judgements do not state facts but express some hope or fear, desire or aversion, love or hate; and that they should, therefore, be enunciated in the imperative or optative moods rather than the indicative.[1] He proceeds to work out the implications of this opinion. But rather more than half way through the book we find him confessing that his own moral judgements sometimes seem to him to be more than mere expressions of emotion. 'When I am compelled,' he notes, 'as happens very frequently in the modern world, to contemplate acts of cruelty which make me shudder with horror, I find myself constantly impelled towards an ethical outlook which I cannot justify intellectually. I find myself thinking, "These men are wicked and what they do is bad in some absolute sense for which my theory has not provided." '[2] Some others, who have felt a similar dissatisfaction with emotivism, have not been able to dispel it as easily as Russell does. For, he goes on to make the surely debatable claim that emotivism is acceptable after all because those who subscribe to it are less likely to make matters worse by

125

inflicting cruel retribution on those who have done cruel things, than people who believe in absolute and objective moral values.

The next important development in moral philosophy was not a revival of belief in absolute values, but it was a recognition that there is more to moral judgements than the venting or arousing of emotion. This new theory is usually called prescriptivism and its principal exponent is R. M. Hare, who became professor of moral philosophy at Oxford in 1966. His ethical theory is to be found in *The Language of Morals* (Oxford, 1952) and *Freedom and Reason* (Oxford, 1963). I shall be mainly concerned with these in this chapter, reserving the consideration of some recent important developments in his theory until chapter 8. Hare's prescriptivism occupies a central place in modern moral philosophy. For the last decade or two, discussion has tended to centre upon it. In my opinion, it is the most clearly stated and comprehensively argued of contemporary ethical theories. I will explain what it is, and show the kind of hostile criticism which it has attracted, in this and subsequent chapters. I have given a fuller treatment to Hare's earlier views in chapter 5 of my *Modern Moral Philosophy* (London, 1970). If the reader has any difficulty in understanding what follows I would refer him to that book in the hope that he may find it useful.

Prescriptivists and emotivists have one thing completely in common. They reject unreservedly any form of descriptivism, whether of the naturalistic or intuitionist variety. They hold that moral judgements do not state facts either about man in the world of nature or moral entities in some metaphysical order of being. Such judgements are *expressive*, not descriptive, in their primary use. Hare has called the theory of morals which he set out to produce as an alternative to emotivism, 'a rationalist kind of non-descriptivism'.[3] In so far as it was non-descriptive, it was intended to preserve the insights of emotivism. But in so far as it was rationalist, it was designed to repair that theory's defects.

There are two further *apparent* similarities between prescriptivism and emotivism. Both theories regard moral judgements, to put matters in a nutshell, as 'action-guiding' and 'reason-giving'. On the one hand, they both see a very close connection between moral judgement and what people do. Moral judgements are thought of as essentially practical; their point, as that of getting something done. On the other hand, both emotivism and prescriptivism take it to be a defining characteristic of moral judgements that they are supported by reasons. That is to say, it is natural in morality to ask, or to give, a reason for what is recommended, and against what is condemned. But, as I say, these two similarities are, at most, superficial. What is meant by 'guiding action' is quite different in the two cases; as is what 'giving a reason' means. Let us consider these differences in turn.

### Two ways of guiding actions

Emotivism, as we saw above (p. 114), regards morality as 'action-guiding' in a causal sense. Stevenson actually wrote, 'to ask whether (a thing) is good is to ask for *influence*' (his italics).[4] Surely that is absurd if it means, as it appears to, that when people seek moral guidance they are deliberately and wittingly asking to be influenced. An inquirer who, having requested moral guidance (e.g. 'Ought I to tell the police what I know?') added a plea for influence (e.g. '... Go on—influence me!') would surely be trivialising his request.

Prescriptivism regards moral judgements as 'action-guiding' in a *logical*, not a causal, sense. It takes a directive to action to be part of their *meaning* (or at least to be implicit in their meaning). In order to appreciate the different ways in which emotivism and prescriptivism are 'action-guiding', we need to bear in mind a distinction which J. L. Austin drew. Both these theories take meaning to be *use* rather than referent. But, as Austin said, 'to speak of the "use" of language can ... blur the distinction between the illocutionary and perlocutionary act.'[5]

A 'locutionary' act, in Austin's terminology, is simply the act of saying something. An '*ill*ocutionary' act is what one is doing *in* saying it. I may, for instance, say 'That horse is the favourite'. *In* saying this I may be doing any one of a number of things— simply conveying information, or advising you to back it, or registering my own decision to do so, etc. The same locution may differ in its illocutionary force from one context to another. By a '*per*locutionary' act, Austin meant what we are doing *by* saying something. The same locution, as we have already noted above (p. 114), can have many different effects on people. *By* saying, 'That horse is the favourite,' I may, according to the circumstances, please you (if you have backed it), frighten you (if you have backed some other), amuse you (if you think the horse no good), etc.

It is important, as Austin's above remark emphasises, to differentiate *per*locution clearly from *ill*ocution. The distinction parallels that drawn above (p. 115) between the *causal* and *logical* explanation of what words mean. Linguistic *rules* constitute illocutionary force, as they do logical explanation. If, *in* saying that a certain horse is the favourite, I am advising you to back it, this will be evident in some way or other. Perhaps because I make it quite explicit—'I advise you to back that horse. It is the favourite.' But alternatively, the illocutionary force may be apparent from my urgent tone of voice; or the knowing expression on my face; or some adjective I use like '*certain* favourite'; or simply from the fact that we are approaching a bookmaker at the time. For all their variety, these factors all constitute rules or norms. What we are doing *in* saying something depends on such rules or conventions, as what we are doing *by* saying it does not.

Emotivism takes moral judgements to guide action by their *per*locutionary force. Prescriptivism, by contrast, takes it to be part of the *ill*ocutionary force of moral judgements that they guide action. Hare, who had been Austin's pupil, thought of the perlocutionary-illocutionary distinction as marking the main difference between emotivism and prescriptivism. What you are doing *in* saying that something is right or good is saying by implication, 'Do it!' or 'Choose it!' No doubt you are saying other things as well. But not to the exclusion of this. The proof of the point lies in the *oddness* of remarks like, 'That is the good life but avoid it!', 'That is the right act but don't do it!' Anyone who said either of these things, though not perhaps formally contradicting himself, would be saying something which we would feel needed explanation. Had he said, 'That's the good life. Choose it'! or 'That's right. Do it!', we may well not have asked 'Why?' But if he tells us not to choose it, or not to do it, when he has called it good or right, we shall very naturally wonder why. We take it as part of what he means, *in* calling it good or right, that we *should* choose it or do it. That, according to prescriptivists is the *logical* way in which moral judgements are action-guiding.

Emotivism also regarded morality as 'reason-giving' in a *causal* rather than a *logical* sense. Stevenson explicitly wrote, 'the reasons which support or attack an ethical judgement ... are related to the judgement psychologically rather than logically.'[6] We saw in the last chapter (p. 119) what he meant by this. He concedes that there are 'exceptions'. Ethical statements have '*some* descriptive meaning' and to that extent they are 'amenable to the usual applications of formal logic'.[7] That is to say, to rules of 'formal consistency'. He gives various examples of inconsistency—e.g. expressing approval of promise-keeping as such and then disapproving of P, which is the keeping of a particular promise.

But whereas the demand for logically consistent reasons is presented by Stevenson as the 'exception' in moral argument, prescriptivists such as Hare conceive it to be the rule. They say that the fact that moral judgements such as 'This is good', 'That is right', are backed up by reasons of a logical kind is what differentiates them from expressions of feeling or taste. To press someone for a reason—in the sense, not of a *cause*, but a justifying ground—when he has purred with pleasure before a warm fire, or groaned with misery when made to eat porridge, is bizarre. One is permitted to express one's feelings or tastes—over a wide area at least—without needing to have justifying reasons for them. It suffices that one's feelings cause one to purr or to groan. But, as justifying reasons are precisely what we do need to have when we utter moral judgements such as 'This is good' or 'That ought to be done', it always makes good sense for someone to ask 'Why?' It is never good sense for us to reply to such a question, 'What do you mean "Why?"? I simply said that e.g. abortion, apartheid, or whatever, is wrong'—as it would be to say, 'What do you mean "Why?"? I simply e.g. purred, or groaned.'

Even those who would not wish to be counted as prescriptivists have criticised emotivists for their short way with logical (as distinct from psychological) reasons. This short way was taken by Ayer, who thought it impossible to argue about value judgements, on the ground that they are incapable of being true or false and so of being either valid or invalid;[8] and also by Stevenson, who was equally sure that differences of moral 'attitude' cannot be resolved by reasoning in the ordinary sense of the term.[9]

J. O. Urmson[10] challenges the view that moral judgements cannot be true and therefore cannot be valid. He thinks we can say, for instance, 'Is it true that killing is wrong?', provided we address the question to some authority. Whether or not there *are* any authorities in morality is a separate issue; the point here is simply that it does not lie in the very nature of morality that there cannot be. As for validity, admittedly questions about the validity of the whole system of morality may not be answerable; but then neither may those about the validity of the whole system of science or mathematics. However, questions about the validity of particular moves within a system can be answered; and this applies as much to morality as to any other universe of discourse. What precisely constitute the 'axioms' of the moral 'system' is, once again another question. But it does not lie in the very nature of morality that there are none. That is the error which we have seen Stevenson made—supposing all moral judgement to be standard-setting and none standard-using (see above p. 121).

Prescriptivists may not wish to be saddled with Urmson's view that moral judgements are true or false; because there is, after all, a difference between authorities whose judgements can be checked independently and those which cannot. However, they would agree that moral principles—which are in effect reasons given for thinking some kind of action or state of affairs good or evil, right or wrong, our duty or otherwise—can be employed in moral thinking in ways not radically dissimilar to those in which scientific hypotheses are used in scientific discovery (see below p. 42). Against Stevenson both G. J. Warnock[11] and J. O. Urmson[12] have said that he speaks of moral *attitudes* as if they were more similar to emotions than in fact they are. Stevenson does draw a distinction between emotions and attitudes, referring to feelings or emotions as 'affective states'[13] which reveal their full nature to immediate introspection; and to attitudes as 'complicated conjunctions of dispositional properties' to feel or act in certain ways.[14] But this distinction does not go far enough for Stevenson's critics. Dispositions are too similar to emotions. Urmson says that attitudes are more like beliefs than emotions. We speak of 'agreement' or 'disagreement' in attitude, as we do, in belief; but with regard to emotions, we speak rather of 'harmony' or 'discord'. The 'category differences' between emotions and attitudes are more marked than between beliefs and attitudes. 'We can call certain differences in attitude disagreements precisely because we can maintain attitudes as we maintain beliefs, because we can be argued out of attitudes as we can be argued out of beliefs, because with reason given we can be expected to abandon attitudes as with reason given we can be expected to abandon beliefs.'[15] To 'abandon' them—not to be 'influenced' out of them.

## Prescriptivity

Hare offers an account of the distinctive meaning of moral judgements mainly in terms of two logical features, which he takes them to possess, namely prescriptivity and universalisability. These two defining characteristics follow on from what has already been said about his conception of moral judgements as 'action-guiding' and 'reason-giving' respectively, in the logical rather than the causal sense. Often Hare speaks in general terms about value-judgements, or ought-judgements. He thinks, by the way, that judgements in terms of 'right' or 'good' can generally be translated into judgements in terms of 'ought' (see final chapter of *The Language of Morals*). The question does arise as to precisely how ought-judgements of a moral kind differ from those of a non-moral and to it we shall return (see below pp. 140 ff.). But our immediate task is to see what Hare meant by prescriptivity and universalisability and to consider some of the criticisms which his claim that they are among the defining characteristics of moral judgement have engendered. I will deal in this section with prescriptivity and in the next with universalisability.

What does it mean to say that moral judgements are 'action-guiding'? Hare's reply is that it 'comes to much the same thing' as saying that they 'entail imperatives'.[16] Moral judgements may be in any of the three persons. Hare makes his points with regard to those which we address to ourselves ('I (or we) ought') but they apply equally *mutatis mutandis* to moral judgements in the second or third persons.

Hare writes, 'I propose to say that the test, whether someone is using the judgement "I ought to do X" as a value-judgement or not is, "Does he or does he not recognise that if he assents to the judgement he must also assent to the command "Let me do X"?'[17] There is a stipulative element in this definition, as Hare readily admits, but he thinks it generally in line with ordinary usage. Anyone who assented to the value-judgement 'I ought to do X', provided he knew the meaning of what he was saying and meant it sincerely, would not dissent from the entailed imperative 'Let me do X'. Notice that the imperative is not said to be what the judgement means, but simply what it entails. Sincere and witting assent to the judgement entails assent to the imperative. And, in its turn, sincere and witting assent to the imperative entails action.

Hare is, of course, aware that some people have weak wills. Indeed, we all do at times. The good we would, we do not; the evil we would not, that we do. This contingency is provided for. Hare explains that his remark, 'it is a tautology to say that we cannot sincerely assent to a command addressed to ourselves, and *at the same time* not perform it,' means that this is so, *subject to the following condition*—'... if now is the occasion for performing it, and it is in our (physical and psychological) power to do so.'[18] The condition may not be fulfilled. All sorts of things may hinder us from doing what we think we ought to do and not least, our own psychological impotence.

The meaning of moral judgements is not, according to Hare, exclusively prescriptive but also descriptive. When I say that something is good or right, I am not simply saying, 'Choose it!' or 'Do it!', I am also saying by implication that it conforms to some standard or criterion; in other words, that there is sometimes good or right *about it*. This is the point at which value-judgements are manifestly different from universal commands. If one door out of six identical doors has on it the sign 'Keep out', it would be absurd of me to say that I had ignored this notice *simply* because I could not see any difference—apart from the 'Keep out' sign— between this door and the others. That is absurd because the 'Keep out' sign suffices to constitute a universal command. But if someone said that out of six men only one was good and I asked what made him different from the rest, it would not suffice to dismiss my question with 'Simply his goodness'. I am entitled to ask, 'What is different about him which provides your *ground* for calling him good?' Goodness and other moral properties are 'supervenient' in this sense, a matter to which I will return in the next section. Here all I want to point out is that, because standards or criteria are inevitably invoked when value-judgements are made, Hare is right to think that the latter have descriptive, as well as prescriptive meaning.[19] If I say to you that a man is good, or his act right, you will often be able to deduce from the circumstances what else I am telling you about him. If, for example, I say that John 'is a good father', you will assume that he clothes and feeds his children as well as he can, etc. Or if I say that Mary 'has been a dutiful daughter' to her recently-widowed mother, you will assume that she has comforted the old lady and helped her with all the legal and domestic matters which had to be settled. Our criteria of goodness in fathers, or of duty in daughters, are likely to be much the same and that is why I can describe John or Mary to you simply by calling them good or dutiful.

What Hare insists upon, however, is the logical priority of the prescriptive meaning of moral judgement. This meaning is 'prior' to the descriptive in the sense that the standards or criteria, in accordance with which moral language is used, can always be changed. This is Hare's version of Moore's 'open question' argument, though, of course, without Moore's intuitionist assumptions (see above p. 100). I can always say, 'But is it good for fathers to clothe and feed their children as well as they can?' or, 'But do daughters have a duty to help their mothers when widowed?' etc. In their primary meaning (as used here) words like 'good' and 'duty' are *constant*. In their secondary, or descriptive, meaning they *change* as standards change. It is a foundation principle of prescriptivism that such change can only come about by using moral terms in their presciptive sense in order to transform their descriptive meaning.[20]

Three main criticisms have been levelled at Hare on account of the views which I have been explaining in this sub-section.

First, the criticism that it is *not* impossible, as Hare mistakenly supposes, to assent to a moral judgement and dissent from the entailed imperative. A. C. MacIntyre[21] and many others have voiced this criticism. Let us suppose all physical or pyschological hinderances to doing what is right are excluded. It is not that John lacks the money to clothe his children, or that Mary is too busy nursing her sick husband to go to her widowed mother—or anything like that. It is not that anybody has a weak will or any other psychological impediment which inhibits them from doing what is right. Leave all that aside and, so we are told, it is still logically possible to assent *sincerely* to the judgement that such-and-such is one's own, or someone else's, duty and *at the same time* to say

'But don't do it!' Well, is this so? Everything turns on what we take 'sincerely' to mean in a context such as this. Hare is accused of *smuggling* the moral judgement that we should live up to our principles into his account of the *logical* structure of value-judgements. But that is not what he does. The point at issue between him and his critics is really this: given what 'sincerely' normally means, would you think that a person, who said 'This is right but don't do it!' was sincere in his judgement that it is right? To me, it seems not.

The second criticism is that Hare is taking too restricted a view, when he regards *all* moral judgements as prescriptive. G. J. Warnock, has written, 'It would be absolutely extraordinary if every member of a class of utterances (sc. value-judgements) subject to no special restrictions as to person or tense or appropriate context or object of utterance, *did* entail some member of another, grammatically wholly dissimilar class of utterances, (sc. imperatives) which are narrowly restricted as to person and tense and context and object of utterance; to make this thesis look plausible would take a good deal of doing; but what reason is there really, for even attempting it?[22] As it stands, there is no denying some force in this criticism. Hare has often been called to task for ignoring the multifarious jobs which moral language does—e.g. 'advising, exhorting, imploring; commanding, condemning, deploring; resolving, confessing, undertaking; and so on, and so on.'[23] But he has replied that all these uses are species of the genus, prescribing.[24] They all imply imperatives. Reflection on the particular list given above would, I think, bear that out. But language is so notoriously loose in its habits that the prescriptivity thesis (if it means that every single instance of an utterance, which the plain man would regard as a moral judgement, will be found to entail an imperative) is likely to be false. But then, any other universal generalisation about the meaning of words is also likely to be false. What is taken to be the definitive use of a piece of language is always to some extent selective. The test of a theory of the meaning of moral language can, therefore, only be: Is it less selective than alternative theories? Does it do fuller justice to the facts? I am inclined to think that prescriptivism passes this test.

A third criticism is, in my opinion, the most telling of all. Again it comes from Warnock. If the primary use of moral terms is prescriptive, then as we said just now (p. 133) standards of moral judgement will be open to unrestricted revision. It will then make perfectly good sense for me to decide that the test of goodness in fathers is *not* whether they feed and clothe their children; or of duty in daughters is *not* whether they care for their widowed mothers; etc. Prescriptivism, so this criticism goes, lets people make up, not only their own minds on moral issues, but their own evidence![25] How can a theory which does that call itself 'a *rationalist* kind of non-descriptivism'?

One reply to this criticism might be that what counts as evidence in any discipline is, in the last analysis, a matter of decision. True, but this does not mean, for instance, that individual scientists can simply decide *individually* what to count as evidence and still be regarded as practising science. It would seem that it is just this which presciptivism permits individuals to do in morality. They can decide, for example, that the criterion of goodness in fathers is how effectively they induce heroin addiction in their children and still be taking a *moral* point of view! We shall come back to this kind of criticism in a later chapter and see how Hare now thinks that it can be rebutted (see below pp. 185ff.).

### Universalisability

The second defining characteristic of moral judgements, according to Hare, is derived from their 'reason-giving' character. We noted above (p.129) that, in normal circumstances, it is *always* logically legitimate to ask a reason for a moral judgement and *never* logically legitimate to decline to give one. All reasons are universal in the sense that, if anything is a reason, then once it has been given, its implications must be adhered to consistently. If I say that abortion is wrong because it is killing babies, I shall expect my opinion to be respected as a morally serious one, even by those who disagree with it. But if I go on to say that I am in favour of deliberately starving to death babies born with certain deformities, I shall not expect to be regarded as a serious moralist —not, at least, until I have given a reason why the two cases are different from one another. This is the kind of thing which is meant by Hare's 'Universalisability Thesis'.[26] He expresses it thus, 'all *moral* valuations are of type U'.[27] We must look more closely at what this means.

First, like all valuations, those of 'type U' are, in Hare's terminology 'supervenient'. If I say that abortion is wrong, then as we have seen, I do not simply open the way to the question 'Why?' but more specifically to 'What is wrong about it?' The answer cannot be 'Simply its wrongness.'

If the reason I give for thinking abortion wrong is that it is killing babies, then, implicit within this reason is the principle, '*All* killing of babies is wrong.' The logical structure of my argument is as follows:

All killing of babies is wrong.
Abortion is killing babies.
So, abortion is wrong.

Notice that the principle, which forms the major premise here, is universal.

But it is not enough for it simply to be universal. It must have a *special* kind of universality, if it is to be a moral principle, according to Hare. It must be what he calls a 'U-type' principle: that is to say, one in which there is *no mention of individuals other than by description*.[28] Compare the following syllogism with the one above:

All killing of a baby of Mary Smith is wrong.
This abortion would be the killing of a baby of Mary Smith.
So, this abortion is wrong.

The major premise is still universal. It applies to *all* actions of a certain kind. But it refers to an individual by name not description (Mary Smith) and so, for all its universality, will not serve as a moral principle, by Hare's criterion. He calls it an E-type judgement, as against U-type. Of course, if you think it wrong to abort Mary's baby *simply because* it is a baby, that is a U-type valuation. But if you think it wrong because it is *her* baby (and so you are not committed to thinking that it would be wrong if it had been someone else's) that is not 'U-type' and your judgement, in Hare's view, is not a moral one at all.

Let us consider two kinds of criticism which have been brought against Hare's universalisability thesis.

The first is that he has confused a moral point with a logical one. The 'U-typeness' which he thinks essential to moral judgements is *not* simply consistency: one could consistently take the view that aborting babies is wrong, if and only if Mary Smith is their mother. But in Hare's opinion that would be an E-type judgement. In order to be U-type it would have to get rid of the proper name 'Mary Smith' and refer to her only by description. That is to say, it would have to be characterised, not only by consistency, but also by impartiality. But impartiality is a moral, not a logical, virtue. Hare has mistaken the fact that he would not wish to make 'It is wrong to abort babies, if and only if Mary Smith is their mother' his own moral judgement for the fact that it would not make sense to regard it as anyone's moral judgement.

I think Hare is right here and his critics wide of the mark. Would not the judgement in question puzzle us? Would we not say, 'What on earth has being Mary Smith's baby got to do with it?', not simply because we disagree with this judgement, but because we do not understand it, and not simply because it is morally objectionable to us, but because it strikes us as logically odd? of course, *why* it is odd is another matter. It remains to be seen whether Hare's view—that it is odd because it is not U-type—is correct or incorrect. But *that* it is logically odd is beyond doubt. Hare has not simply smuggled his *own* moral commitment to impartiality into the analysis of moral judgements, as his critics say. He has raised a genuinely logical question—e.g. Why does being Mary Smith's child not strike us as a morally relevant consideration?—and offered a genuinely logical solution—because moral judgements *qua* moral are U-type. Whatever can be said against this solution, the criticism that it is nothing but a crypto-moral commitment will not stand.

A more effective criticism—or so many have felt—is that Hare's universalisability thesis ignores the *particularity* of real life moral situations. Sartre's famous pupil,[29] who could not decide whether it was his duty to stay with his aged mother in occupied France or come to Britain to join the Free French army, is often quoted in this connection. No universal prescription could help him. Kant says 'Always treat persons as ends never means.' But who is end and who means—his mother, whom he could comfort, or his countrymen, whom he might help to free? Christianity says, 'Love your neighbour.' But which of them is his neighbour? Sartre tells him that all he can do is choose. Without any guiding principle—just choose.

When a man has chosen in a situation such as this and said in effect 'I ought to do X' (so Peter Winch assures us), 'there is nothing in the meaning or use of the word "ought" which logically commits him to accepting as a corollary: "And anyone else in a situation like this ought to do the same" ".[30] Winch refers to Captain Vere's dilemma in Herman Melville's novel *Billy Budd*. Billy has been persecuted and falsely accused of incitement to mutiny by Claggart, the master-at-arms. Frustrated by a speech-impediment which makes him unable to reply, Billy knocks down his accuser, who falls, strikes his head, and dies. Captain Vere, who knows all the facts, is torn between what he calls 'military duty' and 'compassion' but decides that it is his duty to condemn Billy to death. Winch declares himself quite clear that he would find it 'morally impossible'[31] to agree with this judgement. But he is equally clear that he could not bring himself to think that what-ever it would have been right for him to do in Vere's position it would also have been right for Vere to do. In such situations of anguished moral conflict, Winch says in effect, it is manifestly absurd to say that one must (logically) give a reason why one ought to do something, which would apply to everybody else in a similar situation. The way to discover what to do is not to look for any such reason but simply to decide—'... deciding what to do is, in a situation like this, itself a sort of finding out what is the right thing to do ...'[32]

This sort of view is, or was till recently, popular in some quarters, not least in religious ones. It is commonly called 'situation ethics'. I have said elsewhere[33] what I think of it and will not repeat that here. What we must see is how Hare disposes of the criticism that his universalisability thesis does not do justice to the kind of moral dilemma about which we have just been thinking. There are, as I read him, two ways in which he counters such criticism.

First, by suggesting that his critics over-dramatise real life. In fiction, we are always meeting the character who finds it impossible to discern where his duty lies. In real life he is, to say the least, a much rarer bird. Of serious moral dilemmas Hare writes, 'But when a person is in one of these dilemmas, what does he do? If he is on the stage, of course, and if his object is to give his audience their money's worth, he piles on the anguish. But in real life what *should* he do? If one asks those whom one respects and who have been in such situations, they usually reply that they have done the best they could in the circumstances; great harm was bound to ensue in any case, but they tried to minimize it.'[34] People will differ in what they think is best. Everyone must make up his own mind about that. Some—perhaps all—will find it hard to do so; and that, of course, is the heart of the matter. But if I think that, in my own case, an agent ought to do what he thinks is best, it is, *pace* Winch, 'in the meaning and use' of this 'ought' that I am committed to accepting the corollary that anyone else in a moral dilemma ought to do what he thinks is best.

Hare's second line of defence against the charge of ignoring the particularity of moral situations is to draw a very clear distinction between universality and generality; and to show that the one has little or nothing to do with the other.

Generality admits of degrees. Some principles are more general than others: 'a principle *p1* is more general than another principle *p2* if and only if it is analytically true that to break *p2* is, in virtue of that fact, to break *p1*, but the converse is not analytically true.'[35] For example, the following principles are arranged in order of increasing generality: One should not kill babies by abortion; one should not kill babies; one should not kill anybody; one should not kill anything; one should not do anything.[36] But they are *all equally* universal. For, a principle is universal in so far as it requires 'an action of a certain kind' to be performed, or avoided, as the case may be, 'in *all* cases of a certain *kind*, not needing individual references for its determination.'[37] 'Do not kill babies by abortion' is not less universal, though much less general, than 'Do not kill anything'. So, universality is quite different from generality. Principles may have varying degrees of generality whilst having the same degree of universality; indeed, as Hare points out, the notion of varying degrees of universality makes little sense.

Now, the opposite of generality is specificity. The point to take is that universal principles can be very specific. Just because of the complexity and particularity of the situations which confront us in real life, they often have to be. Suppose a certain doctor thinks abortion wrong. He considers it to be killing babies and is totally committed to the principle that one should not kill babies. But then he finds himself in a situation of extreme singularity. Some woman is pregnant. If the pregnancy continues, then she will be unable to do a certain piece of scientific work which will immeasurably increase the happiness of all mankind. There is no other doctor to whom she can go. She asks this doctor for an abortion. He decides that, in this particular instance, it is not wrong to comply and goes ahead. This is just the sort of highly dramatic example with which Hare's critics like to confront the universalisability thesis. Well, no one need deny, or trivialise by lack of respect, the doctor's problem. But, logically speaking, what has happened? It is really quite simple. He has not abandoned his principle that killing babies is morally wrong or his belief that abortion is killing babies. He has *modified* his principle. It now reads something like this, 'It is *always* wrong to kill babies except where an abortion will bring immeasurable benefit to all mankind.' Even if it seems most *improbable* that there has been, is, or will ever be, another pregnant woman in the same situation as the one supposed, this principle is still universal. Even if *as a matter of fact* there never has been, is, or will be, it is still universal. For it applies to hypothetical cases no less than actual ones. If I say, 'It is not wrong to abort this woman's baby, because of her special situation,' I am, in effect, saying that it would not be wrong to abort any woman's baby, *if* she were in this situation. And that I can say. The principle is as universal as before though less general. I am *not* saying that moral principles thus modified can always be clearly verbalised; sometimes I think they cannot. I am *not* saying that I consider the doctor in question to have made the right decision; I am at liberty to think that he would have been a better man had he refused. All I am saying is that he does not provide a counter-example to the universalisability thesis. His situation was exceedingly particular, in the sense of singular or specific. But it admitted of subsumption under a universal principle. Room is left for Hare to say that it had to do so in order to admit of moral judgement. That view may be mistaken. But it is not shown to be so simply by the specificity of the doctor's dilemma.

## Other features of moral judgements

What makes moral value-judgements different from those of other kinds? In his early paper, 'Universalisability' (1955) Hare evidently thought that it was entirely a matter of the 'U-typeness' of moral judgements. In *Freedom and Reason* (1963), however, he appears to have come round to the opinion that 'U-typeness' characterises a larger class of judgements than simply moral ones. He says explicitly, 'it is the logic of the word "ought" in its typical uses that requires universalisability, not that of the word "moral"; the word "moral" needs to be brought in only in order to identify one class of the typical uses, and that with which as moral philosophers we are most concerned.'[38] So what are the other defining characteristics of moral judgements? He lists three 'necessary ingredients', which in combination with prescriptivity and universalisability 'govern' a man's moral opinion on a given matter.[39]

The first of the three is 'an appeal to fact'. We noted above (p. 136) that a judgement such as 'Abortion is wrong because it is killing babies' is, in its logical structure: (i) a major *moral* premise, 'All killing of babies is wrong'; (ii) a minor *factual* premise, 'Abortion is killing babies'; and (iii) a *moral* conclusion, 'Abortion is wrong.' The appeal to fact is in the minor premise. There is always some such appeal in a moral judgement. The particular example which I have just taken shows that this appeal to fact may be itself at times a somewhat complicated matter. If you say, for instance, that fathers of families ought to wear seat-belts because that reduces by such-and-such a degree the probability that they will be killed and leave their dependents in reduced circumstances, the truth or falsity of the minor premise can be tested by a straightforward statistical inquiry. But it is notorious that a premise such as, 'Abortion is killing babies,' raises the question, 'What is meant by a "baby"?' In the end, this will be answered by verbal definition, not empirical investigation. Nevertheless, it is a factual question.

The second ingredient of moral thinking, according to Hare, is 'an appeal to interest or inclination'. They are not quite the same thing: a person may have interests where he has no inclinations, though perhaps not *vice versa*. Both, however, can be called wants and for our present purposes taken together. The fundamental point is that if we had no wants, it would not make any difference to us what happened and so we should see no point in language which commends or discommends. If moral judgements are in this way connected with wants, it is a pertinent question whether any particular judgement is in line with what the person who delivers it *really* wants. He must be made to realise what he is saying, first of all. His judgement is moral and therefore prescriptive and universalisable. If he says that people ought to be punished for stealing, he is saying by implication, (a) 'Punish such

141

people!' (the imperative which the judgement entails); and (b) 'If anyone has stolen, punish him!' (the universalisation of the reason for the judgement). Now, *given* his wants, will the person who has delivered this judgement really be prepared to stand by it, when he understands what it means? Much moral argument, Hare is saying and rightly, is designed to thrust some question of this form on those who have delivered judgements with which others do not agree.

The third 'ingredient' is 'an appeal to imagination'. Hare draws a parallel here between moral and scientific thinking. Just as a scientist tests his hypotheses by deducing from them certain empirically observable predictions and then looking through his telescope, microscope, or whatever, to see if they come true, so, according to Hare, a moralist tests principles by working out what follows from them in supposed situations and seeing whether he can accept them. This exercise of the imagination may have many facets but the one which is most important for Hare's purposes is this. In an example like that of a moment ago—'It is right to punish people for stealing'—assent to this judgement implies assent to prescriptivity and universalisability. This, in turn, implies assent to the imperative 'If *I* steal, punish *me*.' Am I prepared to say that? Only if I am will my judgement that it is right to punish those who steal be a moral one.

Hare's opponents contend that this account of the necessary and sufficient conditions of moral judgement is defective. It does not differentiate moral value-judgements from all those of other kinds. The crucial question is: can we conceive of value-judgements which we would *not* consider to be moral but which are prescriptive and universalisable, based on factual beliefs, concerned with interests and inclinations, and conceived through an exercise of the imagination? Not a few critics have thought that we can. And, in a certain sense, Hare himself thinks that we can. But to this we will return (see p. 149). First I want to complete this sketch of Hare's ethical theory by explaining his view that it provides 'a formal foundation' for utilitarianism.[40]

## A Foundation for Utilitarianism

This 'formal foundation' is as follows. I said a moment ago that when someone has passed a judgement, the question may arise as to whether he is prepared to stand by it as a *moral* judgement. What does that involve, if we go by Hare's 'necessary ingredients'? Take the example, 'Pushers of hard drugs ought to be executed.' Let us suppose that I offer this as my moral opinion. What does that let me in for?

First the judgement will have to be universalisable. Its *universalisability* will require me to recognise that it applies to me as much as to anybody else, if I am a pusher. Then again, it will be prescriptive. Its *prescriptivity* will require me to assent to the entailed imperative, 'If I am a pusher, let me be executed.' This judgement will rest on 'an appeal to fact'; that is to say, it will apply only to people (myself included) if they are *in fact* pushers. Again, it will involve 'an appeal to imagination'. It will require me to go 'round ... all the affected parties' *in my imagination* 'giving equal weight to the interests' of each.[41] This quotation brings out that there is an appeal to *interest and inclination* (wants) also. My wants will come into the judgement because I will have to ask (in Hare's words) 'how much (as I imagine myself in the place of each man in turn) do I want to have this, or to avoid that?'[42] The phrase, 'each man in turn' refers to 'all the affected parties'; and 'this' and 'that' to the content of the imperative entailed by the judgement.

To summarise, what I let myself in for, if I offer 'Pushers of hard drugs ought to be executed' as a moral judgement, is this. Its necessary *universalisability* will require me to exercise my *imagination* by putting myself in the place of all hard drug pushers in turn. As I do so, its necessary *prescriptivity* will require me to decide whether I want it to be implemented (Hare thinks of wanting as assenting to an imperative).

How, then, does all this provide a 'formal foundation' for utilitarianism? The answer lies, I think, in these words of Hare, 'It is in the endeavour to find lines of conduct which we can prescribe universally in a given situation that we find ourselves bound to give equal weight to the desires of all parties ... and this, in turn, *leads* to such views as that we should seek to maximise satisfactions'[43] (italics mine). The 'endeavour' referred to here is, as we have seen, *logically* required by the 'necessary ingredients' which make a judgement a moral one. The 'view' to which this 'endeavour' is said to '*lead*' is a *substantially moral* one, namely that 'We should seek to maximise satisfactions.' What Hare evidently means is that his logical analysis of the defining characteristics of a moral judgement *qua* moral leads to the conclusion that it is not moral unless it is a judgement in accordance with the principle of utility. Universalisability requires us to take account of *all* the affected parties, real or imagined. Prescriptivity, to take account of their *wants*. Thus we arrive at the idea of maximised satisfaction, of the greatest happiness of the greatest number. And not only that. It also follows from this logical analysis of moral judgements that 'everyone is entitled to equal consideration.'[44] So we have a 'formal foundation', not only for Bentham's utility principle but for his equity principle—that everybody should count for one and nobody for more than one—as well.

### The Relationship between Fact and Value

Hare believes in what is commonly called 'the is-ought gap'.[45] He thinks, as many other modern philosophers have done, that factual descriptions are logically quite distinct from evaluative judgements; that, given the facts, it is logically possible to pass any value-judgement upon them. This is the point at which Hare's severest critics join issue with him.

Mrs Philippa Foot points out that there are innumerable words, like 'courageous' or 'father' for examples, which have both factually descriptive, and morally evaluative, meaning.[46] Evidence of this is provided by the logical oddness of saying things like, 'That would be courageous, but don't do it!', or, 'He is her father but it's not her duty to help him.' In special circumstances, such remarks do make sense, but in the ordinary course of events they puzzle us because they block what seems the natural move from the fact that something *is* courageous (or someone our father) to the conclusion that we *ought* to do it (or to help him).

Hare is prepared to admit the naturalness of this move. He explains it as due to generally held moral principles. Most people subscribe to the principle that what is courageous ought to be done, or that children ought to help their parents, and that is why they think it natural to make the moves to which I have just referred. The explanation is not, according to Hare, that we can deduce value from fact, 'ought' from 'is'; it is rather that some general moral principles come to be widely accepted in any given society and it is then contingently improbable, though not logically impossible, that they will be denied.[47] When members of the society hear them denied, they are puzzled.

Hare's critics are not content with this explanation. They cannot share his conviction that it is always logically possible to separate the descriptive element in words like 'courageous' from the evaluative. Hare argues that this is possible from the example of citations accompanying awards for bravery.[48] We can distinguish in such citations between descriptions of what the recipient actually did— e.g. 'he went out under enemy fire and helped two wounded comrades to return to their trench'—from evaluations which the authors of the citation place upon it—e.g. 'his action showed devotion beyond the call of duty and a complete disregard for personal safety.' If Hare's point is accepted, then to call such action 'courageous' is to add to the bare recital of facts an 'extra element'[49] of evaluation. But in what does this extra element consist? Not in the commendation which expresses itself through the imperative 'Let me do likewise!' says Mrs Foot, for I myself may be a complete coward and make no resolution to reform.[50] Nor in any decision of principle on my part to the effect that courage is a virtue, says D. Z. Phillips,[51] for when did I make any such decision?

The way in which some of Hare's critics object to his separation of fact and value is by insisting that there are what they call 'institutional facts',[52] for examples, the fact that I *owe* you a pound or that Jones has *promised* to pay Smith five dollars. Certain facts are, in Miss Anscombe's phrase, 'brute relative' to these facts. The facts for instance that, in the one case, I came to your shop and, in ways which 'ordinarily amount' to doing business with you, asked for a pound's worth of goods; or in the other case, the fact that Jones uttered to Smith, in circumstances which 'ordinarily amount' to making a promise, the words 'I promise to pay you five dollars'. The facts may not be 'ordinary', of course—I may be playing shop with my children or Jones and Smith may be on the stage. But given that the circumstances are ordinary, from the fact that I *owe* you one pound, it follows that I ought to pay you; from the fact that Jones *promised* to pay Smith five dollars, that he ought to do so. J. R. Searle has attempted to show that this move from 'is' to 'ought' can be made with the aid, not of an *evaluative* major premise as Hare supposes, but with that of *factual* premises comprising simply 'empirical assumptions, tautologies and descriptions of word usage'. I have described and discussed this derivation elsewhere.[53] Here it suffices to note Hare's reply. He insists that, in order to be a subscribing member of a society within which promising is an 'institutional' fact, it is necessary to accept 'the non-tautologous principle that one ought to keep one's promises'.[54] He does not mean, of course, that on some specifiable date each of us must have given his assent to this principle; but that acceptance of it is the tacit presupposition of the moves which we so naturally make from the statement that a promise has been made to the judgement that it ought to be kept. Without assent to generally accepted principles which hold any moral community together one cannot (logically) belong to it. Hare's critics take the exactly opposite view that unless one already belongs to a moral community one cannot be conceived (logically) to give assent to a moral principle. In the next chapter, we shall see why they think this; and in the final chapter, we shall consider Hare's recent attempts to build a bridge between his position and theirs.

A further line of criticism, closely related to that which I have been considering against Hare's separation of fact and value, fastens upon his evident assumption that it is logically possible for anyone to choose for himself what the standards or criteria of moral value shall be. If I wish, I can, for example, choose as my criterion of moral goodness in human male progenitors the practice of letting their offspring starve to death. This is, fortunately, an unusual criterion; but there is no reason why it should not be called a moral one.

Mrs Foot retorts[55] that a connection with the speaker's choice is neither a *sufficient*, nor a *necessary* condition for the correct use of value words such as 'good'. It does not follow from the fact that I am ready to choose a certain kind of X that my calling Xs of that kind good will be correct. Nor does it follow that if I am using 'good' correctly, I must be using it in accordance with my own choice of the criteria of goodness. Hare's reply[56] to this criticism is that a distinction must be drawn between a speaker's saying 'X *is good*' and his saying 'I *think X good*'. There are, as he has readily admitted, generally accepted criteria for the use of 'good'. These may not be in line with an individual speaker's idiosyncratic criteria of goodness. But if he uses 'good' in accordance with the generally accepted criteria, his use will not be incorrect. I may, for instance, say that Smith is a good father and thereby convey to my audience the information that he cares for his children even though my own criteria of goodness in fathers are different. But what if I say that I *think* Smith is a good father? By this I imply that I am judging Smith by my own criteria of goodness in fathers. The fact that I am ready to choose fathers who conform to these criteria is both a sufficient and a necessary condition of my saying that I *think* anyone a good father.

Hare's critics would regard this reply to Mrs Foot's criticism as begging the question. He has frequently been condemned for supposing that anyone can be said even to *think* something good if his criteria of goodness are wholly idiosyncratic. D. A. J. Richards, for instance, in his *A Theory of Reasons for Action* (Oxford, 1971) argues that his own 'ideal contract' theory of morality (which resembles Rawls' concept of justice—see below pp. 183 ff.) is preferable to Hare's theory because it 'views the choice of moral principles not, *pace* Hare, as an individual matter, but as a matter of unanimous choice of *all* persons, *qua* rational men ...' (op. cit., p. 84). And as we shall see below (p. 163) Richard Norman in his *Reasons for Action* argues against Hare's individualism that evaluative-descriptive words like 'courageous' are more fundamental in ethics than purely evaluative ones like 'good' or 'right' because the former kind embody public norms, whereas the latter kind are unintelligible when not used in accordance with public norms.

Some of Hare's critics do not regard the criteria in accordance with which value words must be used as simply public. They claim that these criteria have, so to speak, an even more anti-subjective foundation than that. Professor Peter Geach,[57] for example, considers the logical distinction between *attributive* and *predicative* adjectives to be apposite here. *A* is a *predicative* adjective in 'X is an *A*Y' if this sentence can be split up meaningfully into a pair of sentences: 'X is a Y' and 'X is *A*'. For instance, 'This is a red apple' splits up into 'This is an apple' and 'This is red.' *A* is an *attributive* adjective in 'X is an *A*Y', if this sentence cannot meaningfully be split up into 'X is a Y' and 'X is *A*'. For instance, 'That is a big spider' does not split up into 'That is a spider' and 'That is big'. The difference is seen in the fact that 'This is a red apple' implies 'This is a red object', but 'That is a big spider' does not imply 'That is a big creature.' The bigness of the spider is *relative* to that of which it is attributed as the redness of the apple is not.

Geach argues that evaluative adjectives such as 'good', are attributive, not predicative. In order to understand what they mean, you must know to what they are attributed. Goodness in one thing is not the same as goodness in another, any more than bigness is. To the objection that 'good' is sometimes meaningfully predicated of proper name subjects, Geach replies that, in a sentence such as "Bob is good", we do not know what 'good' means until we know whether Bob is a man, a dog, or whatever. A proper name in a sentence such as this always presupposes a continued reference to an individual as being the same X, where X is a common noun.

Since 'good' in a moral sense is attributive, the criteria for its correct use are, according to Geach, necessarily relative to what man is, or is taken to be. Hare[58] concedes that there is a functional sense of 'good' and other such words, which may be applied to men when they are spoken of as filling certain roles, such as that of soldier, servant, etc. A good soldier is one who fights well; a servant who does the right thing is one who answers his master's summons promptly; and so on. But Hare insists that this is a 'non-moral' sense of 'good' or 'ought'. 'Man' in moral contexts means simply 'member of the human species' and 'is not functional'. He suggests[59] that Geach is the latest of a succession of thinkers who confuse two senses of 'function', in thinking of 'man' as a functional word. The former sense is 'what a thing *can* do'; the latter, 'What a thing *ought* to do' (or what it is specifically good for it to do). Man as man has certain capacities. But anyone who thinks that from this we may deduce what constitutes goodness in men should reflect on the fact that slavery and the subjection of women were both justified on this basis by Aristotle.

Geach is not persuaded. In the opening chapter of his book *The Virtues* (Cambridge, 1977) called 'Why Men Need The Virtues' he takes the thoroughly Aristotelian line that man has a final end. The familiar objection that we cannot assume that man has a purpose in the sense in which he may have purposes is swept aside. Geach maintains that the question, 'What are men for?' makes good sense. We may not be as ready with the answer as Aristotle was but Geach thinks Aristotle was right to seek an answer. Just as teleological explanations have heuristic value in biology—'What are hearts for?', 'What are teeth for?', etc.—so they may in morality. Geach is aware that people differ in what they take man's final end to be. But this does not deter him. 'For people whose first practical premises, formulating their ultimate ends, are not only divergent but irreconcilable may nevertheless agree on bringing about some situation which is an indispensable condition of either end being realised, or on avoiding some situation which would prevent the realization of either end.'[60] Geach thinks that the four cardinal virtues—justice, prudence, temperance and courage—are needed for any large-scale, worthy enterprise just as health and sanity are needed. Hare would, no doubt, describe this as falling 'into the trap of supposing that, because the word "good" is logically tied in certain contexts to the *word* "needs", it is therefore logically tied to certain concrete *things* which are generally thought to be needs.'[61] The point can perhaps best be taken by first distinguishing two senses of 'need'. It may mean either the necessary condition of (i) *existence* or (ii) *good existence*. I need air in the former sense; books, in the latter. To call anything a 'need' in this latter sense is to imply that it is good. But notice two things: (i) it does not follow from the fact that anything is a need in the latter sense that it will be one in the former sense; and (ii) there is nothing which I must call a need in the latter sense as I must call some things needs in the former. I cannot live without air. But I can without books. Geach thinks that the virtues are 'needs' in the latter sense. I think Hare would say that he fallaciously seeks to prove this by showing that they are needs in the former sense.

## Form and Content

Perhaps the most common criticism brought against Hare is that, on his analysis of moral judgement, anything goes through. And as I said above (p. 142) he is, in a sense, prepared to concede as much. There are what he calls 'fanatics' and idealists'. An example of a 'fanatic' would be someone who thinks that all Jews should be exterminated: an instance of 'idealism' would be the opinion that all sexual activity, not deliberately intended for the procreation of children, ought to be punishable at law. These judgements would pass Hare's tests for moral ones. A person who held either of them might well be prepared to accept their *universalisability* ('*all* Jews including me if I am one': '*all* sexual activity, mine included'); and their *prescriptivity* ('let me be exterminated if I am *in fact* a Jew': 'let me be punished if *in fact* I engage in the prohibited sexual activity'). He might also be willing to go in *imagination* the round of the affected parties in turn (all *Jews:* all *sexual activists*); and, in each case, to give assent to the entailed imperative ('I *want* to be executed': 'I *want* to be punished'). Hare's 'necessary ingredients' are all there, all *logically* possible of fulfilment in such cases of 'fanaticism' or 'idealism.'

Can these fanatics and idealists pass the greatest happiness criterion to which Hare's analysis 'leads'? Theoretically, yes. If a balance could be made between: (i) the satisfaction which the fanatic (or idealist) would derive from the thought of the extermination of all Jews (or of the cessation of all non-procreatively-intended sexual activity); and (ii) the satisfaction which he would gain from the thought of escaping extermination (or legal punishment) in the case of all affected parties, after imaginatively going round them in turn—then it is *logically possible* that the former should outweigh the latter. The maximisation of satisfaction could conceivably consist in the extermination of all Jews or the prohibition of all non-procreatively-intended sex. Logically, but *not empirically*, thinks Hare! No fanatic or idealist could empirically have such a capacity for satisfaction in his fanaticism or idealism that his delight in seeing all Jews trundled off to gas chambers, or all sexual activisits clapped in goal, could conceivably exceed, as a matter of empirical fact, the summated relief of all Jews in being allowed to live, or the delight of all healthy men and women in being allowed to go to bed together.

Hare's critics are not much moved by these empirical impossibilities. It seems to them to be a fatal defect in prescriptivism that it allows *any content at all* to go through as a moral judgement provided it fulfils the formal conditions, which Hare calls 'necessary ingredients'. Some restriction of *content* seems to them as essential to the definition of morality as any delineation of form. I will consider in the next chapter two such lines of thought. According to the former, the content which can count as moral is limited by considerations of a *psychological* kind; according to the latter, it is limited by considerations of a *social or historical* kind. In both cases the point being made is logical: that, given what 'moral' means, the content of moral judgements must be so restricted.

1. Op. cit., p. 25.
2. Op. cit., p. 128.
3. In unpublished lectures on moral philosophy.
4. 'The Emotive Meaning of Ethical Terms', *Fact and Value*, p. 30.
5. *How To Do Things With Words*, Oxford, 1962, p. 103.
6. *Ethics and Language*, p. 113.
7. Op. cit., p. 116.
8. See above p. 112.
9. See above p. 119.
10. *The Emotive Theory of Ethics*, London, 1963, chapter 7.
11. 'Contemporary Moral Philosophy' in *New Studies in Ethics*, vol. II., p. 451.
12. Op. cit., pp. 38–48.
13. Op. cit., p. 60.
14. Ibid.
15. Op. cit., pp. 43–4.
16. *The Language of Morals*, Oxford, 1952, p. 172.
17. Op. cit., pp. 168–9.
18. *Freedom and Reason*, Oxford, 1963, p. 79; cf. *The Language of Morals*, p. 20.
19. Cf. *Freedom and Reason*, pp. 26–7.
20. Cf. *The Language of Morals*, chapter 7.
21. 'What Morality is Not', *Philosophy*, 1957, p. 330.
22. In a review of my *Modern Moral Philosophy*, *Philosophical Quarterly*, 1971, p. 282.
23. Warnock, 'Contemporary Moral Philosophy', op. cit., p. 457.
24. See *Mind* 1968, p. 438.
25. Op. cit., p. 469.
26. 'Universalisability', *Proceedings of the Aristotelian Society*, 1954–5. He takes the expressions 'U-type' and 'E-type' from E. Gellner, ibid.
27. Hare, op. cit., p. 304.
28. Op. cit., p. 295.
29. *Existentialism and Humanism*, London, 1945, translated by P. Mairet, pp. 35–9.
30. *Ethics and Action*, London, 1972, p. 161.
31. Op. cit., p. 163.
32. Op. cit., p. 165.
33. *Baptist Quarterly*, April, 1966.
34. In 'Moral Philosophy: Some Waymarks', forthcoming.
35. 'Principles' in *Proceedings of the Aristotelian Society*, 1972–3, p. 3.
36. Op. cit., p. 6.
37. Op. cit., p. 5.

38. *Freedom and Reason*, p. 37.
39. Op. cit., pp. 92, 97.
40. *Freedom and Reason*, p. 123.
41. Ibid.
42. Ibid.
43. Ibid.
44. Op. cit., p. 118.
45. Cf. *The Language of Morals*, pp. 27–31.
46. Cf. 'Moral Beliefs', *Proceedings of the Aristotelian Society*, 1958–9, p. 98., reprinted in her *Virtues and Vices*, Oxford, 1978, p. 12.
47. Cf. R. M. Hare 'Descriptivism', *Proceedings of the British* Academy, 1963, reprinted in W. D. Hudson (editor), *The Is-Ought Question*, London, 1969, p. 255.
48. Op. cit., p. 246.
49. Ibid.
50. Ibid.
51. Cf. chapter VII.
52. G. E. M. Anscombe, 'On Brute Facts', *Analysis*, 1957–8; J. R. Searle, 'How to Derive "Ought" from "Is"', *Philosophical Review*, 1964.
53. See articles in Part III of *The Is-Ought Question* and my *Modern Moral Philosophy*, chapter 6, section III.
54. 'The Promising Game', *Revue Internationale de Philosophie*, 1964, reprinted in *The Is-Ought Question*, p. 155.
55. 'Goodness and Choice', *The Aristotelian Society Supplementary Volume*, 1961; reprinted in *The Is-Ought Question*.
56. 'Descriptivism', in *The Is-Ought Question*, pp. 252–4.
57, 'Good and Evil', *Analysis*, 1956, reprinted in P. Foot, *Theories of Ethics*, London, 1967.
58. 'Geach: Good and Evil', *Analysis*, 1957, reprinted in Foot, op. cit.
59. Op. cit., Foot, p. 81n.
60. Op. cit., p. 13.
61. 'Descriptivism', op. cit. p. 256.

# 7

## Has ethics a restricted content?

I shall consider two versions of the opinion that morality has a restricted content. By saying that its content is restricted I mean that, in our moral judgements, it makes good sense to express approval (or disapproval) of certain things but not of others. From this viewpoint, it does not suffice to say that moral judgements *qua* moral have such-and-such a logical form. They must also have such-and-such a substantive content.

The 'must', mark well, is a logical one. There is a difference between making the prediction that moral judgements *will* have a certain content, as a matter of empirical fact, and enunciating the requirement that they *must* have a certain content as a matter of logical fact. We have seen (p.150) that Hare himself made the former of these two moves. He predicted that the content which it is, in practice, possible for a moral judgement to have, will be in some degree, restricted. When anyone tries to meet the demands, first that they should put themselves in the place of everyone who will be affected by their judgement, and then that they should assent in the case of each to the imperative entailed by their judgement, they may find that they simply cannot derive from the thought of their judgement being implemented more satisfaction than from the thought of it not being implemented. They will not then in fact be able to desire the implementation of that judgement. Hare was thinking of judgements of what he called a 'fanatical' or 'idealistic' kind. Judging that all Jews ought to be executed, or that all sexual activity not intended to procreate children should be legally punishable, were given as examples at the end of the last chapter. By contrast, the opinion which I am now going to discuss in this chapter is that there are some judgements which it would be logically impossible to regard as moral ones in view of their content. This is not simply the view that, for psychological reasons, people could not bring themselves to make these judgements as moral ones; it is the view that it would be self-contradictory to say that anyone had done so. In order to be moral, so it is said, a judgement does not simply need, as Hare supposed, to have a certain form, but also a certain content.

Both the versions of this opinion, which I shall consider, have had a considerable influence recently. The former is associated with the names of the Oxford philosophers, Mrs Philippa Foot and G. J. Warnock and also with those of Miss G. E. M. Anscombe of Cambridge and Peter Geach of Leeds. The latter version is to be found in the writings of D. Z. Phillips, H. O. Mounce and R. W. Beardsmore of the University of Wales and Peter Winch of the University of London. I do not wish to suggest that these philosophers form up neatly into two schools of thought but I think there is a good deal of similarity in the opinions of the members of each respective group.

## Morality grounded in Wants

It is said by Mrs Foot and others to be a necessary condition of a judgement being moral that it should commend the satisfaction (or discommend the dissatisfaction) of certain wants which people have. The ways in which these wants can be satisfied vary greatly from case to case. But if anything cannot be thought of as the satisfaction in one way or another of some or all these wants, then it cannot be logically conceived as the content of a moral judgement.

When Mrs Foot began to formulate this opinion, she was sufficiently imbued with the 'action-guiding' and 'reason-giving' conceptions of prescriptivism to start from the assumption that if any judgement is a moral one, it must constitute a reason for action which applies to anyone who may find himself in the relevant situation. What, then, in general terms does a reason for action have to be? The answer, which seemed obvious to her, was this, 'anyone is given a reason for acting when he is shown the way to something he wants.'[1] A moral reason for action, like any other, will have to fulfil this condition. So, moral judgements will need to show men the way to something they want.

What then do they want? It seemed equally obvious to Mrs Foot that their wants can be divided into two kinds, 'for some wants the question "Why do you want that?" will make sense and for others it will not.'[2] No one will be puzzled, for example, by the question, why he wants to do a certain job, or live in a certain place, or receive a certain training, etc. But suppose he is asked why he wants to be free from boredom, or loneliness, or physical injury, or pain, or discomfort, or incapacity. Mrs Foot lists these as conditions from which all men want to be free, not simply as the means to some other end, but as an end in itself. We understand why people want the other things when we are shown that they will be the means to these kinds of freedom. People want certain jobs because these jobs are interesting and if they get them they will not be bored; they want to live in certain places because their friends are there and they will not be lonely; or to receive a certain training because it will free them from some incapacity or other. But if asked why they want to be free from boredom, loneliness, or incapacity, they will say, and rightly, 'We just do.'

As for morality, if its judgements show men the way to something they want, is it something which admits of the question, 'Why should I want that?' or is it not? Mrs Foot thinks that people do not want to be morally good as an end in itself and so must be shown that being morally good is the means to something which they *do* want. She did not think that this is hard to show when she published her paper 'Moral Beliefs' in 1958. The virtues of courage, wisdom and temperance, can be thought of in obvious ways as delivering people from various forms of discomfort or incapacity; and to Mrs Foot's mind at that time, it seemed easy to show that justice, the fourth of the cardinal virtues, frees us from certain forms of loneliness. The unjust man is isolated by his injustice. He has always to be taking others in, or guarding himself against them, for, great tyrants apart, the only effective way to be an unjust man is not to let people suspect, or put it about, that you are one. To Mrs Foot's way of thinking, therefore, a moral judgement is by definition one which commends the satisfaction (or discommends the dissatisfaction) of these wants which all men have. Moral judgements give us reasons for action. But ones which, in the last analysis, come to this—that it pays to be good.

If we do what we ought to do, then we shall satisfy the ultimate wants which inevitably determine what it is reasonable for us to do.

Two questions have been raised against Mrs Foot up to this point.

One is: are there, in fact, any wants which all men are known to have?[3] If we go through Mrs Foot's list (see above p. 155), one by one, we can easily think of people who did *not* want to be free from boredom, loneliness, pain, etc., at least some of the time. They were quite prepared to endure these conditions for the sake of ends which they valued more than having interesting occupations, friends close at hand, good health, etc. Mrs Foot's reply to this criticism has to be that the ends they valued were, in fact, simply other larger scale forms of freedom from boredom, loneliness, pain, etc.—like the advancement of knowledge, the triumph of the proletariat, celestial bliss, or whatever. And that may be arguable. But the other question which was raised against her is not so easy to answer.

Is it consistent with the notion of a morally good man to conceive of him as someone who does what is morally good for his own advantage? Is not a good man courageous, temperate, and even prudent, simply because these are *virtues*, rather than because they yield a heteronomous pay-off in terms of freedom from physical injury, etc.? Must he not—and the 'must' is a logical one—even be prepared to go against his own interests, at any rate in the exercise of justice?[4]

Mrs Foot, looking back in 1978, yields in a degree to this criticism, 'Where I came to grief was, predictably, over justice. It seems obvious that a man who acts justly must on occasion be ready to go against his own interests; but so determined was I to think that every man must have reason to act morally that I was prepared to doubt that justice is a virtue rather than give up that idea.'[5] The clause to fasten on here is, '*every* man must have reason to act morally' (italics mine). This is the opinion which Mrs Foot rejects in her later writings. There are two main ideas, held by all moral philosophers of a kantian turn, which she makes the main target of all her criticism. One is the idea that moral judgements are categorical, that they have what she calls 'automatic reason-giving force'.[6] The other is the idea that moral judgements are universal, that they entail categorical imperatives for all who are in the relevant situations. In her earlier writings Mrs Foot attacked the former idea by her insistence that the reason-giving force of moral judgements is dependent on what people want. This attack is continued in her later writings, but there is also a new 'thrust'. It is against the idea that the wants in which morality is grounded are ones which *all* men have.

When she published her 1972 papers 'Reasons for Action and Desires' and 'Morality as a System of Hypothetical Imperatives', Mrs Foot was ready enough to admit that moral 'oughts' are, in our everyday discourse, treated as categorical. It would be very unusual to hear someone say for instance, 'You ought to tell the truth, *if* you care about such matters and *if* you have no good reasons of your own for not doing so.' We normally speak of what the intuitionists have called *prima facie* obligations, such as telling the truth, in non-hypothetical terms. But Mrs Foot does not think that anyone has offered a valid argument for supposing that moral obligations have the 'special dignity and necessity', the 'inescapability', 'binding force', 'magic force'[7]—as she variously describes it—which our everyday, categorical ways of speaking about them seem to imply. She describes the idea that they have this 'automatic reason-giving force' as a 'fugitive thought'.[8] No one is able to run to ground the considerations which require us to accept it. Is it the 'bindingness' of rational consistency as universal prescriptivism would have us believe? Mrs Foot thinks that she has said enough in her various writings to discredit that idea. We are asked to think of moral considerations as evaluations, which give us reasons for action, which are not dependent on our desires. But are such evaluations even conceivable? Mrs Foot finds the idea incoherent. Just as, if I did not want anything from a motor car, it would be absurd to say that I ought to buy a Rolls Royce, or if I did not forsee any satisfaction in owning works of art, that I ought to collect good ones, so, holds Mrs Foot, it is absurd to think that there are moral 'oughts' which are not grounded in wants.[9] The only explanation which she can imagine for the categorical moral 'ought' in everyday use is social teaching and social demand.[10] We are conditioned by our upbringing to do certain things irrespective of our inclinations: that is where the 'fugitive thought' of categorical obligation must be located. If confirmation that this is all it amounts to is needed, Mrs Foot finds it in the fact that we use the same sort of non-hypothetical 'ought' when we are speaking of the rules of etiquette as we do when invoking moral considerations.

She is quite prepared to accept the full implications of the conclusion that the moral 'ought' is not categorical. She now thinks that it makes perfectly good sense, despite ordinary usage, to say, 'You ought to tell the truth, *if* you care about such matters and have no good reasons of your own for not doing so.' In her 1978 comments on the paper 'Morality as a System of Hypothetical Imperatives' she notes that the 'ought' in 'Ought I to be moral?' has been regarded by many philosophers as 'free floating and unsubscribed', neither a moral 'ought' nor a prudential one. But she has 'never found anyone who could explain the use of the word in such a context'. 'They are apt,' she adds in parenthesis, 'to talk about the expressing of resolves, or of decisions, but it is then not clear why we need the "ought" terminology when "I resolve" and "I've decided" are already in use.'[11] She spells out her own opinion uncompromisingly,

> My own conclusion is that 'One ought to be moral' makes no sense at all unless the 'ought' has the moral subscript, giving a tautology, or else relates morality to some other system such as prudence or etiquette. I am, therefore, putting forward quite seriously a theory that disallows the possibility of saying that a man ought (free unsubscribed 'ought') to have ends other than those he does have, e.g. that the uncaring, amoral man ought to care about the relief of suffering or the protection of the weak. In my view *we must start from the fact that some people do care about such things* and even devote their lives to them; they may therefore talk about what should be done presupposing such common aims. These things are necessary, but only subjectively and conditionally necessary, as Kant would put it[12] (italics mine).

Notice two differences here from Mrs Foot's earlier views. The first, that morality is not now grounded in wants which *all* men are taken to have, but in those which only *some* people have. The second, that these wants are not self-interested ones for freedom from loneliness, boredom, pain, etc., but are such as people have when they 'care about the relief of suffering or the protection of the weak.'

Mrs Foot now thinks of interests and desires as distinct sources of reasons for action;[13] and she thinks of the wants in which morality is grounded as desires rather than interests. A 'moral man', one who is just or benevolent, 'must be ready to go against his interests.' Mrs Foot says explicitly that it may not pay him to be virtuous, as once she thought it would. But this 'moral man', as such, will not have to go against his desires. His reason for acting morally 'will lie rather in what he wants than in what is to his advantage.'[14]

Says Mrs Foot, if a man 'has that basic sense of identification with others that makes him care whether or not they live wretched lives, has he not the best possible reason for charitable action?'[15] Thus benevolence has its place. Justice is more difficult to accommodate, as she recognises, since two different sorts of case have to be comprehended. One, where the life or liberty of an individual is set against the good of the majority; the other, where some obligation is owing but no good can be foreseen from fulfilling it. The former case is covered because those who care for others will not be able to ignore individuals. But what of the latter case? There is a 'love of justice', a 'desire to live a certain kind of life' in the heart of the 'moral man' which covers this also, thinks Mrs Foot.[16] But can he have such desires without the thought that he ought categorically to do so? Mrs Foot thinks so—'without any moral imperatives a man may have such desires.'[17]

The thought running through all this is that 'moral considerations give reasons for action only in ordinary ways,'[18] not in some 'automatic reason-giving' way, that is, but because 'many kind and upright men'[19] *want* to follow the ways of life which we call benevolent or just. You cannot give any man who lacks this desire a reason for being virtuous. A moral imperative is hypothetical: *if* you want to be good, you ought to . . . Kantian philosophers cannot rest here. They think of moral obligations as having an 'automatic reason-giving force' because they cannot endure the thought that anyone can escape these obligations. But Mrs Foot does not see why. She sums up her view, 'Perhaps we should be less troubled than we are by fear of defection from the moral cause; perhaps we should even have less reason to fear it if people thought of themselves as volunteers banded together to fight for liberty and justice and against inhumanity and oppression. It is often felt even if obscurely, that there is an element of deception in the official line about morality. And while some have been persuaded by talk about the authority of the moral law, others have turned away with a sense of distrust.'[20]

From the earlier view that judgements are moral only if they commend the satisfaction (or discommend the dissatisfaction) of certain self-interested wants which all men have, she has come to the conclusion that the wants in question are desires for the well-being of others and for the self-satisfaction which is to be found in caring for them. Only if men have these desires will they have reason to be moral. Mrs Foot evidently thinks that some people are incapable of feeling them, in which case they must be for ever debarred from the moral life. But her talk just now of 'volunteering' for that life suggests that most people are capable of cultivating the appropriate desires. If that is so, does it not make sense to say that they *ought* to cultivate them? This sounds like a moral *ought* but, if so, is it, as Mrs Foot would evidently think, a tautology to say that we ought to cultivate a concern for the oppressed etc.?[21] That does not seem plausible. 'We ought to cultivate such-and-such feelings' could hardly mean, 'If we have such feelings we shall have them.' But if it is not tautological, then the 'ought' will have to be grounded in something other than such-and-such feelings, for the assumption of 'You ought to cultivate them' is that they do not exist. Perhaps Mrs Foot does not think that they can be cultivated. Either you have them or you do not. But, then, what sense is there in talking about 'volunteering' for the moral army? Either you are already in it or you never can be.

*Morality grounded in Tradition*

The second version of the view that morality has a restricted content which I shall consider, put very simply, comes to this: in order to be moral, a judgement must be in accordance with certain judgements which the speaker and his hearers have both been brought up to accept. I will explain what is meant by this version, then I will show how it differs from the version which we were considering a moment ago. We shall see that it does so in two marked respects. Whereas Mrs Foot denies that moral judgements have categorical reason-giving force and affirms that they provide reasons for action only because they are grounded in wants, the philosophers whom we are now to consider deny that moral judgements are grounded in wants and affirm that they are categorical.

To avoid any misunderstanding, a distinction must be drawn at the start between two contrasted ways in which morality can be thought of as grounded in tradition. One is that which F. H. Bradley[22] had in mind when he bade us not think that we know better than the world (cf. above p. 53). The other is often expressed by quoting Wittgenstein's remark that 'if language is to be a means of communication there must be agreement not only in definitions but also (queer as this may sound) in judgements.'[23] Those whose philosophy I am now discussing conceive of morality as grounded in tradition in the latter, not the former, of these two ways.

In the passage from which these words of Wittgenstein are quoted, he has pointed out that a definition of the word 'red', for example, such as ' "red" means the colour that occurs to me when I hear the word "red" ',[24] would be of no use for purposes of communication unless there were general agreement about what things are red. And he goes on to say that it would similarly be of no use to have an agreed method of measuring things unless there was 'a certain constancy in results of measurement'.[25] Similarly, some say we could not communicate with one another morally unless there were some such agreement in judgements. Whether or not Wittgenstein would have gone along with this extension of his point to morality is not certain. He is said[26] to have remarked in his hitherto unpublished manuscripts that the point does not apply to the aesthetically evaluative terms 'pleasant', 'unpleasant', 'beautiful', 'ugly'; in which case it seems unlikely that he would have thought that it applies to morally evaluative words such as 'good' or 'right'. However, those with whose views we are now concerned think that it does. Mr R. W. Beardsmore,[27] for example, insists that there is no sense in supposing that we can each decide for himself what shall count as a moral consideration. If we did that, how could there be any communication between us? We can communicate with each other only as members of a moral community and this community can only be constituted by *some* 'agreement in judgements.' Take this example[28] in order to illustrate the point. Suppose we meet two men. The first says that in his opinion it is morally wrong to wear green on Thursdays. We ask him why and he answers, 'What do you mean "Why?"'? It just is.' The second man says that he has a profound admiration for Nietzsche's 'superman' or Aristotle's 'high-souled man' and when we demur, he replies, 'But they are paragons of courage!' We shall understand the second man's opinion as we do not understand that of the first man—not necessarily because we agree with it any more than with the first man's, but in the sense that we can see why the second man admires the lifestyles concerned. He sees them as demonstrations of courage and we share his admiration of courage. We may think him mistaken in his opinion that Nieztsche's 'superman' or Aristotle's 'high-souled' man were courageous. But we share the moral judgement on which that opinion is based—we, like him, have been brought up to think of courage as a virtue. So, we can have a moral argument with him—are these types *really* courageous? But there can be no such moral communication between us and the first man. He would not point to any ground on which his opinion was based—'It just is.' There is no 'agreement in judgements' and so no communication.

In the Wittgenstein context to which I referred, mention is made of both 'agreement in opinions' and 'agreement in judgements'. Beardsmore takes this over and uses it to differentiate his own view of morality as grounded in tradition from that of a conventionalist such as he takes Bradley to have been. On Beardsmore's view, moral conflict is not as such morally reprehensible. Disagreement in moral 'opinions' is perfectly in order. But it must be based on agreement in some judgements, if those who disagree in their opinions are to understand each other and comprehend what is at issue between them.

The content of moral judgements *qua* moral is restricted, on the present view, in the sense that a judgement cannot (logically) be a moral one, unless what it commends (or discommends) can be—and is—concieved as an instance of something which is commended (or discommended) in certain more fundamental judgements. The behaviour of Nietzsche's 'superman' and Aristotle's 'high-souled' man has enough in common with that of men whom we normally call courageous to make it not altogether absurd to speak of them as courageous. Their behaviour *can* be so conceived. It *is* so conceived in the judgement that these types are admirable because they are courageous. This judgement, therefore, counts as moral because what it commends can be conceived as an instance of that which is commended in the more fundamental judgement that courage is a virtue.

I have already remarked that, whereas Mrs Foot thinks of moral judgements as grounded in wants and as having no automatic reason-giving force, those who think that morality is grounded in tradition take exactly the opposite view on both counts. They deny that moral judgements are grounded in wants and assert that they have automatic reason-giving force. This difference is very clear in Richard Norman's *Reasons for Actions* (Oxford, 1971). He thinks of Mrs Foot and R. M. Hare as both making the same mistake, namely that of supposing a reason for action to be a psychological state of the agent[29]—what he wants in Mrs Foot's case, his pro-attitude in Hare's. Norman allows for the distinction between wanting things as means and as ends, which Mrs Foot draws; but, following Miss Anscombe, points out that things which are wanted as ends are wanted because of some 'desirability-characterisations'[30] which are deemed to apply to them—'comfortable', 'interesting', 'pain-free', etc. It is not a reason for action simply to say that the action will bring about something I want. As Norman puts it,

> Wants have to be backed up by *reasons*. Therefore, not just any assertion of the form 'I want just X' can provide an ultimate reason-for-acting. If it does so, this will be because the description 'X' characterises the thing wanted in such a way that no further reason is necessary. And in that case, it is the fact that the thing is describable as 'X', not the fact that the thing is wanted, that constitutes the reason-for-acting. The notion of 'wanting' can be allowed to fall out altogether[31] (italics mine).

If it is objected that this simply puts wanting one stage further back, since we find the fact that something is 'interesting', etc. a reason for seeking it only because we *want* to be interested, it is open to Norman to reply that such wanting will in its turn depend upon desirability-characterisations and so *ad infinitum*.[32]

All of which is said to apply in the case of ethical characterisations, such as 'courageous', 'dishonest', etc. To give a reason for something, says Norman, is to bring it under a justifying norm. The function of concepts such as courage or honesty is, 'both to characterise an action as being of a certain kind, and at the same time to indicate that its being of that kind constitutes a reason for performing it.'[33] These ethical concepts can fulfil this function because they encapsulate the public norms which determine what counts as a rational action. Just as public norms determine what counts as the rational use of a word, so they determine what counts as a rational thing to do. In so far as they encapsulate public norms, words like 'courage' and 'honesty' stand for that 'agreement in judgements' of which I spoke earlier. Norman thinks that these 'Janus-words'[34] (so-called because their meaning is both evaluative and descriptive) are more 'fundamental ethical words' than purely evaluative terms like 'right' or 'good'. In that they express public norms they give us reasons for action. To say that something is courageous gives 'a perfectly adequate and self-sufficient reason for doing' it;[35] to say that it is cowardly, for not doing it. We do not have to bring in wants. Indeed we cannot do so. There can be no question of norms being constituted by pre-existent wants, for, says Norman, 'it becomes possible to want the thing only when one has already learnt to see it in the relevant way; I can value my home as a "home" only because I have already learnt the concept of a "home" and in learning the concept and its place within a form of social life I have learnt an evaluative norm.'[36]

D. Z. Phillips and H. O. Mounce illustrate the point that morality is not grounded in wants from the case of a man who tried to persuade a Roman Catholic mother that birth-control is morally right because it protects women from the physical harm which having too many children may cause. She was unconvinced and spoke in reply about the honour which bearing children brings. It was not what each of these two wanted which determined their respective moral judgements. Quite the reverse. It was their judgements which determined what they wanted. The mother thought it morally right to submit to the will of God, to accept the responsibilities of motherhood, and so on. Therefore she wanted a large family. The man thought it morally right to provide a high standard of living for one's children, to avoid risks to one's own health, and so on. And so he wanted to limit the size of families. Phillips has also argued in the most uncompromising terms for the view that moral judgements do have what Mrs Foot calls 'automatic reason-giving force'. Though, as we have seen (p. 155), she thought that it pays to be just, she recognised that this is not always true. A man may have to die for justice's sake. Suppose he could save his own life by getting an innocent man killed in his place. If he is just, he will not do so. 'For him,' writes Mrs Foot, 'it turns out that his justice brings disaster on him, and yet like anyone else he had good reason to be a just and not an unjust man.'[37] Phillips fastens on this 'had'. Perhaps he had (past tense), when he started out, because the probability was that justice, rather than injustice, would be to his advantage, as Mrs Foot evidently thinks it would be in nine cases out of ten. But what, now that it has not been in his particular case? Mrs Foot thinks he could not have had it both ways and, while possessing the virtue of justice, hold himself ready to be unjust when things went wrong. But Phillips sees 'a mysterious gap'[38] between this man's beginning and his end. His practice of virtue when he goes to his death rather than be unjust 'is carried on independently'[39] of his initial reason—viz. the likelihood of profit—for adopting justice as his way of life. What fills this gap? Only, thinks Phillips, the thing Mrs Foot fails to see, 'that for anyone concerned about justice, death for the sake of justice is not a disaster.'[40] Justice cannot be justified by anything but itself. Mrs Foot's notion that justice is heteronomously profitable 'has nothing to do with morality.'[41] The just man does what he does because it is just. He cannot be conceived to have any other reason.

Peter Geach[42] dismisses what he describes as this 'high Stoic line' with the comment that 'it is mere sophistry to confuse the thesis that men need the cardinal virtues for their benefit ... with the thesis that being brave or just must pay the individual brave or just man.' The 'benefit' which Geach has in mind is evident in his earlier remark that 'we need justice to secure co-operation and mutual trust among men, without which our lives would be nasty, brutish and short.'[43] *Our* lives? But if I am about to die for justice's sake, my life *is* going to be short from now on. I am not going to have time to satisfy any needs, for private security, for the chance to love others, or anything else. Perhaps my justice now should be thought of as some sort of repayment to society for the security I have hitherto enjoyed through the justice of others? But then why should I repay anybody, unless I think it just to repay? For all Geach's talk of sophistry, it is hard to escape the thought that the just man is the man who loves justice for its own sake.

*Are moral considerations overriding?*

Representatives of these two versions of the view that morality has a restricted content which I have been considering in the present chapter, have recently joined issue on the following question: Are moral considerations overriding?[44] This should not surprise us. Those who think like Phillips believe that nothing could conceivably matter to the just man more than justice as an end in itself. Those who are with Mrs Foot think that justice matters to the just man only because he has certain kindly desires which justice is the means of satisfying. What is at issue between Phillips and Mrs Foot in their recent exchanges is, however, not quite whether we *should* care about morality for its own sake or as a means to some other end. It is the somewhat narrower question, whether or not for a man who *does* care about morality, moral considerations are overriding.

Phillips thinks they are, '... moral considerations are, for the man who cares for them, the most important of all considerations.'[45] The kind of example with which he backs up this opinion is that often used to illustrate the graciousness of the high-born. When etiquette requires a bow and some ignoramus offers to shake hands, your great man, in order not to hurt the other's feelings, will shake hands. Etiquette takes second place to morality. But Mrs Foot points out that this is not always so and thinks that no one would expect it to be. The graciousness, even of the high-born, has its limits. If not hurting someone else's feelings is going to cost you an awful lot of money, then, usually if not invariably, no one will think the worse of you if you go ahead regardless. Phillips' assumption, that to say of a man that he cares about morality is to say that for him moral considerations are always overriding, is false.

Mrs Foot advances her own illustration to show that people who do care about morality sometimes let etiquette override it. If your guests at a party are drinking too much and it occurs to you that in consequence they may have an accident on the way home, it will nevertheless be thought boorish if you tell them that they have had enough and put the drink away. The fact that someone may get hurt or killed if you go on topping up their glasses, is undoubtedly a moral consideration. But in such a situation, you are expected to give etiquette precedence over morality, says Mrs Foot. At any rate, you are in the circles with which she is familiar.

She adds immediately, 'But to say that no one in these circles "cares about" morality would be a bit stiff.'[46] What is at issue, then, between her and Phillips is quite clearly the meaning of 'cares about' when it comes to caring about moral considerations. Mrs Foot contends that Phillips can only deny that the host in her illustration cares about morality either, (a) by placing his own stipulative definition on 'cares about', thus making his thesis 'uninterestingly trivial', or (b) by assuming that such a host will inevitably feel remorse, if he hears that any of the guests has been involved in an accident, thus rendering the thesis untrue.[47] Phillips is prepared to concede that such a host might well not feel any remorse and so that leaves only Mrs Foot's former alternative. But why should she think that Phillips is placing his own meaning on 'cares about'? He is perfectly entitled to press upon Mrs Foot—as he does—the question, 'What does the care consist in?'[48] There is nothing bizarre or in the least unusual about the content which he himself gives to caring. If the host puts the drinks away, impolite or not, he cares. If afterwards, he feels some remorse about, or some responsibility for, the accident, he cares. But if all such content is excluded, as it appears to be by Mrs Foot, what is caring? Hosts can, according to Mrs Foot, care about moral considerations even though they put etiquette before morality at the party and feel no remorse or responsibility for what may happen afterwards. She ventures the opinion that Martians who took their ideas of human nature from Phillips would be very surprised when they got here.[49] But he replies[50] that if they came armed with testimonials exclusively from Mrs Foot, they would be even more surprised, for they would find that amongst humans anything at all evidently counts as caring for moral considerations.

Why do so many of us have this idea that moral considerations are overriding? Mrs Foot finds the answer in our upbringing. We are taught etiquette 'as a rigid set of rules which are on occasion to be broken.' But we are taught morality as a set of rules some of which it is sometimes *'morally permissible'*[51] to break. The point is that we are taught to think that other considerations sometimes override good manners. But nothing overrides duty. Built into the system of morality there is provision for conflict between one moral consideration and another—the duty not to tell lies may be outweighed by that to be kind and so on. The exceptions to any moral rule are thus, to echo Mrs Foot, 'accommodated' within morality.[52] What this means is that there are guidelines for resolving conflicts. It is, for instance, required of us that we take special pains to be sure of the facts, to let our imagination comprehend all the possibilities, etc. when the issue is a *moral* one. I am not sure that the rules of etiquette may not similarly conflict; and be weighed against each other within etiquette; and it still be true that weighing considerations of etiquette takes second place to weighing moral ones. But let that pass. The mere fact that moral considerations belong to a system of morality with its own guide-lines for resolving conflicts does not show anything which is relevant to the controversy between Phillips and Mrs Foot. Those who care about moral considerations may still be recognised by their overriding concern to solve the moral problems before anything else. And surely they *are* so recognised. Phillips, for his part, takes the pessimistic line. He subscribes to the view, which is so fashionable now, that moral conflicts are frequently insoluble and consequently the man who cares for moral considerations spends a lot of his time in anguish. It is the vogue to think of the moral life as full of remorse. But I am not so sure of this. I seem to know rather a lot of people who sleep easy because they believe that they have done the best they could. And I feel no compulsion to tell them they should not.

1. 'Moral Beliefs', *Proceedings of the Aristotelian Society*, 1958–9, reprinted W. D. Hudson (editor), *The Is-Ought Question*, p. 211.
2. Ibid.
3. Cf. D. Z. Phillips and H. O. Mounce, 'On Morality's Having a Point', *Philosophy*, 1965, reprinted in *The Is-Ought Question*, pp. 236–8.
4. Cf. D. Z. Phillips, 'Does it Pay to be Good?', *Proceedings of the Aristotelian Society*, 1964–5.
5. *Virtues and Vices*, p. xiii.
6. 'Morality as a System of Hypothetical Imperatives', *Philosophical Review*, 1972; reprinted in *Virtues and Vices*.
7. Ibid.
8. Op. cit., p. 163.
9. 'Goodness and Choice', *Proceedings of the Aristotelian Society*, Supp. Vol. 1961., reprinted in *The Is-Ought Question*, pp. 220–1.
10. 'Morality as a System of Hypothetical Imperatives', op. cit., p. 162.
11. Op. cit., pp. 169.
12. Op. cit., pp. 169–70.
13. Cf. her remarks on the difference between interests and desires in 'Reasons for Action and Desires', *Proceedings of the Aristotelian Society*, Supp. Vol., 1972, reprinted in *Virtue and Vices*, p. 156.
14. Op. cit., p. 154.
15. Op. cit., p. 155.
16. Cf. Ibid.
17. Ibid.
18. Op. cit., p. 154.
19. Ibid.
20. 'Morality as a System of Hypothetical Imperatives', op. cit., p. 167.
21. Cf. op. cit., p. 169.

22. Cf. *Ethical Studies*, Essay V.
23. *Philosophical Investigations*, I. 242.
24. Op. cit., I. 239.
25. Op. cit., I. 242.
26. See G. Hallett, A Companion to Wittgenstein's *'Philosophical Investigations'*, London, 1977, pp. 304–5.
27. *Moral Reasoning*, London, 1969, especially chapter 10. I discuss Beardsmore's views in *Modern Moral Philosophy*, pp. 307–11.
28. Cf. Beardsmore, op. cit., chapter 5.
29. Op. cit., p. 15.
30. Op. cit., p. 53. Cf. Anscombe, *Intention*, Oxford, 1957.
31. Op. cit., p. 63.
32. Op. cit., p. 65.
33. Op. cit., p. 66.
34. Ibid. The expression is borrowed from P. H. Nowell-Smith, *Ethics*, London, 1954; cf. R. M. Hare, *Freedom and Reason*, p. 75.
35. Op. cit., p. 81.
36. Op. cit., p. 76.
37. 'Moral Beliefs', in *The Is-Ought Question*, p. 213.
38. 'Does it Pay to be Good', *Proceedings of the Aristotelian Society*, 1964–5, p. 50.
39. Ibid.
40. Ibid.
41. Op. cit., p. 55.
42. P. T. Geach, *The Virtues*, Cambridge, 1977, pp. 16–17.
43. Op. cit., p. 16.
44. P. Foot, 'Are Moral Considerations Overriding?' in *Virtues and Vices*; and D. Z. Phillips, 'Do Moral Considerations Override Others?' in *Philosophical Quarterly*, 1979.
45. 'In Search of the Moral "Must"', *Philosophical Quarterly*, 1977, p. 150.
46. Op. cit., p. 184.
47. Op. cit., pp. 184–6.
48. 'Do Moral Considerations Override Others?', op. cit., p. 252.
49. Op. cit., p. 186.
50. Ibid.
51. Ibid.
52. Op. cit., p. 187.

# 8

# Two schools of thought still conflicting

At the beginning of our story we saw utilitarians and intuitionists in confrontation. At the end of it we once again see them so. There are still philosophers—like J. J. C. Smart[1] or R. M. Hare[2]—who argue the case for utilitarianism. And even amongst philosophers who are not as convinced as they are of utilitarianism's correctness, there has recently been considerable interest in the analysis of the notion of utility. Whether we think of it with hedonistic utilatarians such as Bentham entirely in terms of pleasure and pain, or with ideal utilitarians like Moore in terms of aesthetic enjoyments and personal affections, certain questions arise—e.g. How are the consequences of actions—whether hedonistic or ideal—to be measured against each other? Must we consider the consequences of individual acts or of the rules of action? etc. Books like David Lyons, *Forms and Limits of Utilitarianism* (Oxford, 1965), reflect the interest which there has been in such questions recently.

But one of the most remarkable features of modern moral philosophy has been a revival of a form of intuitionism. I shall refer to the philosophers concerned as neo-intuitionists, though they may not care for the title. Of course, I am not attributing to them all the beliefs of the classical intuitionists. Most, if not all, of them would reject the view that there are self-evident moral truths which we know through a special faculty of conscience, at least in the forms in which 'moral sense' and rational intuitionists once held it. What they have in common with those philosophers, however, is the opinion that there are some moral convictions which are logically irreducible—and morally non-subordinate—to the principle of utility; and that, if we ignore these 'intuitions' we shall misrepresent the nature of morality.

## The Rejection of Consequentialism

The beginning of the contemporary neo-intuitionist rejection of utilitarianism can, I think, be identified as the appearance of Miss G. E. M. Anscombe's uncompromising paper 'Modern Moral Philosophy' in 1958.[3] She complains[4] that every one of the best-known English academic moral philosophers since Sidgwick has put out a philosophy according to which it could conceivably be right to kill the innocent as a means to some desirable end. In this they have all been at variance with 'the Hebrew-Christian ethic', according to which 'there are certain things forbidden whatever *consequences* threaten, such as, choosing to kill the innocent for any purpose, however good; vicarious punishment; treachery (by which I mean obtaining a man's confidence in a grave matter by promises of trustworthy friendship and then betraying him to his enemies); idolatory; sodomy; adultery; making a false profession of faith.' The whole point of the strictness of such prohibitions, according to Miss Anscombe, is that we are not to be tempted by fear or hope of consequences. She accuses the philosophers concerned of starting out from a denial that 'right' has any descriptive meaning and then taking a roundabout route through logical analysis to the conclusion—which comes to the same thing and is often 'urged upon men by wives'—that 'the right action is the one productive of the best consequences'.

In concrete situations we may be tempted to listen to our wives but, says Miss Anscombe, if anyone *really* thinks in his cool hours that it is open to question whether such an action as the judicial execution of the innocent could be right, then 'I do not want to argue with him; he shows a corrupt mind.'[5] It is, of course, debatable whether Miss Anscombe has got even Christianity right, let alone moral philosophy. But her kind of view has certainly become popular in recent years, and not least among philosophers who would dismiss any theological considerations as irrelevant. I will show that this is so by referring to five modern philosophers.

G. J. Warnock in his *The Object of Morality* (London, 1971)[6] takes the view that, in order to understand the particular kind of appraisal or evaluation which is commonly called moral, we must recognise that the 'object of morality'—its 'proper business'—is 'to countervail "limited sympathies" and their potentially most damaging effects.'[7] He defines what he means by 'limited sympathies' in this way: 'the propensity, natural to some degree in all human beings, not to care about, to be indifferent or even actively hostile to, the welfare, needs, wants, interests, of other humans, and conversely to be concerned about, if not exclusively their own, yet those of some more or less restricted group.'

How then, are we to achieve this object of countervailing limited sympathies? Warnock takes the answer, which utilitarians would give, to be that we should do so 'directly and head-on' by inculcating the principle that each individual ought to have a concern for the welfare, needs, wants, interests *of all*. His criticism of this recommendation is twofold. He thinks it runs counter to our ordinary moral convictions; and that it is, in effect, self-defeating.

Warnock brushes aside many of the usual objections which are made to utilitarian consequentialism. Its critics often point out that we cannot foresee our own future wants, let alone everyone else's and that, even if we could, we would not be able to foresee for more than a little way ahead and afield what consequences any action of ours will be likely to have. But, of course, says he, utilitarians have always been aware of such objections and their prescription has simply been that we should aim at the greatest happiness of those whose lives we can affect as far as we can foresee what will cause it. They have simply held that it is right to get as near as we can to the goal of universal happiness and Warnock sees nothing wrong with that—on *two* conditions.

The first is that we do not regard such beneficence as the whole of virtue, like the utilitarians. 'There are other virtues,' he insists, 'not reducible to specialised forms of beneficence.' It is conceivable—and most of us have experience of instances where it would have been highly probable—that an unjust act, a lie, a broken promise, should maximise happiness. But merely pointing this out does not suffice to convince the plain man that in such circumstances the unjust act should be committed, the lie told, or the promise broken. Our intuitions are likely to be to the contrary. Of course, a utilitarian's reply will be that our intuitions are mere prejudices surviving from a less enlightened age in human history; the belief that universal benevolence is the whole of justice may not be one which we *do* have, but it is one which we *ought* to have. In order to block any such move on the utilitarian's part, Warnock advances his second criticism.

It is, as he acknowledges, similar to that which D. H. Hodgson develops with much more detail in his *Consequences of Utilitarianism* (Oxford, 1967) in order to show that utilitarianism is self-defeating. The argument probably applies, in the last analysis, to utilitarians of all kinds but it is easiest to illustrate with reference to act-utilitarians. An act-utilitarian, as such, believes that the greatest happiness of the greatest number can most effectively be achieved by each of us performing the individual acts which, in their several situations, effect the greatest general happiness. But it is obvious even to act-utilitarians that some degree of co-operation between individuals is necessary, if mankind is to march forward to the utilitarian millenium. Co-operation is not conceivable, however, unless individuals are prepared to enter into certain mutually binding undertakings, such as to tell each other the truth, to keep their promises, etc. Act-utilitarians, as such, will, therefore, be prepared to enter into some such undertakings. They will perform this act of commitment to each other because they believe that it will make for the greatest happiness of all in the long run. However, after they have entered into these undertakings, they will, *qua* act-utilitarians, be obliged to stand by them *only* in so far as they believe that doing so will be optimific. On occasion they may not think this and then they will, from their own point of view, be fully justified in departing from their undertakings.

Well now, suppose we were all act-utilitarians. Any one of us would be obliged to fulfil his undertakings to the others only in so far as he thought it would be for the general good. The rest of us would know that he might pull out of them at any time and so we would have to ensure that the undertakings, on which our co-operation was based, were such that repudiations of them on the part of individuals could not have effects which were too disastrous. But we would all know that the undertakings had been determined by this consideration and that would make us think that it mattered less if we ourselves departed from them. In which case we would be less likely to stand by them. This fact would also have to be taken into account in deciding what the undertakings should be. And so *ad infinitum*. It is easy to see that a point would soon be reached at which the undertakings had become such that departures from them made no material difference at all; and that would be tantamount to there being none at all. Suppose an act-utilitarian makes me a promise. I know that he will keep it only if he thinks it will serve utility to do so; consequently, I will rely upon it that much less. But he will know this and consequently will have that much less compunction about breaking his promise. But I, in turn, will know that he will have that much less compunction and therefore I will rely on his promise even less. But he will know that I will, and so he will feel even less compunction at the thought of breaking his promise. And so on to a point, soon reached, where his promise counts for nothing between us. Act-utilitarianism necessarily defeats itself in this way. If the act-utilitarian undertakes obligations to others because he thinks this is the right thing to do, his very act-utilitarianism makes it inevitable that he will stultify what he has done. Act-utilitarians cannot (logically) co-operate. But without co-operation what hope is there, asks Warnock, of 'countervailing "limited sympathies"'?

It seems a little odd that Warnock should find this argument as conclusive as he evidently does. For, is it not really much the same sort of criticism of utilarianism as that which he dismissed? Of course, as Warnock said, if utilitarianism required us to foresee *all* the consequences of our actions for *everybody*, it would be impossible; but, said he, it does not require us to do that most of the time. Well, having said this, ought he not to say in the same tone of voice that, of course, act-utilitarianism would be self-defeating, if it consistently required people to go back on their undertakings, but in fact, act-utilitarians, who opt for co-operation with each other, do not necessarily defeat their own purpose simply because their act-utilitarianism does not require them to go back on that option most of the time?

*Utilitarianism and Vicarious Affects*

Warnock sees the object of morality as that of countervailing limited sympathies. But some neo-intuitionist philosophers do not take such a poor view of limited sympathies, or as they call them 'vicarious affects'. They see, in the very fact that there are such 'affects' evidence that utilitarianism is both contrary to our ordinary intuitions and self-defeating. I take Nicholas Rescher's *Selfishness: The Role of Vicarious Affects in Moral Philosophy and Social Theory*, (Pittsburgh, 1975) as representative of this view.

With due acknowledgement to Adam Smith, Schopenhauer and Spinoza, Rescher explains what he means by vicarious affects. He describes them thus, 'Our own satisfactions and dissatisfactions are ... in substantial measure composed of reactions not to developments that affect us directly and personally, but to our indirect and vicarious participation in the welfare and happiness of other people.'[8] These vicarious affects may be either 'positive' and 'sympathetic' (i.e. deriving pleasure from other people's pleasure and displeasure from their displeasure) or 'negative' and 'antipathetic' (i.e. deriving pleasure from other people's displeasure and displeasure from their pleasure). Each class of vicarious affect includes a range of sentiments: people stand at varying 'affective distances' from us and our feelings vary accordingly. If we love people very much, it gives us intense pleasure (or displeasure) to hear of their good (or ill) fortune; and if we hate them very much, then vice versa. The less closely connected with us by the ties of love or hatred people are, the less intense proportionately these vicarious affects will be. In all cases, however, Rescher is thinking of the satisfaction or dissatisfaction which we find in what happens to certain people *rather than* to others.

The *moral* significance of vicarious affects is expressed by Rescher in this way, 'The positive (that is, sympathetic) vicarious affects in fact represent worthy, morally commendable attitudes: sympathy, fellow-feeling, human solidarity and the like. There is no question that they merit recognition and approval from an ethical point of view ... the negative (that is, antipathetic) vicarious affects in fact represent unworthy, morally negative attitudes: hostility, malice, envy, jealousy, *schadenfreude* and the like.'[9]

Received moral opinion finds moral value in vicarious affects. The positive ones it regards as morally good; the negative ones, as morally evil. A man is a better man if he feels delighted when his children are happy and depressed when they are sad, than he would be if he simply did his duty by them dispassionately. He is a worse man if he takes malicious delight in a friend's misfortune than he would be if he simply did not care two straws about it.

We must now consider Rescher's two criticisms of utilitarianism.

First, how are vicarious affects supposed to show utilitarianism to be contrary to our ordinary moral intuitions? In two ways. One, because the *utility* principle *lets in* the possibility that *negative* vicarious affects will make a state of affairs morally better and that is something which our ordinary moral intuitions cannot accept. The utility principle assesses the rightness or wrongness of actions solely by the pleasure or pain which they cause. Other things being equal therefore, a utilitarian would have to say that an action was right if he believed that it would increase the general happiness simply by causing someone to take malicious pleasure in someone else's misfortune. The utility principle cannot take any account of differences in the *moral* quality of the pleasures or pains which actions cause. But our ordinary moral intuitions can—and do. We want to know, not simply whether people will be made happy or miserable, but *how* they will get that way.

Then again, utilitarianism's *equity* principle *excludes* the possibility of *positive* vicarious affects making a state of affairs morally better and this too is contrary to our ordinary intuitions. The equity principle requires us to be impartial in our dealings with others. But, as Rescher remarks, 'the central facet of the vicarious affects is that when they come in the door, *impartiality* flies out the window.'[10] It may be that 'a small handful of philosophers and theologians' have thought such impartiality morally desirable. Rescher amusingly quotes a letter, written by William James' father, in which he describes his attempts to pray impartially for his children! But plain men do not regard impartiality towards one's children as virtuous. Even though positive vicarious affects are essentially partial, our ordinary moral intuitions tell us that they are a great good.

The second criticism of utilitarianism mentioned just now was that vicarious affects show it to be self-defeating. They are said to do so by bringing to light a fatal contradiction which lies at the heart of it. Vicarious affects increase the pleasure or pain of those who experience them; this being so, the *utility* principle bids us take account of them in the hedonic calculus. But the occurrence of vicarious affects is contingent upon partiality felt towards certain people; and this being so, the principle of *equity* bids us take no account of them. Bentham's two principles—utility and equity—are thus at variance. Utilitarianism defeats itself.

Can any effective reply be made on behalf of utilitarianism to these two criticisms?

We may wonder concerning the first of them whether the positive vicarious affects are regarded by ordinary people with such unqualified approval as Rescher takes for granted. Plain men approve of family affection but not of nepotism. Quite where the one ends and the other begins is, of course, hard to say. Each of us will draw his own line between them. But not simply anything in the way of partiality towards one's friends or kin is approved by our moral intuitions. The trend is for honourable men to be required to show less and less of it, in practice, if not in feelings. So the utilitarian could, with some plausibility, reply that our ordinary moral intuitions are moving in his direction. And he could, of course, always add, so much the worse for them if they are not!

What of the criticism that the vicarious affects show utilitarianism to be self-defeating? It could be argued that the equity principle does *not* condemn them. It does not prescribe *simpliciter* that we must treat everyone in the same way. Utilitarianism's leading exponents, like Mill or Sidgwick,[11] have always recognised that the greatest happiness may be achieved by people taking special care of those closely related to them. It demands equity only in ways consistent with that recognition. The happiness *consequent upon* people having a special care for those near to them must be equitably distributed in so far as that can be done. If, for example, it is a fact that a country prospers better when its businesses can be handed down from father to son, that additional prosperity must be used to benefit all. This may be a very artificial conception but that is not the point. The point is that the equity principle does not condemn the partiality of the vicarious affects as such. It is, therefore, not at variance with the utility principle, which welcomes them. Utilitarianism may have many defects but it is not self-defeating in the way Rescher suggests.

### Intuitions and Ways of Life

Stuart Hampshire offered a neo-intuitionist critique of utilitarianism in his Leslie Stephen Lecture, called 'Morality and

Pessimism', delivered at Cambridge in 1972. He said, 'the notion of morality requires that there be some strong barriers against the taking of life, against some varieties of sexual and family relations, against some forms of trial and punishment, some taking of property, and against some distributions of rewards and benefits.'[12] His basic idea seems to be that anything appropriately called morality will consist in the last analysis of certain unconditional prohibitions, having to do with some or all of these areas of human life. Of course, the content of such prohibitions—or as he does not hesitate to call them, intuitions—will vary from society to society and even from individual to individual; but some such set of 'moral impossibilities'[13] there must be, if there is to be morality at all. Utilitarians, he concedes, do not deny that there are these varied 'absolutes' at the primitive, pre-rational stages of moral experience;[14] but they think that by rational reflection our several intuitions can be 'systematically connected' and rendered 'not absolute but conditional'[15] by bringing them all under the authority of the utility principle. And that, in Hampshire's view, is where they make their fatal mistake because rational reflection shows certain things to be essential to the concept of morality, which are incompatible with this utilitarian craving for subordination and unity. Hampshire writes eloquently of the prohibitions, or intuitions, which he takes to be essential to the idea of morality; but I do not find it easy to fasten with complete confidence upon what he would say are his main points against the utilitarians. However, I will venture the opinion that there are three.

For one, the different sorts of character—or as Hampshire calls them 'ways of life'—which we encounter in different people can only be adequately understood when they are seen as differing 'mixes', so to speak, of the intuitive prohibitions to which I have been referring. These 'ways of life' must be seen as 'sets' of virtues or vices, says Hampshire.[16] 'Each society, each generation within it, and, in the last resort, each reflective individual, *accepts*, and *amends*, an established morality expressed in rituals and manners, and in explicit prohibitions; and he will do this in determining what kind of person he aspires to be and what are the necessary features of a desirable and admirable way of life as he conceives it.'[17] The point is evidently that these differing 'ways of life', in their rich and subtle variety, cannot all be conceived as variations upon the one theme of impartial benevolence. There are virtues and vices which are not logically reducible to the mere fulfilment or non-fulfilment of the utility principle.

A second point which Hampshire appears to be making is that morality is misconceived, if the essence of it is taken to be—as it is by a utilitarian such as Hare—universal prescription. He says, 'The absolute moral prohibitions, which I am defending, are not to be identified with Kant's categorical moral injunctions; for they are not to be picked out by the logical feature of being universal in form. Nor are they prescriptions that must be affirmed ... just because they are principles of rationality, and because any contrary principles would involve a form of contradiction. They are indeed judgements of unconditional necessity, in the sense that they imply that what must be done is not necessary because it is a means to some independently valued end, but because the action is a necessary part of a way of life and ideal of conduct.'[18] The point seems to be that the consistency required of a moral agent is consistency with his own intuitions. But how could he achieve that without taking these intuitions (allowing of course for any conceivable degree of specificity) to be universal prescriptions? Hampshire's subsequent remark,[19] that one does not expect everybody to recognise the same moral necessities but simply to recognise some, certainly dissociates him from all utilitarians; but it does not shed much light on precisely how his conception of moral consistency differs from that of a universal prescriptivist.

There is, however, no doubt at all about the third way in which Hampshire thinks that utilitarians misconceive of morality. They fail to see that conflict is of its very essence. We have a plurality of intuitions and we can never guarantee that they will not clash. When they do, we often find that no amount of reflection will resolve the conflict. In such a situation, a moral agent 'has to make a choice, and to bring himself to do one of the normally forbidden things, in order to avoid doing the other.'[20] Hampshire, in a subsequent paper, insists that 'a conflict of moral claims is natural to us';[21] that 'unavoidable conflict of principles of conduct, and not a harmony of purposes, is the stuff of morality, as we ordinarily experience it.'[22] His point is not simply that moral conflicts occur. If it were simply that, it would be uncontestable. But what he clearly wishes to say is that we cannot conceive of what is normally meant by morality without conceiving of it as a conflict. The only kind of evidence which he seems to have for this opinion is, again, uncontestable but hardly relevant. Conflict may be, as he says, 'a condition of continuing moral development';[23] but the mere fact that we have to learn the hard way how to solve our moral problems does not in itself prove that they admit of no solution except arbitrary choice. Hampshire does not seem to me to have offered any conclusive proof of his contention that, when moral issues arise, we must (logically) always be in a dilemma to which there is 'no rational solution.'[24]

## Integrity and Conflict

Bernard Williams, like the other philosophers whom I have chosen to call neo-intuitionists, thinks that we misconceive of morality unless we recognise that it may lay claims upon us which cannot be logically reduced—nor made morally subordinate—to the one principle of utility. I shall extract from some of his writings[25] two lines of argument which he thinks lead to this conclusion, one concerning moral integrity, the other moral conflict.

To begin with the former, imagine a poor out-of-work scientist who is offered a well-paid job researching into bio-chemical warfare. He thinks such research morally wrong and will suffer miseries of guilt if he accepts the job. A utilitarian, according to Williams, will have to tell him that he ought to take it, if he thinks that the happiness, which the high salary will give to himself and his family, is likely to outweigh any unhappiness which his bad conscience will cause him. Such a view, says Williams, is 'absurd' because it 'alienates' a man from his own moral feelings and actions.[26] We cannot, as moral agents, regard our moral feelings merely as objects of utilitarian value, says Williams,[27] 'because our moral relation to the world is partly given by such feelings.' We cannot—and I think he intends to indicate a logical, as well as an empirical, impossibility—regard such feelings simply as 'happenings outside one's moral self', to be thrown into the hedonic scales along with all other pains or pleasures, when we are deciding what we ought to do. How can a man, in deciding this, be expected to step aside from what he thinks is right? This is 'to alienate him in a real sense from his actions and the source of his action in his own convictions'.[28] If they are *his* actions, then they must (logically) flow from *his* convictions. Williams speaks, in the same context, of a man's actions as flowing from his own 'projects' and this perhaps accounts for Hare's[29] seemingly in-sensitive criticism that he has persuasively redefined 'integrity' to mean self-centredness. I take it that Williams is in fact thinking only of feelings and actions which are rooted in sincerely held moral convictions and that he is making this point: there is some-thing self-contradictory, as well as morally offensive, in trying to convince a man, on utilitarian grounds, that he should think it right to do something whilst thinking it wrong; that he should have a concern for morality which counts the satisfaction of this concern as just one more pleasure, evaluatively on the same level as all other pleasures. The utilitarian defence will be, of course, that this is not what the man is being persuaded to do. Let him by all means retain his feelings that what matters most for him is to do what he thinks right. But let him recognise that either, (a) his moral convictions are really instances of the utility principle, or (b) he is mistaken in what he supposes to be right. Neither of these is an invitation to forsake his integrity—only to enlighten it.

The second line of argument which I find in Williams concerns moral conflicts. Though he does not speak of intuitions, he, like Hampshire and the other philosophers we are now considering, regards conflict as of the essence of morality. He is thinking of cases where either there are two things, both of which we cannot do, but both of which we think we ought to do; or of cases where there is one thing, certain features of which make us think we ought to do it, and certain other features of which, that we ought not.

Williams offers three different sorts of example of such conflicts. One sort he calls emergencies. Suppose, for instance, we are on our way to fulfil a routine promise to meet somebody and we see a child in danger of drowning. Of course, it is our duty to save the child although it means breaking the promise. Williams comments that even in such a case it is not as if the promise had never existed—we still have an obligation to explain why we broke it—but he acknowledges that it would be 'utterly unreasonable' to doubt that we ought to break the promise or to feel bad about it afterwards.[30] A second kind of example Williams calls tragedies. His illustration here is Agamemnon at Aulis, having to choose between killing his daughter or failing in his duty as a commander. In such a case Williams does not think it at all unreasonable for the agent concerned to agonise about what he ought to do, or to feel bad about it afterwards whichever of the courses open to him he may take. This rational feeling of remorse will not, says Williams, be due to a persistent doubt that he may not have chosen the better course (as a utilitarian would have to suppose) but will be due to 'a clear conviction that he has not done the better thing because there was no better thing to be done.'[31] His third sort of example is of politicians who have to do something 'morally disagreeable'[32] because—not too often one hopes but inevitably from time to time—this is 'part of the business' of a politician.[33] In some such cases, although there is a moral justification for the act, it may leave with the politician concerned a 'moral remainder' in the form of remorse. Utilitarianism, says Williams, could not regard such a man as reasonable 'because it lacks any sense of *moral* cost, as opposed to costs of some other kind (such as utility) which have to be considered in arriving at the moral decision.'[34]

Williams will have none of the reply that in all these sorts of example the people who have been involved in the moral conflict have feelings of 'natural', as distinct from 'moral', regret for the ill which they have had to inflict in resolving their conflict and this is why they feel bad. It is, he contends, 'absurdly unrealistic to try to prise apart a man's feeling regrets about what he has done and his thinking that what he has done is something that he ought not to have done, or constituted a failure to do what he ought to have done.'[35] If this means that it is realistic to recognise that a man's 'natural' and 'moral' feelings of regret are usually intermingled, it is no doubt true. But, as R. F. Atkinson pointed out in reply to Williams, this does not settle the matter. The only kind of case which will test Williams' view is one in which 'the regret was determined *exclusively* by a moral thought.'[36] Not by the thought that one took the wrong decision, or that the conflict only arose because one is unfortunately so stupid as to have got into it, or that what one had to do has hurt other people—all of which may occasion 'natural' feelings of regret; but simply by the thought that one has had to do something which one would normally consider wrong. One must be in no doubt that what one did was unavoidable, that one did not simply blunder into the conflict, and that no one has been hurt. Then all one will have to contemplate is the fact that, in doing what one thought best, one did something which one would normally consider wrong. Now, does it constitute a failure to understand the nature of morality, if we say that there would be no occasion for remorse in such a case? Atkinson's opinion that it does not is surely persuasive.

Williams builds his whole case on the following foundation, 'The notion of a moral claim is of something that I may not ignore: hence it is not up to me to give myself a life free from conflict by withdrawing my interest from such claims.'[37] He means that if I give one moral claim precedence over another without remorse then I am, in effect, saying that the latter was not a moral claim at all.[38] However, he does not seem to hold to this ground quite consistently for, as we have seen, he considers that it would be unreasonable to feel uneasy about ignoring a moral claim in his first sort of example. As for the other two sorts of example, he may well be right as to the psychological facts—to the extent that we have been accustomed to regard certain courses of action as wrong, we shall feel repugnance when we adopt them. But what Williams does not seem to consider for a moment is the possibility that, whilst morality may be in part the recognition of claims which cannot be ignored, it may also be in part the determination of what these claims should be. To this possibility we must give some further consideration in a moment.

## Justice and the Veil of Ignorance

John Rawls of Harvard published his discursive but influential book *A Concept of Justice* in 1972. He expressly states[39] that it is his intention to show that 'the conception of justice as fairness' is 'a viable alternative to the utilitarian tradition'. This intention he proposes to fulfil by carrying the social contract theory to a higher level of abstraction than did any of its classical exponents, such as Locke or Rousseau.[40]

We are asked[41] to imagine an 'original position', in which people come together to arrive at an agreement concerning the principles which shall henceforth determine 'the kinds of social co-operation that can be entered into and the forms of government that can be established'. It is important to notice that Rawls' social contract is not an agreement to enter into a particular society or set up a particular form of government, but to decide *what shall count as just or unjust*. He does not think of the 'original position' as a historical state of affairs, of course, but as a 'purely hypothetical situation', set up to show what is involved in the concept of justice as fairness, i.e. as 'the result of a fair agreement or bargain'.

This agreement or bargain is fair because 'all are similarly situated and no one is able to design principles to favour his particular condition.' How so? According to Rawls, all the people in the original position enjoy equal liberty, are self-interested and mutually disinterested, lack envy, and are rational. They are characterised by a further feature which is central to Rawl's theory—they all have to agree upon principles of justice behind 'a veil of ignorance'. None of them knows who or what he is. That is to say, they are ignorant of their class, social status, fortune, natural assets and abilities, intelligence, strength, psychological propensities, and even of their own conception of the good. All this ensures that they have to decide what counts as just or unjust without having any idea of what will—or even probably will—be to their own advantage as distinct from that of others.

What principles of justice will such people choose? Rawls, having consulted his own intuitions, comes up with the answer[42] that they will choose two, viz:

*The First Principle:* Each person is to have an equal right to the most extensive total system of equal basic liberties compatible with a similar system of liberty for all.

*The Second Principle:* Social and economic inequalities are to be arranged so that they are both: (a) to the greatest benefit of the least advantaged, consistent with the just savings principle, and (b) attached to offices and positions open to all under conditions of fair equality of opportunity.

(The just savings principle is based on a recognition that each generation has a duty to bear its share of the burden of realising and preserving a just society.)[43] Rawls evidently thinks that his readers will all concur with his view that these are principles of justice which will win the assent of people in the original position when they exercise their self-interest and rationality behind the veil of ignorance.

There is no denying the interest which his book aroused. I have given no more than the barest impression of its contents; many are the convolutions and involvements of its argument. Philosophers differ in their estimate of its worth. The professor of jurisprudence at Oxford describes Rawls' ideas as 'very important to me';[44] the professor of moral philosophy complains that he has found the effort to grasp them through all Rawls' confusions 'really

... painful.'[45] Dworkin, however, sees as plainly as Hare that Rawls has mistakenly proceeded on the assumption that his own intuitions about justice are equally self-evident to other reasonable men. The *second principle* above has implications with which many would not concur. It implies, for example, that in the 'original position' all rational beings would hedge against the possibility of the worst happening to themselves. But there are situations in which some people would think it rational to gamble on a happier outcome.[46] Again, according to this *second principle*, any social or economic disadvantage to the better-off is just, if it improves the lot of the worse-off. By no means all people would agree that social and economic justice demands that degree of egalitarianism.[47] Yet again, the assumption of the *second principle* seems to be that justice is entirely a matter of the distribution of social and economic benefits. But what of cultural ones? The impoverishment of the rich, who patronise arts and letters, may result in the cultural decline of a society. If so, is that just? Rawls evidently thinks so. Dworkin, however, for all his admiration of Rawls, thinks it less than self-evident. Indeed, he suggests that the importance of Rawls' book for him lies, not so much in the answers it gives, but in the questions which it raises—in particular the question, can the concept of justice be explained apart from all considerations about what constitutes the good life, except those of fairness?[48] Whatever its other merits, when seen as an exercise in what I have called neo-intuitionism, Rawls' book has some fairly obvious defects.

*Are there two levels of moral thinking?*

With regard to the two types of ethical theory which we have been considering—utilitarianism and neo-intuitionism—Hare makes this observation: 'It is impossible to understand the issue between utilitarians and their opponents without distinguishing the different levels of moral thinking as I have tried to do in several papers.'[49] This notion, that there are different *levels* of moral thinking, is predominant in his most recent writings. What he has particularly in mind is the difference—as he calls it—between 'intuitive' (or 'level-1') and 'critical' (or 'level-2') thinking. In order to explain precisely what is meant by these two levels it is necessary to start with two other distinctions which Hare draws.

One is that between normative ethics and metaethics, to which I made some reference myself in the *Introduction*. Normative ethics is the concern of moralists, who try to answer such questions as 'Is abortion wrong?', 'Should apartheid be abolished?', etc. Metaethics is the pursuit of moral philosophers, who try to understand what logical features a judgement must have in order to be a moral one.

From the metaethical point of view, according to Hare, a second distinction can be drawn. It is that between two parts, or elements, of which any doctrine in normative ethics—such as utilitarianism or intuitionism, for example—consists.[50] One element he calls the 'formal': it is the 'abstract or theoretical' account which the doctrine in question gives of morality in any logically possible world. The other element Hare calls the 'substantial', or 'material': it is the 'concrete or practical' account which the doctrine gives of morality in the world as we know it. The 'formal' element in utilitarianism, for example, is impartial benevolence (we ought to do what will bring about the greatest happiness of the greatest number, each person counting for one and nobody for more than one). The 'substantial' element is whatever is thought to fulfil this principle, given the nature and circumstances of human beings in the world as it is.

What, then, is the crucial distinction between 'intuitive' and 'critical' thinking? The first thing to notice is that Hare draws this distinction *within substantial normative ethics*. The second, that he does not regard these two levels of thinking as rivals or alternatives. 'They are,' he says, 'elements in a common structure, each with its part to play.'[51] He adopts the names 'archangel' for someone who thinks in an exclusively critical way and 'prole' for someone whose thinking is exclusively intuitive, but says that 'we all share the characteristics of both to limited and varying degrees and at different times'.[52] One hardly need say that Hare does not mean by 'intuitive' thinking all that some classical moral philosophers have meant by it. He is not making the logical point that there are some moral propositions which we know to be true because they are self-evident; but rather the psychological point, that there are certain moral judgements which, most of the time, seem to most of us to be beyond question. He describes these judgements as 'habits of mind, dispositions, intuitions, principles, rules, or whatever one cares to call them;' and he says that it is by applying them to particular cases that 'nearly all of us do nearly all of our (moral) thinking'.[53] We feel extremely reluctant, for instance, to tell lies; we find it hard to condone cruelty; and so on. If we were 'archangels', omniscient, clear-headed and free from the temptation to make exceptions in our own case, we might safely be left to judge what is right or wrong in every situation as it arises. But, being human, we do not have the time, information, or freedom from self-deception and self-interest to do this.[54] And so 'we need dispositions'.[55] These dispositions, or intuitions, are formed as the result of education and experience. Our upbringing implants in us the moral precepts and principles of which our parents and teachers approve. This, Hare now says, is 'highly desirable'.[56] His earlier writings on moral education have been criticised for placing too great an emphasis upon teaching children to think for themselves about moral issues;[57] but those to which I am now referring leave us in no doubt that he thinks a child 'lucky' to have had implanted within it 'a good set of moral dispositions'.[58] A person's own experience will, of course, add further 'intuitions' to those which he derives from his education. Experience should not be conceived simply as empirical observation, according to Hare, but as reflection upon what happens to us, leading to the adoption of precepts or principles of conduct.[59] All these intuitions, or *prima facie* principles, as Hare sometimes calls them following W. D. Ross, are 'overridable', i.e. they can be held whilst allowing that in particular cases one may break them.[60]

There is one feature which is essential to intuitions, if they are to be implanted in children and to serve as useful guides for plain men. They must be comparatively simple and general. If they are too complicated and specific, children will fail to grasp them and ordinary people will not have the time or subtlety of mind to see whether or not they apply in a given situation.[61] The simpler and more general they are the easier it is to recommend their unswerving practice. Hare is not against doing so. He says quite explicitly that unless the circumstances are 'most unusual' our 'best chance of acting for the best' is to be guided by our intuitions.[62] He quotes approvingly both Butler and Moore to the effect that there are some rules which we must regard as binding; and he expresses some sympathy with Miss Anscombe's view, noted above, that anyone who thinks it possible to question an intuition as fundamental as that the judicial execution of the innocent is wrong thereby shows a corrupt mind.[63] However, unlike Moore and Miss Anscombe, Hare recognises that there do come, now and then, what Butler called 'cool hours', when the question rears its head, 'Are the intuitions I have the ones I ought to have?'[64] It is this question, which lifts us onto the 'critical' level. At the intuitive level we apply simple general *prima facie* principles without question. But that level of thinking 'cannot be self-sustaining'.[65] In order to answer the above question we have to engage in a kind of critical reasoning which is different from that which takes our intuitions for granted.

Notice, to begin with, the three sorts of circumstance in which, according to Hare,[66] we are compelled to engage in critical thinking. Firstly, when two or more of our intuitions *conflict* in a particular situation. In chapter 4 we took note of W. D. Ross's view that we sometimes have to 'weigh' *prima facie* obligations against one another; and it is much the same idea which Hare has in mind here. Unlike some moral philosophers, who think that the moral life is full of such conflicts,[67] Hare thinks that, if we are fortunate, they will not often occur. But sometimes they will and then we shall need a way of settling them. Secondly, a situation may be so *unusual* that it makes us doubt whether our intuitions are really well fitted to guide us. It is not now that they conflict but simply that they seem to be wholly inadequate to the facts of the case. Anti-abortionists, for example, may find themselves in this position, as we supposed above (p. 130); people, who strongly approve of fidelity in marriage may sometimes feel compelled to approve of adultery in a particular case; and so on. Hare thinks that these 'unusual' cases will be rarer than those of conflict; but I wonder if that is so in our day, when so many people would be very uncertain if asked what their basic moral intuitions are. Thirdly, and most important of all in Hare's estimation, there are occasions when we have to *select* the intuitions which we will teach to this and succeeding generations. A person of strong and stable character will not feel disposed to question his intuitions all that often but even he cannot prevent environmental changes of the kind which call for some reassessment of moral beliefs or moral education.

Situations of the three kinds, which I have just listed, call for some criterion by which to judge intuitions. It must be one which enables us to decide between them when they conflict; to determine whether they should be ignored in highly unusual circumstances; and to select, or to change, some but not others, when we reflect upon new developments affecting our own present or our children's future. These situations inevitably arise. If we do not think that we can deal with them by critical thinking, says Hare, then we will have to suppose that a Butlerian God does it for us and reveals the results to our conscience.[68] Although critical thinking concerns the substantial part of normative ethics (cf. above p. 186) the move which has to be made is an appeal to what was described earlier as the 'formal' element in any normative ethical doctrine. The conflicts, unusual cases and demands for selection, which occasion critical thinking, all present themselves as questions about what must be done in the world as it is but, in order to solve them, an appeal must be made to that which, according to the ethical doctrine concerned, differentiates moral right from wrong in any logically possible world. For a utilitarian this will be the principle of impartial benevolence; for an intuitionist, it is, presumably, some or all of his intuitions.

We pass then, from Hare's general differentiation of critical and intuitive thinking to the case which he presents, on the basis of this differentiation, for utilitarianism. One thing seems certain. It is no use looking to our intuitions *as a whole* to supply the criterion which will enable us to settle conflicts, unusual cases or problems of selection. Hare dismisses any such view as 'laughably circular'.[69] He is, of course, right to insist that it is a 'tautological question' whether our intuitions require us to obey them.[70] Inevitably, they do. But, even so, it is not circular to appeal from some intuitions to others. This, I take it, is what the neo-intuitionists would claim to be doing: settling conflicts, unusual cases, and problems of selection, by spotting which intuitions are beyond all question and which are not.[71] In order to fault such neo-intuitionists Hare needs to show that they are either not consistent, or not convincing, in their view. They will not be consistent if, having taken any intuition to be beyond question, they proceed to question it. Whether they do this or not, I cannot say, but probably not. However, they will fail to convince, if the intuitions which they take to be beyond all question are not ones which the great majority of people would so regard. There are, I think, grounds for saying that some of them are unconvincing in this way. For example, P. T. Geach's view that 'fixing our attention on Original Sin is the

189

best way to begin the consideration of sexual morality',[72] leads him to the conclusion that 'man's generative powers and appetites are of necessity specially corrupted'; that all sex outside marriage is 'an enormous evil,' is 'poison', and so on—conclusions which very many, even within the Christian tradition, would not share. If Geach's reply is, that this 'shows a corrupt mind' (cf. above p. 171) then all hope of settling the matter by argument is at an end.

Hare concentrates his attention on those who are prepared to argue. He asks them to consider the possibility that all moral intuitions must yield in the end to the principle of impartial benevolence. We can perhaps best understand his argument by noting how he disposes of various possible objections.

It may be said, first of all, that taking the utilitarian principle as one's criterion in critical moral thinking is simply selecting, without justification, one intuition from amongst all the rest, as the final arbiter of right and wrong. Hare's reply is that the 'formal' element in utilitarianism—viz. the principle of impartial benevolence—restates the logical properties of universalisability and prescriptivity, which he has shown to be defining characteristics of any judgement which is moral. If he has shown this, then it does indeed follow, as he claims, that utilitarianism is not just one conceivable doctrine amongst many others in normative ethics but is the one whose 'formal' component is analytically true. For, as Hare argues, if universalisability and prescriptivity constitute morality, a judgement will have to be in accordance with the principle of impartial benevolence in order to be moral in any logically possible world.[73] Of course, Hare's opponents do not accept the antecedent in his argument and therefore reject the consequent.

A second objection which may be raised to Hare's utilitarian principle of impartial benevolence is that it has unacceptable implications, when taken to be the criterion of critical moral thinking. Two sorts of example are commonly quoted against it. One is that of the fanatical individual. Suppose someone, having gone the round of all the affected parties, as Hare says he must (cf. above p. 143), *is* prepared to prescribe and universalise his fanatical opinions. Then, if Hare is right, we will have to say that it would be morally right for this individual to put them into practice. The other sort of example used against Hare is that of the fantastic situation. Suppose some person *could* bring about the greatest happiness by killing somebody in order to use his organs for spare part surgery, etc. Then, if Hare is right, we will have to say that this person would be doing right to act accordingly. These implications run counter to received moral opinion. The plain man's intuitions tell him that what is imagined could not be right.

Hare, I take it, is ready to concede that there are such objectionable implications in his utilitarian principle, considered simply as that which determines what is right or wrong in any logically possible world. *If* anyone could derive more satisfaction from the thought of the extermination of all Jews than from that of his own survival after putting himself in the place of each of them in turn, then it would be right for him to exterminate Jews. *If* there were a world in which the greatest happiness would be achieved by letting sadists run amok, then it would be right in that world to let them. But Hare would say that all this is beside the point. In order to see why, we must remind ourselves of what is at issue. It is not simply the *formal* component in Hare's ethical doctrine which is under consideration. What is at issue is whether or not his utilitarian principle serves well as a criterion in what he calls *critical* moral thinking. And, as I emphasised above, he takes this critical thinking to be about the *substantial* component in normative ethics. That is why he can remark, as he does, that 'the most important thing' to bear in mind is that 'it is enough' if the deliverances of critical thinking 'can be justified in the world as it actually is, among people as they actually are'.[74] It is not apposite, when we are considering the merits of impartial benevolence as a criterion of critical thinking, to consider what its implications might be in some other, logically possible but fantastic world. All we need worry about is how it works in this world. Hare is confident that, people being what they actually are, we are never likely to encounter fanatics 'heroic' enough to pass the 'universalise and prescribe' test referred to just now; or, the world being what it actually is, to find ourselves in situations where, by chopping people up for spare parts, shooting one man to save nineteen, or strangling an awakening baby in order to escape detection, etc., etc., we can increase the long-term sum of human happiness.[75] It is, therefore, no defect in a criterion, designed to guide our thinking about *substantial* moral conflicts, uncertainties, or changes, that its deliverances, in a world radically different from this, would shock us.

I think Hare would add that even if it is empirically possible on rare occasions for isolated people to meet the sort of fanatical individual, or find themselves in the sort of fantastic situation of which I have been speaking, no allowances for this possibility should be made in the critical thinking which selects *prima facie* principles. The object of critical thinking is to settle conflicts, uncertainties and changes in our intuitions by working out what will bring about the greatest 'acceptance utility' as Hare calls it.[76] That is to say, by working out that, the general acceptance of which will be for the best. The operative word here is 'general'. The object of the exercise is to affect the general intuitive level of moral thinking in a society. This can only be done if the results of critical thinking are such as can be easily taught and widely understood. They have to be, as Hare puts it, 'sufficiently general for the ordinary man to build them into his character and into those of his children in such a way that they will not be in doubt as to what they should do in the moral situations that they are likely to meet with, unless they are rather unfortunate.'[77] They can fulfil this condition only if they take no account of very rare, and merely possible, individuals or situations.

A third objection, which might be raised to Hare's utilitarian criterion of critical thinking, is that it gives no indication of how we are to spot a genuine, as distinct from a spurious, conflict, uncertainty, or need for change at the intuitive level. Individuals may *feel* torn between two duties, uncertain what they ought to do, or weary of their nagging conscience, but this may be due simply to their lack of moral fibre, not to any defect in their intuitions. How can we tell when it is a genuine case which calls for critical thinking? Hare dismisses this as 'not a philosophical question' and concludes that failure to answer it is 'no objection to a philosophical position'. We simply 'have to ask ourselves which procedure (sc. intuitive or critical thinking) is likely to approximate to the result which would be achieved by a reasoner not hampered by our human frailties.'[78] I suppose Hare's point is that there is no philosophical technique for ensuring that we have given the correct answer to that question. We simply have to use our own judgement. But I would have thought it a philosophical question how we are to manage to think like people who think more clearly than we do ourselves.

Hare sees in his distinction between the intuitive and critical levels of moral thinking the way to reconcile utilitarianism and intuitionism in their contemporary forms. He takes all neo-intuitionists to be descriptivists; and all utilitarians to be prescriptivists. The two schools of thought are 'incompatible only if they claim to state the whole truth about our moral language'.[79] In fact, both views are needed for a full understanding of it. The things which descriptivists say about moral discourse as a whole are certainly true at the intuitive level. At this level people agree in their judgements and so there is no need to distinguish linguistic from moral intuitions. Keeping promises and so on can be taken for what 'right' means because there is such general agreement about moral standards that if I say something is 'right', I in effect describe it, according to the situation, as the keeping of a promise, or whatever. But conflicts, uncertainties and the need for change, arise. Hare agrees that, when we 'find two people saying in the same sense of "wrong", one of them that an act is wrong, and the other that it is not, although they agree about the non-moral facts' we must realise that 'this could not be so, if moral intuitions were a species of linguistic intuitions',[80] as descriptivists would have us believe. Some recognition that what is meant by moral terms such as 'right' is logically distinct from the standards in accordance with which we use them is needed. Without this logical distinction there would be no possibility of critical thinking. Hare would now say that the descriptivism of Mrs Foot and his other critics is acceptable as an account of the intuitive element in moral thinking; but that only his own prescriptivism adequately provides for both the intuitive and the critical elements which are essential to moral thinking.

It is interesting to note in conclusion that Hare's 'two levels' idea is paralleled in a number of other moral philosophers. As Hare himself says, a form of it is at least as old as Plato, who differentiated the *knowledge* which his Guardians needed to have, from the *right opinion* which sufficed for his Auxiliaries.[81] Aristotle, in turn, distinguished the *that* of morality (the intuitive judgements that certain acts are right) from the *why* (the critical reflection which discerns the reasons for these intuitive judgements).[82] In the earlier chapters of this book we have encountered something very like Hare's 'two levels' idea a number of times. We noted Whewell's distinction between 'subordinate rules' and a 'supreme rule' of morality (above p. 3); Sidgwick's between 'germinal' and 'adult' ways of moral thinking (above p. 36); and Urmson's between

193

'standard using' and 'standard setting' (above p. 121). Hare himself acknowledges[83] that he owes something to W. D. Ross's distinction between *prima facie* obligations and obligations *sans phrase* (cf. above p. 97), and to Rawls', between 'justifying a principle' and 'justifying a particular action falling under it.'[84] In a lengthy footnote Rawls lists a number of parallels to his own distinction in philosophers ranging from Hume to Anthony Quinton and P. H. Nowell-Smith.

Critics of Hare's 'two level' (or 'two tier') theory accuse him of introducing an unwarranted tension into the concept of morality. How can moral obligation be both unconditional and subject to revision? R. B. Brandt expresses this criticism, 'the two-tier theory tears "morally wrong" and "morally bad" apart.'[85] Brandt's assumption appears to be that conformity and revision cannot subsist together in any rational discipline. So far from finding this criticism compelling, it seems to me to be a point in Hare's favour that his theory sets tension between conformity and revision at the heart of morality. For, as I have tried to argue elsewhere, such tension is of the essence of rationality.[86]

1. Cf. his *An Outline of a System of Utilitarian Ethics*, London, 1961, and (with Bernard Williams) *Utilitarianism: For and Against*, Cambridge, 1973.
2. Cf. above pp. 142–44.
3. *Philosophy*, 1958, reprinted in *The Is-Ought Question*, W. D. Hudson (editor), London, 1969.
4. *The Is-Ought Question*, pp. 184–7.
5. Op. cit., p. 192.
6. Op. cit., pp. 27–34.
7. Op. cit., p. 26.
8. Op. cit., p. 5.
9. Op. cit., pp. 15–16.
10. Op. cit., p. 8.
11. J. S. Mill, *Utilitarianism*, Everyman edition p. 17. H. Sidgwick, *The Methods of Ethics* (seventh edition) pp. 241–2.
12. Op. cit., reprinted in S. Hampshire and others, *Public and Private Morality*, Cambridge, 1978 p. 7.
13. Cf. op. cit., p. 9.
14. Op. cit., p. 10.
15. Op. cit., p. 8.

16. Op. cit., p. 13.
17. Op. cit., p. 19, italics mine.
18. Op. cit., p. 13.
19. Op. cit., p. 15.
20. Op. cit., p. 14.
21. 'Public and Private Morality' in S. Hampshire and others, op. cit., p. 43.
22. Op. cit., p. 42.
23. Op. cit., p. 44.
24. Op. cit., p. 47.
25. Symposium with R. F. Atkinson, 'Ethical Consistency', *Proceedings of the Aristotelian Society*, supplementary volume No. 39, 1965; *Morality*, London, 1973; *Utilitarianism: For and Against*, (with J. J. C. Smart), London, 1973; 'Politics and Moral Character' in S. Hampshire and others, op. cit.
26. Cf. *Utilitarianism: For and Against*, p. 104.
27. Op. cit., pp. 103–4.
28. Op. cit., pp. 116–17.
29. See his 'Ethical Theory and Utilitarianism' in *Contemporary British Philosophy*, volume 4, edited by H. D. Lewis, London, 1976, p. 120.
30. 'Politics and Moral Character', op. cit., p. 61.
31. 'Ethical Consistency', op. cit., p. 111.
32. 'Politics and Moral Character', op. cit., p. 55.
33. Op. cit., p. 62.
34. Op. cit., p. 65.
35. 'Ethical Consistency', op. cit., p. 112.
36. Op. cit., p. 131.
37. Op. cit., p. 116.
38. Op. cit., p. 117.
39. Op. cit., p. 150.
40. Op. cit., p. 11.
41. See op. cit., pp. 11–12.
42. Op. cit., p. 302.
43. See op. cit., pp. 284–93.
44. R. Dworkin in B. Magee, *Men of Ideas*, London, 1978, p. 250.
45. Cf. R. M. Hare's review of Rawls' *A Concept of Justice* in *The Philosophical Quarterly*, 1973, p. 251.
46. Cf. Dworkin, op. cit., p. 251; Hare, op. cit., p. 250.
47. Cf. Dworkin, ibid,; Hare, ibid.
48. Ibid.
49. 'Utilitarianism and the Vicarious Affects' in *The Philosophy of Nicholas Rescher*, edited by E. Sosa, p. 146.
50. Op. cit., pp. 143–4; 'Justice and Equality' in *Justice and Economic Distribution*, edited by John Arthur and William Shaw, 1978, pp. 117–18.
51. 'Moral Conflicts', Tanner Lecture at Utah State University to be published in volume of Tanner Lectures edited by S. McMurrin.
52. Ibid.

53. 'Utilitarianism and the Vicarious Affects', op. cit., p. 146.
54. 'Ethical Theory and Utilitarianism', op. cit., p. 124.
55. 'Utilitarianism and the Vicarious Affects', op. cit., p. 147.
56. 'Moral Philosophy', interview with B. Magee in his *Men of Ideas*, p. 161.
57. I venture this criticism in my 'Trusting to Reason: an unfashionable view of Political, Moral and Religious Education', *New Universities Quarterly*, 1980.
58. 'Utilitarianism and the Vicarious Affects', op. cit., p. 148.
59. 'Principles', *Proceedings of the Aristotelian Society*, 1972, pp. 7–8.
60. 'Moral Conflicts', op. cit.
61. Cf. 'Principles', op. cit., pp. 14 and 16.
62. 'Utilitarianism and the Vicarious Affects', op. cit., p. 148.
63. 'Principles', op. cit., pp. 10–11, 7, and 4–5; cf. above p. 171.
64. 'Utilitarianism and the Vicarious Affects', op. cit., p. 151.
65. 'Justice and Equality', op. cit., p. 117.
66. 'Ethical Theory and Utilitarianism', op. cit., p. 124.
67. See above on Hampshire and Williams, pp. 179, 181.
68. 'Moral Conflicts', op. cit.
69. 'Utilitarianism and the Vicarious Affects', op. cit., p. 146; cf. also 'Moral Conflicts'.
70. 'Justice and Equality', op. cit., p. 129.
71. Cf. S. Hampshire, 'Morality and Pessimism', op. cit., p. 19.
72. *The Virtues*, pp. 145–6.
73. 'Utilitarianism and the Vicarious Affects', op. cit., pp. 143–5.
74. 'Justice and Equality', op. cit., p. 125.
75. These are typical counter-examples used against Hare.
76. 'Utilitarianism and the Vicarious Affects', op. cit., p. 149; 'Moral Philosophy', op. cit., p. 164; Ethical Theory and Utilitarianism', op. cit., p. 123; 'Rules of War and Moral Reasoning' in *War and Moral Responsibility*, edited by M. Cohen, T. Nagel and T. Scanlon, 1974, p. 57.
77. 'Principles', op. cit., p. 16.
78. 'Rules of War and Moral Reasoning', op. cit., p. 58; cf. 'Moral Conflicts'.
79. 'Moral Philosophy: Some Waymarks' as yet unpublished paper.
80. Ibid.
81. 'Principles', op. cit., p. 12; 'Utilitarianism and the Vicarious Affects', op. cit., p. 146; 'Moral Philosophy: Some Waymarks.'
82. 'Moral Philosophy: Some Waymarks.'
83. 'Ethical Theory of Utilitarianism', op. cit., p. 122.
84. 'Two Concepts of Rules', reprinted in P. Foot, *Theories of Ethics*.
85. See *A Theory of the Good and the Right*, Oxford, 1979, p. 233.
86. 'Learning to be Rational', *Proceedings of the Philosophy of Education Society of Great Britain*, vol. XI, 1977.

# Index